Orchids
of Indiana

Orchids
of Indiana

Michael A. Homoya

PUBLISHED BY THE INDIANA ACADEMY OF SCIENCE

DISTRIBUTED BY INDIANA UNIVERSITY PRESS

BLOOMINGTON & INDIANAPOLIS

Printed in Hong Kong

Library of Congress Cataloging-in-Publication Data
Homoya, Michael A. (Michael Allison), date.
    Orchids of Indiana / Michael A. Homoya.
        p.   cm.
    Includes bibliographical references (p.   ) and index.
    ISBN 0-253-32864-0 (cloth)
    1. Orchids—Indiana.   I. Title.
QK495.O64H66   1993
584′.15′09772—dc20   92-34139

1 2 3 4 5 97 96 95 94 93

FRONTISPIECE: *Cypripedium candidum* (white lady's-slipper). May 1986, Porter Co. Lee Casebere. x1¼.

Dedicated to the memory of my parents

Peter F. Homoya, Sr., 1919–1991

Marcia K. Homoya, 1921–1992

HE rules the skies and in his hands upholds
The solar Worlds: while from his breath divine
Spring living souls, that men and beings move.
By him alone the trees and shrubs are set,
And with the lesser plants, the spark of life

Receive, imbibing solar heat and light.
Then to the Sun their leafy limbs expand,
And nuptial buds with dazzling beauties bloom
Of thousand shapes and hues, or sweet perfumes;
The Earth adorning with a verdant dress,
Sprinkled with floral gems like lucid stars,
Sparkling throughout the skies, adorned all
By gilding light, with colors of the prism:
Thus they delight the human senses, showing
The deeds of GOD in floral wonders growing.

—C. S. Rafinesque, *Flora Telluriana* (1836)

CONTENTS

Orchids
of Indiana

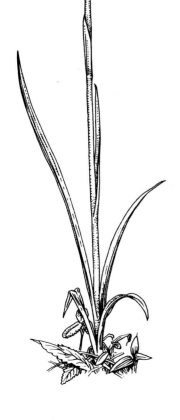

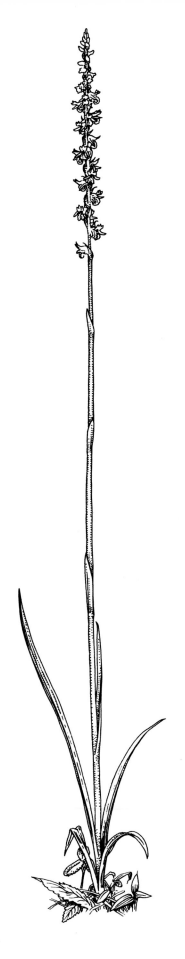

List of Figures

List of Tables

Foreword

The Indiana Academy of Science, which was founded in 1885, is a nonprofit organization dedicated to promoting scientific research and the diffusion of scientific information; encouraging communication and cooperation among scientists; and improving education while stimulating interest in the sciences. One of the ways it accomplishes these goals is through publications. Accordingly, the Publications Committee and the IAS are excited to be able to present this attractive and informative book.

Orchids of Indiana, the twelfth book produced by the Academy, represents the culmination of many years of investigation by the author and those who assisted him. Considerable effort was expended to make the book useful to both the interested amateur and the professional botanist. We think you will find the format easy to follow and the writing style enjoyable. One of the format decisions, to use an alphabetic rather than a phylogenetic arrangement, may cause some purists to pout, but we decided it made the book more user-friendly. As you explore the book, the author's attention to detail as well as his understanding of the ecology of our orchids will be obvious. Mike, like myself a native of southern Illinois, is one of the best plantsmen ever to walk the Indiana landscape. The introduction, which contains descriptions of the natural regions of Indiana and a first-class color map to augment the text, is the embodiment of thousands of hours of careful field observations. The well-researched distribution maps may be the best available, and provide an opportunity to see the geographic affinities of the taxa that reside in Indiana. The inclusion of illustrations of orchid fruits is a unique and beautiful element that I believe will help make this publication more beneficial; floristic treatments often ignore reproductive features such as fruits, which are often more persistent than flowers or leaves, even though they may provide diagnostic characteristics through nondestructive analysis. Also helpful is the phonetic table for pronunciation of scientific names.

This book could not have been published without the assistance of many. Special thanks are due to Lee Casebere and others who provided the excellent photographs. The lifelike illustrations were drawn by Paul Nelson, while John Wyatt drafted the range maps. Excellent editorial comments were offered by Marlin Bowles and Floyd Swink of The Morton Arboretum, Charles Sheviak of the New York State Museum, Paul Catling of Agriculture Canada, and Roberta Diehl of Indiana University Press. On behalf of the Academy, I would like to acknowledge their important contribution. I would particularly like to extend my gratitude to John Gallman, Director of Indiana University Press. His patience, assistance, and willingness to cooperate with the Academy helped make this publication possible. We applaud Sharon Sklar and her associates at the Press for producing a gorgeous publication. My colleagues in the Academy, especially members of the Publications Committee, Executive Committee, and Budget Committee, are to be commended for their continuing support and assistance. They made it possible to produce this book "the right way," i.e., with color plates, cloth binding, larger trim size, figures with corresponding text, etc. Finally, we congratulate the author for creating a lovely and interesting book that will help us to better understand and appreciate one of the most peculiar groups in our biota, the orchids.

BILL N. MCKNIGHT
Chair, IAS Publications Committee
Park Tudor School

Preface

I vividly recall the day I met my first wild orchid. It was a mild winter day in 1970, and a grand old gentleman named Russell Riepe was taking my mother and me and some friends on an excursion into Jackson Hollow, a deep sandstone gorge in southern Illinois. All day the fog was exceptionally thick, creating for us what seemed a dreamlike journey into a forgotten land. Russell knew the territory well, however; he flawlessly guided our descent into the white, silent hollow. At one point, while pausing beside a detached boulder the size of a two-story house, Russell directed our attention to a rosette of spoon-shaped green leaves handsomely patterned with white veins. That, he declared, was a rattlesnake plantain, a wild orchid. Such a sight astonished me, because like most people, I had believed that orchids were inhabitants only of the mystical and distant lands of the equator. That small, seemingly insignificant plant was clearly not growing in a jungle; it illustrated that wild orchids do indeed occur in our temperate soil. Although I saw many other spectacular things that day, including rare ferns and phenomenal rock formations, it was the rattlesnake orchid that so transfixed me. My passion for those magnificent monocots was born.

Orchids are and have been the passion of countless others, whether it entails cultivating the tropical kinds or attempting to observe as many native species as possible growing in their natural habitats. The latter activity, known as orchid botanizing, is my particular affair, as a major portion of this book attests. I find it exhilarating to sight a new species, like a birder observing an unfamiliar bird, or an art connoisseur encountering a "lost" Renoir. As for the orchid botanizer, each has a wish list of desired species. My Indiana list includes, in addition to those orchids extirpated from the state, species never known to have occurred here that perhaps do: those that grow in locales not too distant from our southern border, such as *Cypripedium kentuckiense, Listera australis,* and *Spiranthes odorata,* and those near our northern border, like *Goodyera repens, Malaxis monophyllos,* and *Platanthera blephariglottis.* Discoveries of any of these species, or others new to the state, should be reported to the Division of Nature Preserves, Indiana Department of Natural Resources.

I wrote this book with two objectives in mind. One was to create a work that would instill an interest in orchids and nature. For that reason, I attempted to write in a style that would appeal to the amateur nature enthusiast (even though, first and foremost, this book is intended to be an accurate and scientific account of Indiana orchids). The other objective was to generate concern for and an improved performance of our earthkeeping responsibilities. It is my hope that readers will embrace this call to a better understanding of all our fellow creatures, and then to enjoy them, appreciate them, and become participants in their stewardship. Consider the consequences if we don't. How impoverished we will be when that last wild orchid blooms for the final time.

Acknowledgments

Being an author is hardly possible without the generous assistance of others. There are a great number of people to whom I am grateful for their generosity. Although I have attempted to document all contributors, I may have unintentionally omitted some of them. In such cases, I offer my sincere apologies.

Assistance in numerous ways, from identifying a bee to translating a German text to providing orchid location data, was provided by a host of contributors. For such assistance I offer my gratitude to Kate and Brian Abrell, Delano Arvin, Colleen Baker, Bob Ballantyne, Roger Beckman, John Bogucki, Ron Campbell, Paul Carmony, Fred Case, Lee Casebere, Leland Chandler, Greg Croy, Allison Cusick, Tammy Darr, Jeff Dillon, Mary Drippé, Rich Dunbar, Jackie Eichhorn, Judy Esterline, John Gallman, Lois Gray, Nancy and Brad Grenard, Cloyce Hedge, Roger Hedge, Ron Hellmich, Hank Huffman, Marion Jackson, Ken Klick, Ken Landes, DeAda Mally, Michelle Martin, Dick Maxwell, Denny McGrath, Max Medley, Andrew Methven, Bev Morganett, Steve Olson, Bill Overlease, Tom Post, Tony Reznicek, Vic Riemenschneider, Doug Rood, Lise Schools, John Schwegman, Art Spingarn, Helene Starcs, Jerry Sweeten, Terrie Temple, Byron Torke, Sue Ulrich, Michael Vincent, Fred and Maryrose Wampler, Juanita Webster, Sally Weeks, Mark Weldon, Winona Welch, Jerry Wilhelm, Fred Wooley, George Yatskievych, and Dan Zay.

Orchid location data for areas outside Indiana, which were useful in creating the range maps, were provided in part by the following: Robert Haynes and Robert Kral (Alabama), Bruce Palmer (Arizona), Bert Pittman (Arkansas), Heather Townsend (California), Mike Oldham (Canada), Tamara Naumann (Colorado), Richard Wunderlin (Florida), Bob Moseley (Idaho), Mark Loeschke and Dean Roosa (Iowa), Marc Evans (Kentucky), Karen Johnson (Manitoba), Rodney Bartgis (Maryland and West Virginia), Chris Ludwig (Maryland), Welby Smith (Minnesota), Kenneth Gordon and Will McDearman (Mississippi), Don Kurz (Missouri), Loyal Mehrhoff (Montana), Michael Fritz (Nebraska), Teri Knight (Nevada), Harold Hinds (New Brunswick), Paul Martin Brown (New England), Frankie Brackley (New Hampshire), Anne Cully (New Mexico), Richard Mitchell (New York), Larry Magrath and Linda Watson (Oklahoma), Paul Catling (Ontario), Tom Smith (Pennsylvania), Stuart Hay (Quebec), Vernon Harms (Saskatchewan), Paul Sommers (Tennessee), Steve Orzell (Texas), Ben Franklin (Utah), John Gamon (Washington), and Mary Neighbours (Wyoming). To all of them I offer my appreciation.

I wish to thank the directors, curators, and staff of the herbaria that provided loans of specimens and use of their facilities (see Distribution Maps, in the Guide to Species Accounts, for the list of herbaria). I am especially grateful to Nancy Andrews, Rebecca Dolan, Barbara Hellenthal, Joseph Hennen, and Lewis Johnson for their efforts in this regard. The value of herbaria and their workers cannot be overstated. Without them this work would be very impoverished.

I am pleased and proud to have the high-quality photographs and illustrations offered here, and most of the credit is due to the work and skill of those other than myself. For the most part, the excellent photographs are those of Lee Casebere, who spent many hours in the field to get slides specifically for this work. I am also indebted to Jim Aldrich, Marlin Bowles, Don Kurz, Valdemar Schwarz, and Perry Scott for their fine photo contributions. The top-quality illustrations and graphics are the work of Cheryl LeBlanc, Paul Nelson, Roger Purcell, and John Wyatt. It is particularly gratifying to include Paul's work, as he—being my cousin—has made this book somewhat of a family project.

My sincere thanks to John Bacone, Director of the Division of Nature Preserves, Indiana Department of Natural Resources, and his staff for providing the time, resources, and encouragement required to prepare this manuscript. I am additionally grateful to Cloyce Hedge for supplying the framework for the discussion of *Platanthera flava* var. *flava*, and to Cheryl LeBlanc, who spent many hours in the production of tables, maps, and illustrations, as well as providing major word processing assistance.

I am extremely privileged and thankful to have had expert, critical review of my manuscript prior to publication. These reviewers, Marlin Bowles, Paul Catling, Bobbi Diehl, Bill McKnight, Charles Sheviak, and Floyd Swink (he reviewed two separate drafts!), have been invaluable. Charles Sheviak was also very helpful, viewing and identifying a number of difficult *Spiranthes* specimens.

I cannot overemphasize the importance of the Indiana Academy of Science in the production of this book. Aside from its most obvious contribution of being publisher, the Academy's members, especially those of the Publications, Budget, and Executive committees, have provided assistance in numerous ways. I am particularly indebted to Bill McKnight, chairman of the Publications Committee. Without his scientific and organizational skills, as well as his enthusiasm, encouragement, and patience, this book might not have reached fruition.

To those who took an interest in and helped train a young, "budding" botanist, I offer my sincere appreciation. This group includes many dear friends and their families, including Don Autry, Max Hutchison, Robert Mohlenbrock, Russell Riepe, Phil Robertson, John Schwegman, Julius Swayne, and Jack White. There have been many others along the way who have inspired, assisted, taught, and prayed for me, too many to include here. Nevertheless, be assured that I am forever grateful.

Parents and family always merit more gratitude than they get, and mine are no exception. Thanks, Mom and Dad, for all that you did for me; I never adequately thanked you. My warmest thanks also to Pete, Bruce, Chris, and Rebecca—you have helped me in ways that you have never known.

The writing of this book was a labor of love, but it also involved considerable sacrifice. Late weeknight hours and Saturdays, too many to count, were spent cloistered away at my cobwebby basement desk. But the greatest sacrifice was made not by me, but by my family. My wife, Barbara, and sons, Aaron and Wesley, not only tolerated my absence and occasional bouts of frustration, but they faithfully encouraged and prayed for me throughout the book's creation. For this I am most grateful, and thank God to have been blessed by them.

Orchids
of Indiana

Introduction

O*rchids*—marvelously beautiful, mysterious, and complex—grace our world as few other plants can. They are, so to speak, floral royalty in the kingdom of plants. And with over 30,000 orchid species known worldwide, they reign supreme not only in elegance, but in variety as well. Consider, for example, the Central American *Platystele jungermannioides*, whose flowers are no larger than the head of a pin, or, at the opposite extreme, the giant *Grammatophyllum papuanum* of New Guinea, with stems 15 feet in length. Consider also the tropical American *Vanilla planifolia*, from which we get vanilla extract, and *Cattleya*, the beautiful orchid of the florist trade. And not to be overlooked are the rare and bizarre, such as that ghostly denizen of Florida's swamps, *Polyrrhiza lindenii*, whose body consists only of epiphytic, photosynthetic roots, and perhaps most unusual of all, the Australian *Rhizanthella gardneri*, which lives and flowers completely "down under" the surface of the earth!

To many people the mention of orchids evokes thoughts of a steamy hothouse or a remote tropical paradise, and rightly so, because along with being popular greenhouse plants, orchids are most common in the tropical regions of the world. However, orchids are not confined to life under glass, or a misty jungle. They occur in virtually all terrestrial environments hospitable to life, from the Arctic tundra to hot, desert-like scrub forests. Within this range of environments is Indiana, with its rich soil, ample rainfall, and temperate climate. Some might think these conditions produce only soybeans, corn, and hogs, and indeed, that is much of what Indiana is about; but Indiana also is orchid country. In fact, a number of orchids—forty-three species in all—adorn the Hoosier landscape. True, most of these wild orchids may not be as suitable for homecoming corsages as their greenhouse cousins, but there is no question that, on a small scale, they are as fascinating and beautiful. This book is about those orchids.

History of Indiana Orchidology

Unlike some of the larger groups of organisms in Indiana, the orchid family has received relatively little attention. The Orchidaceae were not ignored, however, as botanists with a variety of botanical interests collected

3

orchids in their mission to document the state's flora. During Indiana's grand era of field botany from 1850 to 1950, many botanists made specimens of or studied Indiana orchids. Some of the more notable, all now deceased, include Charles Barnes, Albert Bechtel, Willis Blatchley, E. Lucy Braun, Asahel Clapp, Howard Clark, John Coulter, Stanley Coulter, Charles Deam, Edward Eames, Barton Evermann, Ray Friesner, Frederick Hermann, Ellsworth Hill, Ralph Kriebel, Marcus Lyon, Scott McCoy, Frank Morris, Julius Nieuwland, Donald Peattie, Herman Pepoon, John Potzger, Jacob Schneck, Julian Steyermark, Levi Umbach, William Van Gorder, Winona Welch, Edgar Wherry, and Allen Young.

Perhaps the earliest list of Indiana orchids was produced by Asahel Clapp, a New Albany physician with a keen knowledge of the native flora. On interleaves within his copy of *A Synopsis of the Flora of the Western States* (Riddell, 1835) Clapp penned a list of the flora that he observed and collected in the New Albany area from about 1830 to 1860. He entitled his list: "A Catalogue of the Native and Naturalized Flowering and Filicoid Plants Found on the North Side of the Ohio Since [unintelligible, but apparently the early 1830s] and within 20 Miles of New Albany, Indiana." Although Clapp's list was regional in scope, it reflected the extent of knowledge about Indiana plants at that time, and was in effect the first flora of the state. In his catalogue Clapp listed eleven genera and seventeen taxa of orchids, but in an updated version of his catalogue, which he kept in his *Manual of the Botany of the Northern United States* (Gray, 1848), he listed twelve genera and nineteen taxa.

Following Clapp's work many additional regional and county floristic publications have been made, mostly in the *Proceedings* of the Indiana Academy of Science and Indiana Geological Survey reports. A compilation of those reports and other data was utilized in the creation of the first statewide flora of Indiana. The flora, written by J. M. Coulter, S. Coulter, and C. R. Barnes (1881), listed twenty-eight orchid taxa in twelve genera, or roughly one-half of the taxa known to occur in Indiana today. At the turn of the century a more complete orchid list was available in an updated state flora by S. Coulter (1900), which included thirty-seven taxa in twelve genera.

The most authoritative flora produced for the state was the *Flora of Indiana*, by C. C. Deam (1940), which listed forty-one orchid taxa in seventeen genera. Unlike the preceding state floras, Deam included only those plants that could be verified by a voucher specimen. Consequently, he omitted some of the earlier reported orchid taxa, such as *Spiranthes praecox*, and thus the difference in numbers between his flora and that of earlier ones represents a greater addition of new taxa than might be apparent.

Crovello, Keller, and Kartesz (1983) listed forty-one species of orchids in eighteen genera (forty-three taxa) for the state in *The Vascular Plants of Indiana: A Computer-based Checklist*.

The most recent botanical work on the Indiana flora, the *Manual of the Seed Plants of Indiana* (Crankshaw, 1989), lists forty orchid taxa (all at species level) in seventeen genera.

There are four publications that deal specifically with the occurrence and distribution of orchids in Indiana. These are, in order of their appearance: "The Orchidaceae of Northern Indiana" (Steele, 1881); "Distribution of the Orchidaceae in Indiana" (Cunningham, 1896); "Distribution of Indiana Orchidaceae" (Brunson, 1942); and "Orchids of the Indiana Dune Region" (Swink, 1966). All are good though brief summaries of the orchid flora as it was known at the time. The paper by Cunningham is perhaps the most comprehensive statewide treatment of the family, but Swink and Steele provide the best ecological information for specific species. Brunson provides an interesting account of orchid distribution in the state with regard to geographic affinities and occurrence in botanical areas.

Orchid Morphology and Reproduction

"What makes an orchid an orchid?" The answer is simple yet complex, because orchids, although possessing rather complicated reproductive structures and exhibiting tremendous variation in design, are strikingly different from other plants, and with minimal training one can quickly distinguish an orchid from other members of the vegetable kingdom.

Orchids are more easily identifiable if one understands some basic plant morphology and classification. Orchids are perennial, vascular plants belonging to the class of angiosperms (flowering plants) called monocotyledons. Monocots, meaning literally "one seed-leaf," include such familiar plants as lilies, irises, cat-tails, grasses, and orchids. Two of the features shared by almost all of these plants are parallel leaf venation and flower parts in cycles of three. The other major class of flowering plants, the dicotyledons ("two seed-leaves"), differs in that it typically has a network of veins branching in various directions throughout its leaves, and possesses flower parts mostly in cycles of four or five or multiples thereof.

Orchids are obviously monocots, as *Aplectrum hyemale* so perfectly illustrates (see Fig. 1 and photo of leaf in species account). Note the six (2 x 3) flower parts consisting of three sepals and three petals, and the conspicuous parallel venation of the leaf. Note also that one of the petals is unlike the other two. The differentiated third petal, called the lip, or labellum, is a major morphological trait and key character of the orchid family. It gives the orchid flower a look and a symmetry (bilateral) unlike plants with repetitive floral segments, such as the lily.

In most orchids the lip is the largest of the floral segments, as well as the most variable in shape and color. Typically the lip is resupinate, that is, "turned upside down," so that it is the lowermost positioned of the petals. There are notable exceptions to this rule, however, including *Calopogon tuberosus*. Interestingly, the arrangement of the lip in the lowermost position does not appear in the initial development of the floral buds, but occurs after a 180–degree twist of the pedicel (flower stalk) and ovary. The lip position is necessary for a variety of reasons, the most important being to provide a target and landing platform for pollinating insects.

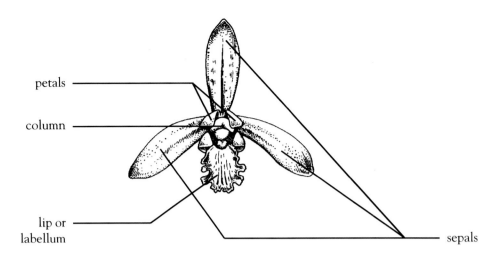

FIGURE 1. *Aplectrum hyemale* flower showing
the principal components of orchid
floral morphology

Orchids also are characterized by a reproductive structure known as a column (see Fig. 2). Of all the morphological features characterizing an orchid, perhaps the column is most significant. A column is a columnar structure that supports reproductive organs positioned in proximity to one another. It is a fusion of reproductive structures (anthers, filaments, stigmas, and styles) that normally are separate in other plants. In many orchids the column is an unimposing structure protruding from the ovary and hidden in an envelope of petals and sepals. But in some, such as *Calopogon, Cypripedium,* and *Liparis,* the column is quite conspicuous. Typically the apex of the column consists of a single stamen possessing one fertile anther. These orchids are referred to as monandrous. The remaining stamens are sterile and modified and incorporated into the body of the column (remember that orchids are monocots, and the "missing" stamens must be accounted for somewhere!).

In diandrous orchids two fertile stamens are present. Each stamen has an anther positioned laterally on the column behind a modified sterile stamen known as a staminode (see Fig. 3). The staminode is a shield-like structure positioned at the tip of the column, above the opening of the slipper-shaped lip. *Cypripedium* is the only Indiana orchid genus belonging to this group.

Enclosed within the anther cavity of the column are egg-shaped masses of pollen grains known as pollinia (see Fig. 2). Pollinia (singular: pollinium) typically occur in pairs, and are either granular with loosely attached pollen grains, or hard and waxy with pollen grains tightly packed. The pollen provides the sperm to the fertilization process.

Located beneath and posterior to the anther is the stigma, or stigmatic surface. Because orchids are monocotyledons, and there are typically three stigmas in a monocot flower, the presence of only one stigmatic surface evidently represents an absence, or a fusion of, the second and third stigmas. In

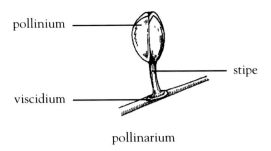

pollinium

stipe

viscidium

pollinarium

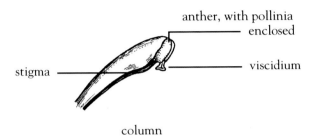

anther, with pollinia
enclosed

stigma

viscidium

column

FIGURE 2. Column and removed pollinarium
of *Tipularia discolor* (with anther-
cap removed)

Cypripedium all three stigmas are fused and functional, but in many of our genera two are fused, with the third being sterile. The sterile stigma, called the rostellum, is located between the stigmatic surface and the anther. It is thought to be functionless in some species, but in others assists in the pollination process by producing a sticky glue-like material that cements pollinia to the bodies of visiting pollinators. In some species the rostellum is in the form of a viscidium, a sticky pad that is connected to a pollinium by a stipe, and serves the aforementioned purpose as pollinia cement. The pollinium, stipe, and viscidium are collectively referred to as a pollinarium (Fig. 2).

In addition to the presence of a column and lip, there are other significant features that help distinguish orchids. All orchids have inferior ovaries; that is, each flower's ovary is positioned below the flower parts. Multitudes of ovules are produced in the ovary, and if they become fertilized, an equally large number of tiny, dust-like seeds without endosperm are formed. A ripened orchid ovary, its fruit, is classified as a capsule. Capsules, by their shape and position, are quite distinctive and useful as a diagnostic tool (see Fig. 4).

Orchid flowers also have a quality and substance not found in the flowers of many other plants. Their seemingly wet, crystalline texture commonly appears like a collection of polished quartz beads, a condition I refer to as "jewelaceous." This quality is best seen under the magnification provided by a good stereo microscope, but a hand magnifying lens with bright light will do.

Although not normally observed because of their subterranean existence, terrestrial orchid roots are also diagnostic. For example, many orchid roots

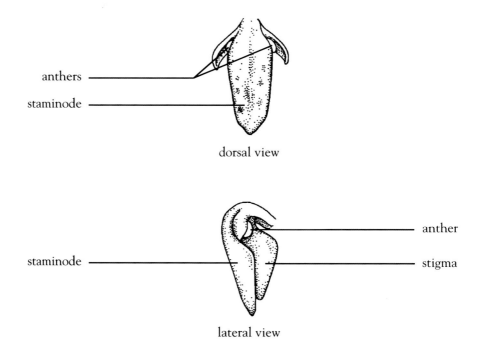

anthers

staminode

dorsal view

staminode

anther

stigma

lateral view

FIGURE 3. Column of *Cypripedium candidum*

are typically rather thick, fleshy, pale, and commonly brittle. Some are tuberously thickened, while others are fibrous. They are attached to a variety of modified stems, such as pseudobulbs in *Liparis* and the subterranean, horizontal rhizomes of *Cypripedium*. Spherical and oval corms are present in *Aplectrum* and *Tipularia*, respectively. Roots may be absent altogether in some, such as *Corallorhiza* and *Hexalectris*.

ORCHID REPRODUCTION

All organisms must reproduce to perpetuate their kind. To ensure reproductive success, plants have available to them a variety of strategies. These strategies fall within two major categories: sexual and asexual. Sexual reproduction involves the production of seed, resulting from the union of egg and sperm. For most plants, this is the principal mode of reproduction. It brings about mixing of genetic material and the benefits that it provides. Asexual reproduction, or apomixis, is a means of propagation without the union of egg and sperm. This is accomplished through vegetative means, such as with stolons, rhizomes, and bulbils; or by parthenogenesis, as in the development of viable seed from unfertilized ovules (agamospermy). Asexual reproduction normally produces genetically identical individuals (clones).

Most orchids are prime examples of outcrossing, sexually reproducing plants, but many North American orchids are also self-fertilized (autogamous). Catling (1983c) states that as many as 37 percent of eastern Can-

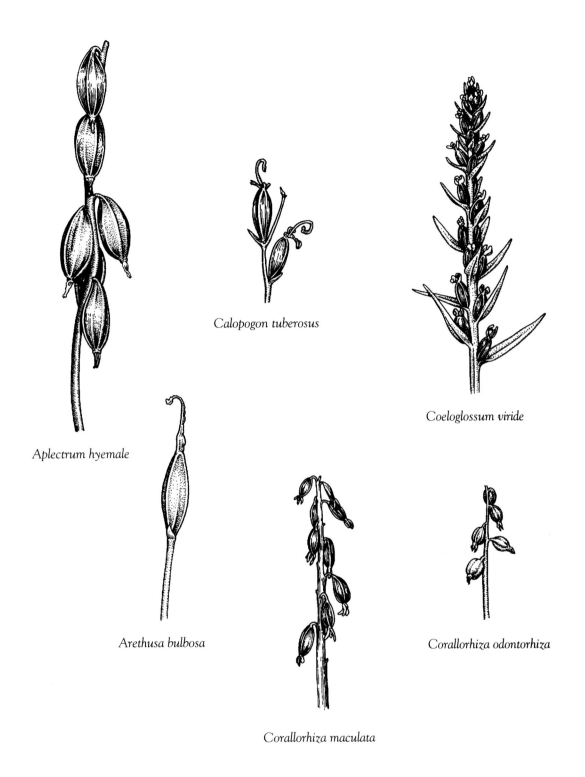

Calopogon tuberosus

Coeloglossum viride

Aplectrum hyemale

Arethusa bulbosa

Corallorhiza odontorhiza

Corallorhiza maculata

FIGURE 4. Capsules of various Indiana orchids,
approximately life size

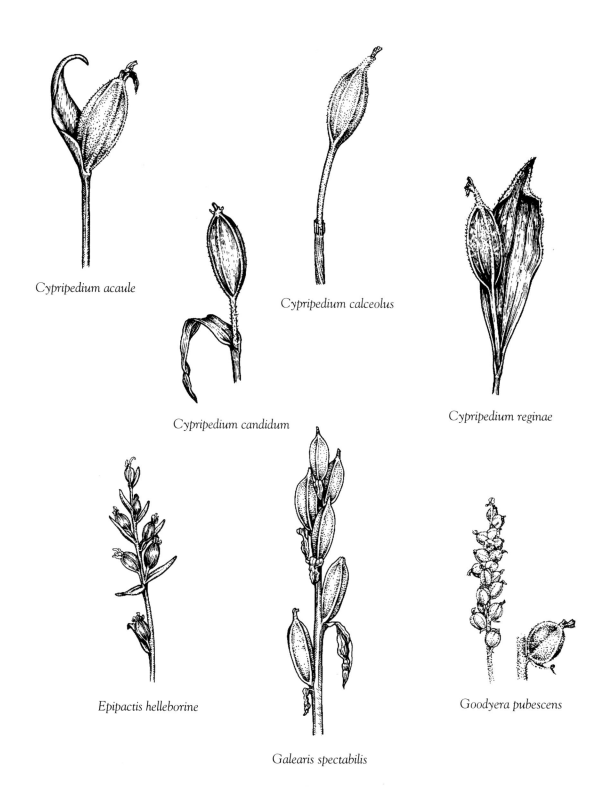

Cypripedium acaule

Cypripedium candidum

Cypripedium calceolus

Cypripedium reginae

Epipactis helleborine

Galearis spectabilis

Goodyera pubescens

FIGURE 4. continued

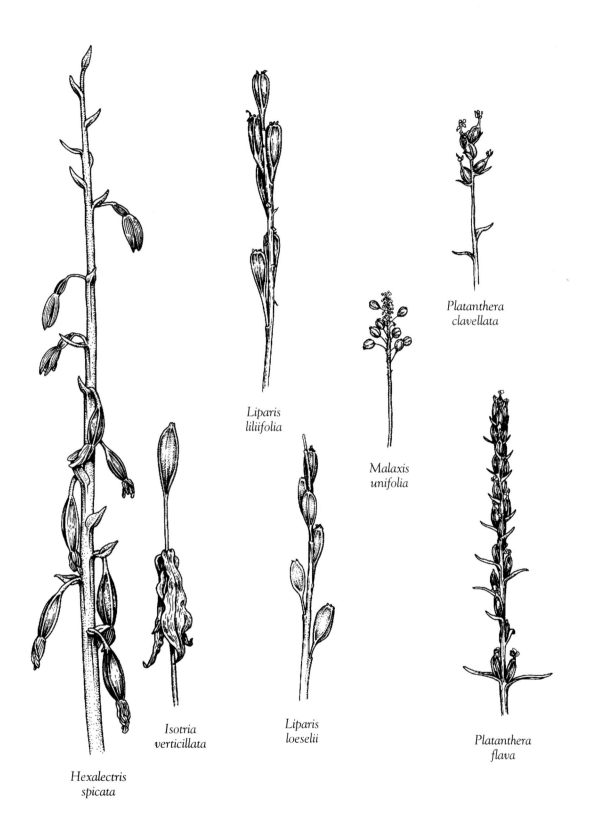

*Liparis
liliifolia*

*Platanthera
clavellata*

*Malaxis
unifolia*

*Liparis
loeselii*

*Isotria
verticillata*

*Platanthera
flava*

*Hexalectris
spicata*

FIGURE 4. continued

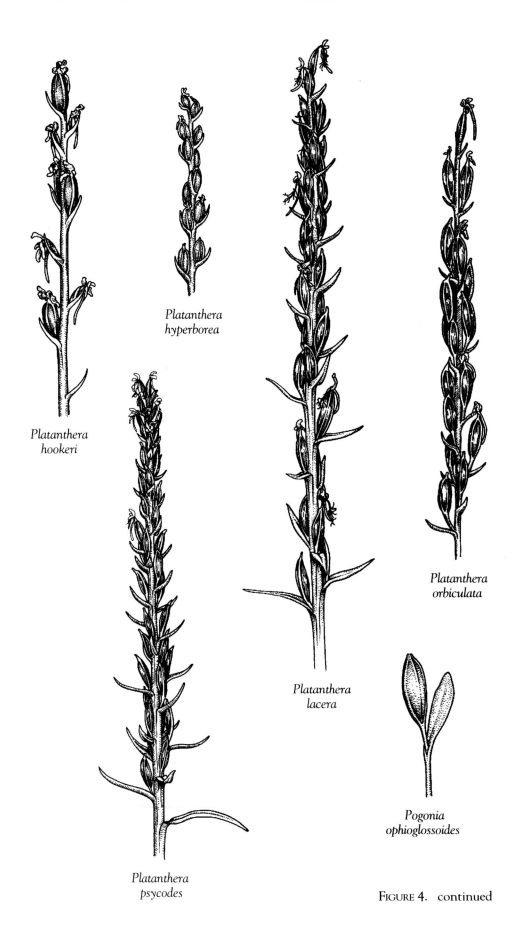

Platanthera
hyperborea

Platanthera
hookeri

Platanthera
orbiculata

Platanthera
lacera

Pogonia
ophioglossoides

Platanthera
psycodes

FIGURE 4. continued

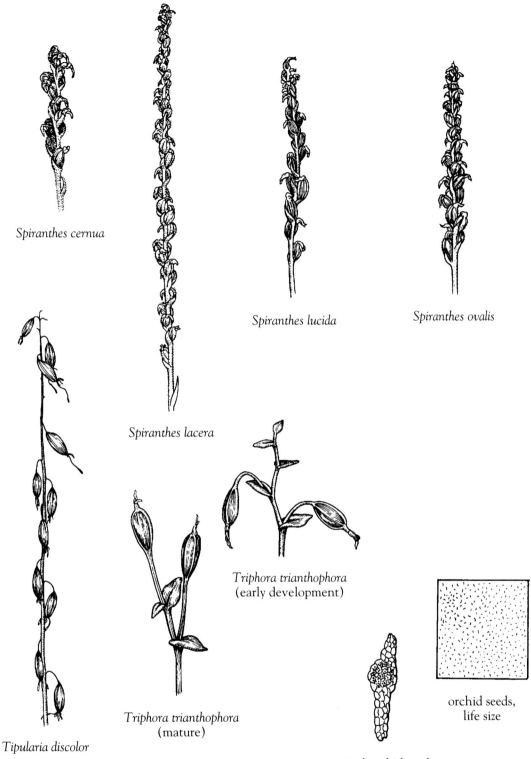

Spiranthes cernua

Spiranthes lucida

Spiranthes ovalis

Spiranthes lacera

Tipularia discolor

Triphora trianthophora
(mature)

Triphora trianthophora
(early development)

typical orchid seed,
greatly enlarged

orchid seeds,
life size

FIGURE 4. continued

ada's orchids are autogamous. *Aplectrum hyemale, Corallorhiza odontorhiza, Liparis loeselii,* and *Spiranthes ovalis* var. *erostellata* are some that belong to this category. In individuals of some species, such as *C. odontorhiza,* autogamy is necessitated by the fact that their flowers do not open, but are fertilized in bud (cleistogamy). In some of the native Indiana orchids, such as *Cypripedium, Goodyera, Isotria,* some *Platanthera,* and *Pogonia,* vegetative reproduction is common. Agamospermy occurs in the various races of *Spiranthes cernua,* and possibly in *Aplectrum* and some *Platanthera* as well.

ORCHID POLLINATION

Although some orchids are self-pollinating (see Orchid Reproduction), the majority are cross-pollinated, and few plants exhibit the contrivances utilized by orchids in the transfer of pollen. Typically, each orchid has a "strategy" to get its pollinia attached to a pollinator's body, relying on certain specific pollinator(s) to execute the process—bees, butterflies, mosquitoes, and a host of other insects are involved. Rarely is it possible, if ever, for an orchid to "exchange" pollinator types. For example, a butterfly-pollinated orchid normally cannot be successfully pollinated by a wasp, nor can a wasp-pollinated flower be pollinated by a butterfly.

There are several pollination scenarios possible among Indiana's variety of orchids, too many to include in this work. The following two examples illustrate orchid pollination in general. The first example depicts the pollination process of diandrous species, which in our state are represented solely by members of the genus *Cypripedium.* The pollination mechanics of monandrous species (which includes all of Indiana's orchids except *Cypripedium*) are typified in the second example, using here *Platanthera psycodes* pollination. The majority of the information presented regarding these two examples comes from Stoutamire (1967, 1974) and Luer (1975). For a synopsis of breeding systems and pollination for all North American orchids, consult Catling and Catling (1991b).

The story of *Cypripedium* pollination is a classic one. It begins when an insect, such as a nectar-seeking bee, enters the slipper through the relatively large opening situated in front of the staminode. Upon discovery that no reward of nectar exists, the bee attempts a departure only to find that exiting via the entry route is difficult, this due to inwardly pointing hairs and an infolded margin at its opening. Facing two options of either perishing or escaping, the bee crawls to the back of the slipper to two small openings positioned on each side of the staminode. The openings allow escape to the outside world (if the bee is not too big), but not before it brushes first against the stigma, and then the anther; from the latter it collects pollen on its head or thorax. Once free, the bee, if not wiser for the experience, will initiate the process again, depositing acquired pollen onto the stigma of the next flower visited, and thus bringing about cross-pollination. Pollination in many species of *Cypripedium* is an uncommon phenomenon, as evidenced by the relatively few capsules present in a population. Stoutamire (1971) pointed out that bumblebees (*Bombus*), after their initial visit to a *C. acaule* flower, quickly learn that no reward is present inside the slipper and thus avoid entering additional flowers, leaving only a few naive bees to carry out the pollination process. Low frequency of capsule production is offset, however, by the great quantities of seed produced.

The means of accomplishing pollen transfer in *Platanthera psycodes* is noticeably different from that of *Cypripedium*. *Platanthera psycodes* lures nectar-seeking pollinators, primarily butterflies and diurnal moths, that are attracted by scent and color. The nectar is located in the spur of the labellum (see Fig. 5). As the insect's proboscis shaft is inserted into the spur, it comes in contact with the sticky viscidium. If a firm contact is made, the viscidium and its connected pollinium are securely cemented to the proboscis. After the moth procures the desired nectar it withdraws its proboscis along with the attached hemipollinarium, and moves to another flower. Following removal of the hemipollinarium a fascinating phenomenon of plant animation occurs. Upon leaving the flower the pollinium and the supporting stalk are positioned vertically on the moth's proboscis, but within 3 to 10 seconds the stalk visibly bends forward to a position horizontal and parallel to the proboscis. This movement favorably positions the pollinium so that upon insertion of the moth's proboscis into the spur of the next flower, the pollinium will be at the correct angle to make contact with the stigma. Without the repositioning the pollinium would collide with the anther, and consequently avert pollination.

PHENOLOGY

Indiana's wild orchids normally bloom within certain specific periods of time during the growing season. But because of variation in environmental

FIGURE 5. Removal of hemipollinarium from *Platanthera psycodes* by a hummingbird clear-wing hawkmoth (*Hemaris thysbe*). The directional movement of the pollinium to the horizontal position occurs within seconds after removal from the column. This movement positions the pollinium for attachment to the stigma of the subsequently visited flower.

factors, especially climate, the blooming period of a given species may be different from one year to the next (consider the drought of 1988, when many orchids apparently did not bloom at all, or were delayed, or the early onset of spring in 1991, when many plants bloomed much earlier than normal). This is true also of individuals within an orchid population, as even slight differences in habitat and exposure may cause one individual to bloom at a time different from others of the same population. For example, individuals of sun-loving species occurring in light shade will normally flower somewhat later than those in full sun. Conversely, shade-loving species may bloom earlier if exposed to an above normal intensity of light (but too great an intensity can cause scorching). These time differences are normally not great, but do provide a greater range of blooming than might occur under homogeneous conditions.

Because of this variability, the flowering chart presented in Table 1 presents a range of blooming dates for a given orchid species. The range reflects a compilation of blooming dates taken from approximately 3,000 herbarium specimens, as well as personal observations of plants in the field. The blooming dates as determined from the above data are indicated by solid circles. The time period indicated by the large circles depicts the flowering dates of the majority of individuals of that species examined. The smaller solid circles represent a flowering period of a lesser number of individuals observed of the species. The latter period is not the most likely time to find prime flowering individuals.

It is evident from the chart that some species bloom over a longer period of time than do others. This disparity between species is the result of a number of factors, including the overall range of a species. Those that have statewide ranges will normally have a greater range of blooming dates than those found only regionally, because of the climatic differences between northern and southern Indiana; individuals of a given species at one end of the state will normally bloom at a time different from those at the other. For example, *Galearis spectabilis* commonly blooms in April and early May in southern Indiana, but may not bloom in northern Indiana until late May or early June. Interestingly, this north-south disparity of blooming is reversed in the autumn-flowering orchids, with the northern populations of a species blooming before the southern ones. This reversal may seem illogical until one realizes that an orchid must have sufficient time to ripen its capsules before the first killing frost, and frost comes earlier in the north.

Another reason for differences in blooming periods is the number of flowers produced by the plant. Unifloral orchids such as *Arethusa bulbosa, Isotria verticillata,* and *Cypripedium* spp. normally do not remain in bloom as long as one possessing 15 to 20 buds that open successively over a period of days, such as in *Spiranthes* spp., *Platanthera* spp., and others.

In some orchids apparent blooming is extended due to the persistence of flowers on the developing ovaries. Although these plants may not technically be "in bloom," in appearance they are, because many of their flower parts are in nearly as good a condition as they were when they first opened. The only visible differences in the older flowers are deteriorated columns,

TABLE 1. Range of Flowering Dates for Orchids of Indiana

Taxon	Apr	May	Jun	Jul	Aug	Sep	Oct	Nov
Aplectrum								
A. hyemale		•••••••	•••					
Arethusa								
A. bulbosa		••••						
Calopogon								
C. tuberosus		•••••	•••••••	••••				
Coeloglossum								
C. viride	••	••••••••	•••					
Corallorhiza								
C. maculata				••••••••	•••••			
C. odontorhiza					•••••••••	••••••	•••	
C. trifida		••••	••••					
C. wisteriana	••••••	•••••						
Cypripedium								
C. acaule		••••	•••••					
C. x andrewsii		•••••						
C. calceolus parviflorum		•••••						
C. calceolus pubescens	••••	•••••						
C. candidum		••••	•••••					
C. reginae		••••	•••••					
Epipactis								
E. helleborine			••••	••••				
Galearis								
G. spectabilis	•••••	••••••••	••					
Goodyera								
G. pubescens				••••••	•••••			
Hexalectris								
H. spicata				•••••	••••••			
Isotria								
I. verticillata		••••••••	••••					
Liparis	?							
L. liliifolia		•••••••	•••••					
L. loeselii		••••	•••••					
Malaxis						?		
M. unifolia			•••••••	••••				
Platanthera								
P. ciliaris				•••••••	••••••			
P. clavellata				•••••	•••••			
P. dilatata		••	•••••					
P. flava flava				••••••••	•••••	•••••		
P. flava herbiola		••••	•••••••					
P. hookeri		•••••	•••••					
P. hyperborea			••••••	•••••				
P. lacera			•••••••	•••••		?		
P. leucophaea			•••••	••••				
P. orbiculata			•••					
P. peramoena				••••••	•••••			
P. psycodes			•••••	•••••				
Pogonia						?		
P. ophioglossoides			•••••••	••••				
Spiranthes								
S. cernua					•••••••	•••••••	•••	
S. lacera (cf. v. lacera)			••••••	•••••••				
S. lacera (cf. v. gracilis)					•••••	•••••	•••	
S. lucida		•••••••	•••					
S. magnicamporum						•••••••	••••••	••
S. ochroleuca						••••••	•••••	
S. ovalis					••••••	•••••		
S. romanzoffiana				••••••	•••••			
S. tuberosa					•••••	•••••		
S. vernalis			•••••••					
Tipularia								
T. discolor				•••••••	•••			
Triphora								
T. trianthophora				••••••••	•••••	•••		

shriveled lips, and swollen ovaries. Apparently these flowers persist because of their fleshiness and possession of at least limited amounts of chlorophyll. Examples of orchids with these traits include *Coeloglossum viride* and *Platanthera flava*.

CLASSIFICATION

The intent of a natural classification scheme is to show relationships between organisms as determined by similarities in genetic and morphological traits. Determining relationships is more difficult than it might sound; it is simply not a matter of stating "If it flies like a duck, walks like a duck, and looks like a duck, then it must be a duck!" Indeed, because of a lack of agreement among scientists on definitive guidelines in segregating taxonomic groups, classification is far from an exact science. As might be expected, several classification schemes have been devised over the years to depict relationships of organisms, and not surprisingly there are many disagreements regarding which scheme is "correct." The classification of orchids is no exception. Ask botanists whether our "rein orchids" should be *Habenaria* or *Platanthera*, and observe the disparity of opinions! Fortunately, there is little disagreement about the taxonomic treatment of the orchids of Indiana's flora, although no classification scheme is free from future revision.

It is far beyond my intent to debate the merits of the various classification schemes. The following arrangement by Dressler (1981) is one of the commonly referenced treatments of the various subgroups within the orchid family. For elaboration on the characters used in defining the various levels of the hierarchy, the reader is referred to Dressler (op. cit.).

PHYLOGENETIC ARRANGEMENT OF INDIANA ORCHIDS

(ADAPTED FROM DRESSLER, 1981)

FAMILY *Orchidaceae*
    SUBFAMILY Cypripedioideae
        GENUS *Cypripedium*
    SUBFAMILY Spiranthoideae
      TRIBE Erythrodeae
        SUBTRIBE Goodyerinae
          GENUS *Goodyera*
      TRIBE Cranichideae
        SUBTRIBE Spiranthinae
          GENUS *Spiranthes*
    SUBFAMILY Orchidoideae
      TRIBE Neottieae
        SUBTRIBE Limodorinae
          GENUS *Epipactis*

TRIBE Orchideae
    SUBTRIBE Orchidinae
        GENERA *Coeloglossum, Galearis, Platanthera*
SUBFAMILY Epidendroideae
    TRIBE Vanilleae
        SUBTRIBE Pogoniinae
            GENERA *Isotria, Pogonia*
    TRIBE Arethuseae
        SUBTRIBE Arethusinae
            GENUS *Arethusa*
        SUBTRIBE Bletiinae
            GENERA *Calopogon, Hexalectris*
    TRIBE Malaxideae
        GENERA *Liparis, Malaxis*
SUBFAMILY Vandoideae
    TRIBE Maxillarieae
        SUBTRIBE Corallorhizinae
            GENERA *Aplectrum, Corallorhiza, Tipularia*
ANOMALOUS TRIBE (as of yet not associated with any subfamily)
    TRIBE Triphoreae
        GENUS *Triphora*

Orchid Ecology and Distribution

Simply put, orchid ecology is the study of orchids in relation to their environment. This is a vast, complex topic, as everything about an orchid's life history involves the orchid and its surroundings. For our purposes here, the discussion will concentrate on the basic environmental requirements of an orchid from germination to adulthood. Readers are referred to other works for in-depth accounts of the subject (see especially Stoutamire, 1974; Withner, 1974; Sheviak, 1974; Luer, 1975; Dressler, 1981; and Case, 1987). The following information was derived from both the above references and the author's knowledge as gained through field experience.

SEEDLING DEVELOPMENT AND MYCORRHIZAE

Determining all of the conditions necessary for a terrestrial orchid to develop from seed to mature plant is one of the greatest challenges to orchidologists. This is particularly evident in our failure to understand the requirements necessary to cultivate successfully these orchids from seed. Orchids produce a great number of seeds; some estimates suggest tens and even hundreds of thousands of seeds per capsule in some species! The seeds are tiny, dust-like packages that, unlike seeds of most plants, lack an endosperm (the stored food available for a seedling's initial growth). Developing orchid embryos and seedlings must therefore get their nutrition from some other source. That source in most cases is decaying organic matter, or in some species, another plant. However, because orchids are incapable of true saprophytism and parasitism (although these terms are commonly used for convenience), their nutrition is provided through mycorrhiza(e), a symbiotic relationship between vascular plants and saprophytic or parasitic fungi. The fungus involved may be one of several taxa; the symbiosis between north temperate orchids and their mycorrhizal fungi is not highly specific (Harley and Smith, 1983). The development of mycorrhiza(e) between orchid and fungus occurs after the orchid embryo is invaded by a non-pathogenic fungal partner. The developing embryo obtains nutrition from the fungal hyphae through the process of digestion (the orchid cells digesting the fungus cells), and in return the orchid is thought to contribute substances to the fungus that it cannot manufacture itself (Withner, 1974). The relationship with the fungus is tenuous at best, however, as the fungus may overtake the developing embryo and act as a pathogen rather than a provider. Actually, the fungus as a pathogen may be the norm, because of the millions of orchid seeds broadcast into the environment each season, only a few develop into mature plants. Although seeds fail to develop for a variety of reasons, many probably succumb to lethal associations with fungi.

THE ENVIRONMENT AND ITS EFFECT ON POPULATION DYNAMICS AND DISTRIBUTION

An established orchid seedling develops properly only if the environment is suitable for the orchid and, perhaps more importantly, the symbiotic fungi. This may seem obvious, but it is not totally understood, as many questions remain unanswered regarding the relationship between orchids, their symbiotic fungi, and their occurrence on the landscape. There are many factors that we can partially understand and measure, however. Soil moisture, nutrients, temperature, light levels, and competition are just a few of the factors that we know are involved in an orchid's success (or lack thereof) at a given site. For this discussion, the most important of these factors can be summarized in two words: *light* and *substrate*. With the exception of a few nonphotosynthetic species, orchids must have light in order to carry out the food-producing process of photosynthesis. This need for light is fundamental; the intensity of light greatly impacts an orchid's vigor, health, and ability to reproduce, and thus its success in the landscape. Light needs differ between species; some plants need long periods of exposure to full sunlight, while others are successful in low light (and in fact may require it). Note: Achlorophyllous (albino) individuals in at least three leafy orchid genera (*Epipactis, Platanthera, Triphora*) have been discovered in North America (Light and MacConaill, 1989). These unusual and sporadically occurring plants obviously have no need for light, apparently getting their nutrition through mycorrhizae.

The importance of light as it relates to the different needs between species is particularly evident in the vegetation dynamics of a site. With soil conditions more or less constant, a given site may yield over time a great diversity of orchid species simply due to the changing light intensities caused by disturbance and succession. For example, an abandoned field, if not swamped by dense growths of early successional weeds, might soon harbor a number of *Spiranthes* species, most notably our most common ladies'-tresses, *S. cernua*. Later, as shrubs and saplings invade and provide shade, other orchids, such as *Liparis liliifolia* and *Spiranthes ovalis* var. *erostellata*, may enter the scene. At this stage *Spiranthes cernua* declines, because too little light reaches it to produce flowering spikes. Eventually, *S. cernua* is unable to capture enough energy to stay alive, and ultimately disappears altogether. As shade levels increase with the appearance of forest trees, *Liparis* and *Spiranthes ovalis* var. *erostellata* also wane, and may be replaced by others such as *Cypripedium calceolus* var. *pubescens* and *Galearis spectabilis*. Normally the latter also lose vigor when a dense forest canopy develops, leaving only nonphotosynthetic orchids and those capable of winter photosynthesis to thrive.

Although light is obviously a significant variable in orchid ecology and distribution, it is substrate that is perhaps the most important determinant in an orchid's presence or absence at a site. Soil, with its associated mycorrhizal fungi, is the "life blood" of terrestrial orchids, and our knowledge of it is fundamental to understanding orchid ecology. The following is a brief discussion of soils as they relate to orchid ecology; the reader is referred to the species accounts for information on soil preferences of specific orchids. A soil's mineral content, pH, moisture content, composition and size of soil particles, degree of organic matter, and temperature all play important roles in satisfying an orchid's needs. Naturally, different species have different soil requirements and tolerances. Even seemingly closely related species may have very different soil requirements. For example, *Platanthera psycodes* occurs in neutral to slightly acidic, highly organic soils saturated with cool ground water, whereas *P. peramoena* prefers rather acidic, low organic silt-loam soils that are only ephemerally wet.

Some species are tolerant of a wide range of soil conditions (e.g., *Spiranthes cernua*), occurring in soils that are dry or wet, organic or nonorganic, acidic or basic. Why some species have very exacting soil requirements and others do not has no simple answer, but the logical conclusion with respect to orchid abundance and distribution is clear. Exacting species are typically more range restricted and generally less common than widely tolerant ones. It is therefore no surprise that *Spiranthes cernua* is perhaps the most common Indiana orchid, while in contrast its relative *S. magnicamporum*, a ladies'-tresses of dry, calcareous substrates only, is one of the rarest.

By learning the soil requirements of an orchid and by knowing the distribution of the soil that satisfies the requirements, one can get a good idea of the range and/or potential range of the species. For example, the crested coral-root orchid (*Hexalectris spicata*) is a strong calciphile occurring only where limestone bedrock crops out at the surface. Not coincidentally, then, *Hexalectris* is restricted to areas of the state with limestone outcrops, thereby eliminating noncalcareous regions as potential for discovery.

EFFECTS OF DISTURBANCE

Contrary to popular belief, orchids are not plants that shun disturbance; in fact, most species appear to require disturbance at some point in their life cycle, and some, particularly the ladies'-tresses, would be quite rare or absent without it. Even the lady's-slippers, plants commonly thought to inhabit only untouched, pristine sites, respond favorably and thrive under certain types of disturbance. Beneficial disturbances to which some orchids favorably respond include partial thinning of a dense tree canopy, small patchy soil disturbance, light browsing and grazing, periodic mowing, and fire.

Obviously not all disturbances are beneficial to orchids. Wholesale conversion of the landscape to agriculture or development certainly is detrimental, although even here if the land is allowed to revegetate naturally, some orchids may soon recolonize. Abandoned sand scrapes, quarries, and old fields are examples of ruderal environments where some orchids thrive. The key word here is "abandoned." Annual soil disturbance, or a substrate buried by concrete, prevents the establishment and growth of orchids.

Disturbance appears to satisfy two primary needs of orchids: preparation of the substrate for seed germination, and reduction of competition for light and nutrients. For example, some orchid seeds apparently do not germinate or develop into seedlings in thick turf or heavy leaf litter, as evidenced by low numbers under such conditions, whereas higher numbers may be evident in similar areas where reductions of the turf or litter have taken place. The dynamics of *Spiranthes lucida* populations exemplify this perfectly. The great majority of individuals that I have encountered occur in fens where the soil has been exposed. In fact, the largest population that I am aware of in Indiana occurs in a fen where soil has been exposed in an old tire rut!

Similarly, greater vigor and reproductive potential (and thus normally greater numbers of individuals) are characteristic of mature plants occurring in areas where competing vegetation has been removed or suppressed. This is quite noticeable in grassland communities where a "flush" of blooming *Spiranthes cernua* may appear after an earlier dormant-season fire.

Disturbance also plays an important role in orchid distribution. Major disturbance, such as total landscape conversion, eliminates available orchid habitat and increases the distance between existing populations and suitable habitat, thereby reducing colonization opportunities. Conversely, mild disturbance has the opposite effect, allowing for range expansions of some species, and enhancing populations of others locally within range. This is most noticeable in the range expansions of *Spiranthes ovalis* var. *erostellata* and *Liparis liliifolia* following the Great Depression, when the two species colonized young regrowth forests on land abandoned by destitute farmers. Were it not for the increased area of these young forests, it is quite likely that these orchids would not be as widespread as they are in Indiana today.

One major historical disturbance that has played an extremely important role in determining orchid distribution is continental glaciation. The reworking of the landscape by those prehistoric ice sheets is a disturbance beyond compare, and we can only speculate what it must have been like during the actual event. Their effect on orchid distribution is without question, however. The orchid habitats present today in the glaciated parts of the state are obviously a direct result of the ice sheets, not only by the glaciers' shaping of the land surface, but also by their impact on drainage, groundwater flow, and soils they left behind.

This is seen clearly in a comparison of the area north and south of the Shelbyville Moraine, the southern terminus of Wisconsinan glaciation. North of the moraine surface soils are principally neutral to alkaline in pH, have a relatively high fertility, and are underlain by deep layers of till composed of great quantities of sand and gravel. Most of the bogs, fens, and sedge meadows are confined to areas north of the moraine. South of the moraine, into either unglaciated terrain or areas of pre-Wisconsinan glaciation, the substrate is quite different, typically having leached, acidic soils of low fertility with little sand or gravel in the subsurface. Few seepage communities are present, and no true bogs or fens are known. Consequently, many orchids, especially those with affinities to the north or south, reach the limit of their range at or near the moraine. Species with northern affinities that occur only north of the moraine (in Indiana) include *Coeloglossum viride*, *Cypripedium reginae*, *Platanthera leucophaea*, *P. psycodes*, and *Pogonia ophioglossoides*. Species confined mostly south of the moraine include *Hexalectris spicata*, *Platanthera flava* var. *flava*, *P. peramoena*, *Spiranthes vernalis*, and *Tipularia discolor*.

Indiana as Orchid Habitat

"Probably as good a place to study or collect hardy Orchids as there is in America, is the low and wet prairies of the Kankakee, Calumet, St. Joseph, and other rivers of Northern Indiana . . . " (L. B. Case, 1881). This quotation illustrates how important Indiana, particularly northern Indiana, once was as orchid habitat. Over a century later, Indiana is one of the most altered landscapes of any state in the U.S., and its national significance for orchid habitat no longer applies. However, with the few existing natural communities in the state, ranging from sphagnum bogs in the northern counties to cypress swamps in the south, Indiana continues to provide a variety of good habitats for orchids. To get an idea of what and where these remaining communities are, the following text and map (Fig. 6) of the natural regions of Indiana (condensed from Homoya et al., 1985), and a list of Indiana's major natural communities and their descriptions, are provided.

Located in the heart of temperate North America, Indiana is generally

FIGURE 6. **The natural regions of Indiana**

EXPLANATION

 1 Lake Michigan Natural Region

 2 Northwestern Morainal Natural Region
A, Valparaiso Moraine Section
B, Chicago Lake Plain Section
C, Lake Michigan Border Section

 3 Grand Prairie Natural Region
A, Grand Prairie Section
B, Kankakee Sand Section
C, Kankakee Marsh Section

 4 Northern Lakes Natural Region

 5 Central Till Plain Natural Region
A, Entrenched Valley Section
B, Tipton Till Plain Section
C, Bluffton Till Plain Section

 6 Black Swamp Natural Region

 7 Southwestern Lowlands Natural Region
A, Plainville Sand Section
B, Glaciated Section
C, Driftless Section

 8 Southern Bottomlands Natural Region

 9 Shawnee Hills Natural Region
A, Crawford Upland Section
B, Escarpment Section

 10 Highland Rim Natural Region
A, Mitchell Karst Plain Section
B, Brown County Hills Section
C, Knobstone Escarpment Section

11 Bluegrass Natural Region
A, Scottsburg Lowland Section
B, Muscatatuck Flats and Canyons Section
C, Switzerland Hills Section

12 Big Rivers Natural Region

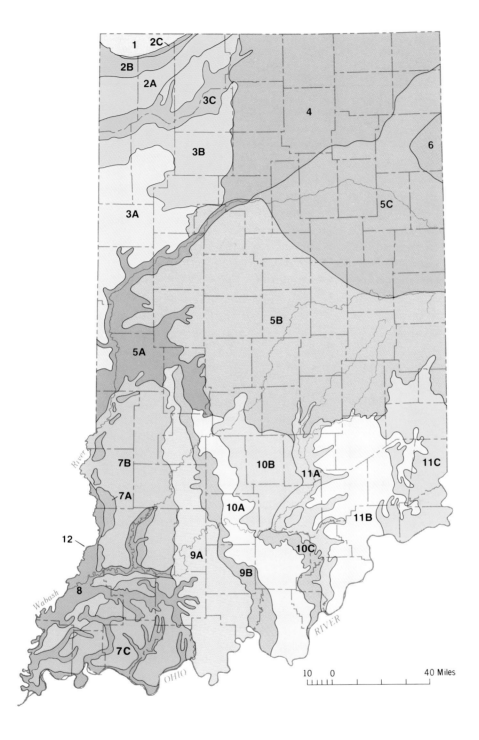

1

2C

2B

2A

3C

4

6

3B

5C

3A

5B

5A

7B

10B

11A

11C

7A

10A

11B

12

9A

10C

8

9B

Wabash River

7C

OHIO

RIVER

10 0   40 Miles

considered a land of level till plains, generous rainfall, and moderate temperatures, and such is indeed true for much of the state. However, Indiana is also a land of diversity, with a surprisingly rich variety of contrasting landforms and vegetation types.

One way to look at Indiana's diversity is to organize the state into large, discrete units and characterize them by the predominant natural features present. These units are called natural regions. There are twelve natural regions recognized in Indiana (see Fig. 6), each identified by a combination of natural features, such as climate, soils, glacial history, topography, exposed bedrock, vegetation, animal life, and physiography. The combination of features differs from region to region. For example, dry upland forest dominated by chestnut oak with a ground layer of painted sedge (*Carex picta*), all overlying Mississippian siltstone, is a common combination that identifies part of a major region of Indiana known as the Highland Rim Natural Region. Although each feature taken separately occurs in other parts of the state, their combination, especially to the extent of coverage of the landscape in which they occur, is distinctive only to the Highland Rim.

Natural regions are composed of landscape units called natural communities. Although natural communities are similar to natural regions in that they are landscape units, they are normally considered on a smaller scale, and oriented to a specific site. They are not as generalized and conceptualized as natural regions; they are reality on the land. A natural community is a group of organisms that are interrelated with each other and their environment (White and Madany, 1978). Important characteristics used to identify natural communities include soil moisture and reaction, substrate, species composition, vegetation structure, and topographic position.

A good example of a natural community that illustrates these features is dry upland forest. The community name quickly provides a considerable amount of information, telling us that the community is dry, that it is on an upland site, and that it has trees. If we include information about soil characteristics, such as texture and parent material, we can, with some field experience, predict the floristic composition of the community. For example, most dry upland forests on limestone in southern Indiana have chinquapin oak, blue ash, red cedar, redbud, southern black haw (*Viburnum rufidulum*), beak grass (*Diarrhena americana*), and yellow pimpernel (*Taenidia integerrima*), among many others. This exercise can be conducted for any natural community type in the state.

The advantages of knowing and recognizing natural communities for the purposes of botanizing for orchids are great. For example, the dry upland forest example mentioned above is an excellent habitat for *Hexalectris spicata*. However, a dry upland forest over sandstone or shale provides a very different environment, better suited for orchids other than *Hexalectris*, such as *Isotria verticillata*.

Knowing within which natural region the dry upland forest is located is also important. Consider again the dry upland forest habitat of *Isotria*. Dry upland forests over sandstone and shale commonly occur in both the Shawnee Hills and Highland Rim natural regions. Interestingly, even though these dry forests generally appear indistinguishable, only the Highland Rim, with one exception, possesses *Isotria*. Why this is so is not clear, but it shows the importance and utility of recognizing natural regions.

The Natural Regions of Indiana

REGION I—LAKE MICHIGAN NATURAL REGION

This natural region consists of the water and lake bed of Lake Michigan. Obviously, no orchids occur there. The lake's presence is nonetheless an important factor in orchid distribution, as the climatic effects produced by its large body of water may be requisite for the occurrence of *Platanthera hookeri* and *Corallorhiza trifida* in the Dunes region. Quite possibly these two orchids would never have occurred in Indiana were it not for the lake's cooling effects on the region's summer temperatures.

REGION II—NORTHWESTERN MORAINAL NATURAL REGION

This natural region was formed in part by the latest advances of the Lake Michigan Lobe of the Wisconsinan ice sheet. Subsequent factors contributing to shaping the landscape include normal erosional processes along with major fluctuations in the pool level of Lake Michigan. It is divided into three sections: the Valparaiso Moraine Section, the Chicago Lake Plain Section, and the Lake Michigan Border Section.

A tremendous diversity of natural communities is present for such a small region; floristically, no other can compare with it, at least on an acre-for-acre basis. This is due in part to the merging of several major vegetation types, these being the eastern deciduous forest, the tall grass prairie, and the northern forest and wetlands. In addition, there is an interesting assemblage of Atlantic Coastal Plain species along with Lake Michigan shoreline endemics. It is certainly one of the best for native orchids, both in numbers and species diversity. It is particularly good for *Cypripedium* spp., *Platanthera* spp., and *Spiranthes* spp. Two orchids known in Indiana from this region only are *Corallorhiza trifida* and *Platanthera hookeri*.

The Valparaiso Moraine Section is a large moraine characterized in part by forested knob-and-kettle topography with beech and sugar maple on the mesic sites, and white oak, black oak, red oak, and shagbark hickory on the drier sites. A gently rolling till plain characterizes other parts of the moraine, where tall-grass prairie was the predominant vegetation. Kettle lakes, fens, bogs, and seep springs are characteristic and important aquatic and wetland communities of the area.

The Chicago Lake Plain Section is identified by the ridge and swale and lacustrine plain topography that occurs between the Valparaiso Moraine and the Lake Michigan Border Section. The Plain is located on the former site of Lake Chicago, and the ridge-and-swale topography is a remnant of water level fluctuations of that glacial lake. Almost all of the natural communities are on acidic sands, although areas of calcareous substrate occur locally. Major natural communities include marsh, lake, oak barrens (savanna), sand prairie, seep spring, and scattered areas of mesic, dry-mesic, and dry forest communities.

The Lake Michigan Border Section consists of a strip of dunes, interdunal ponds (pannes), and beach that borders Lake Michigan. The dunes, some of them quite large, are composed of a mosaic of oak barrens, jack pine barrens, dry to mesic forest of black oak, white oak, red oak, basswood, red maple, and some white pine, and sand prairie. On the windward side of the dunes is a variety of shrubs and herbs tolerant of the strong winds, such as longleaf reedgrass (*Calamovilfa longifolia* var. *magna*), fragrant sumac (*Rhus aromatica*), and common juniper (*Juniperus communis* var. *depressa*). The beach community, an area of shifting sands and periodic flooding, has interesting pioneer species such as sea rocket (*Cakile edentula* var. *lacustris*), beachgrass (*Ammophila breviligulata*), and bug-seed (*Corispermum hyssopifolium*).

REGION III—GRAND PRAIRIE NATURAL REGION

The name "Grand Prairie" is applied in reference to the large expanse of tall-grass prairie that occurred in this region. Unfortunately, virtually all of the prairie is gone today, so it is difficult to describe the natural state of the landscape. Small remnants can still be found along railroad rights-of-way and in nature preserves and other areas protected from agriculture, which give some idea of the region's former glory. Although the Grand Prairie was certainly rich in orchid numbers, it probably was not particularly diverse in species. Orchids that probably were once common include *Cypripedium candidum*, *Platanthera leucophaea*, and possibly *Spiranthes magnicamporum*. Three subsections of the region are recognized: the Grand Prairie Section; the Kankakee Sand Section; and the Kankakee Marsh Section.

The Grand Prairie Section is distinguished by the predominance of rich, loamy soil (as opposed to the sandy and highly organic soils of the remaining sections of the region). This area was the epitome of the vast tall-grass prairie of presettlement times. From its remnants it appears that some characteristic plants included leadplant (*Amorpha canescens*), little bluestem (*Andropogon scoparius*), big bluestem (*Andropogon gerardii*), rattlesnake master (*Eryngium yuccifolium*), yellow coneflower (*Ratibida pinnata*), compass plant (*Silphium laciniatum*), prairie dock (*S. terebinthinaceum*), prairie goldenrod (*Solidago rigida*), Indian grass (*Sorghastrum nutans*), and many others.

The Kankakee Sand Section is characterized by the presence of prairie and oak barrens community types associated with sandy soil. The soil consists mostly of acidic dune sand and outwash plain sediments. Although many of the plants present also occur in the Grand Prairie Section, several are confined mostly to the sandy substrates found in this section. These include longleaf reedgrass (*Calamovilfa longifolia* var. *magna*), June grass (*Koeleria pyramidata*), hairy puccoon (*Lithospermum caroliniense*), lupine (*Lupinus perennis*), fame flower (*Talinum rugospermum*), and primrose violet (*Viola primulifolia*). A remarkable assemblage of coastal plain disjuncts also occurs in this section, especially in the wet swales. Examples include flax (*Linum intercursum*), bugleweed (*Lycopus amplectens*), panic grass (*Panicum verrucosum*), nutrush (*Scleria reticularis*), and bladderwort (*Utricularia radiata*).

The Kankakee Marsh Section is identified by the predominance of marsh, lake, and wet prairie communities that previously existed along the Kankakee River. This complex of communities was formerly quite extensive, extending for several miles on both sides of the river for most of its length in Indiana. Little is left today. Plants typical of marsh and wet prairie that probably occurred commonly in the area include blue joint grass (*Calamagrostis canadensis*), swamp loosestrife (*Decodon verticillatus*), spatterdock (*Nuphar advena*), reed canary grass (*Phalaris arundinacea*), hardstemmed bulrush (*Scirpus acutus*), giant bur-reed (*Sparganium eurycarpum*), and prairie cord grass (*Spartina pectinata*).

REGION IV—NORTHERN LAKES NATURAL REGION

This natural region is identified by the presence of numerous fresh-water lakes of glacial origin. It is covered with a thick deposit of glacial material which, in places, is over 450 feet thick. The topography is complex, characterized by knobs, kettles, kames, valley trains, and out-wash plains. Much of the surface is quite sandy and gravelly. Many types of natural communities, especially wetlands, are present, including bog, fen, marsh, prairie, sedge meadow, swamp, seep spring, and lake. Bog, fen, and marsh communities are more numerous here than in any other natural region. Various deciduous forest types compose the upland sites. Oak and hickory species dominate the dry and dry-mesic upland forests, while the mesic sites have American beech, sugar maple, black maple, and tulip tree.

The Northern Lakes region is exceptionally favorable for orchids, especially the wetland species, such as *Calopogon tuberosus*, *Liparis loeselii*, *Platanthera hyperborea*, *Platanthera psycodes*, and *Pogonia ophioglossoides*.

REGION V—CENTRAL TILL PLAIN NATURAL REGION

This natural region is the largest in the state. It spans most of central Indiana between Illinois and Ohio from the Wabash and Eel rivers south to the extent of Wisconsinan glaciation along the Shelbyville Moraine. Except for a section in the western part, it is relatively flat, consisting of a formerly forested till plain composed of flatwoods, ephemeral swamps, and mesic upland forest. Additional communities, particularly wetland types, occur along river valleys. Three sections compose the natural region: Entrenched Valley Section; Tipton Till Plain Section; and Bluffton Till Plain Section.

With respect to orchids, the Central Till Plain, with the exception of the Entrenched Valley Section, is not particularly noteworthy. Because of the region's location in the middle of the state, it is more of a "melting pot" of orchid distribution than are the other regions; no orchid species are confined exclusively to it.

The Entrenched Valley Section is quite unlike the other sections. It consists primarily of deeply entrenched valleys with steep, forested slopes and, in places, massive cliffs composed of sandstone and, to a lesser extent, limestone. Because of the topographic diversity caused by the entrenchment, many natural communities are present, including cliffs, hill prairies, seep springs, fens, and numerous forest types (but predominantly beech/sugar maple/red oak forest). The community diversity allows a great variety of plants to occur in this section, many of which are at the edges of their ranges, particularly from the south or north. Of special interest are the northern disjuncts, such as eastern hemlock, white pine, northern enchanter's nightshade (*Circaea alpina*), large-leaved shinleaf (*Pyrola elliptica*), and Canada yew (*Taxus canadensis*). Of the orchids, *Coeloglossum viride* and *Triphora trianthophora* occur in this section possibly in greater numbers than elsewhere in the state.

The Tipton Till Plain Section is a broad, relatively flat area formerly covered by an extensive beech-maple-oak forest. It is naturally poorly drained, with a substrate of neutral silt and silty-clay loams. Red maple, pin oak, bur oak, swamp white oak, Shumard oak, American elm, and green ash are important trees in the ephemerally wet depressions, whereas American beech, sugar maple, white oak, red oak, shagbark hickory, tulip tree, and white ash are characteristic of the better drained sites. With the exception of a few woodland species, most of this section is not particularly good for orchids.

The Bluffton Till Plain Section is similar in all respects to the Tipton Till Plain, except that in the former a predominance of clay-rich soils produced greater areas of swampland and poorly drained flatwoods. Also, because of its more northerly location, greater numbers of species with northern affinities occur or did occur in the Bluffton Till Plain, including *Platanthera orbiculata*.

REGION VI—BLACK SWAMP NATURAL REGION

This is the western lobe of a large lacustrine plain named the Black Swamp by early settlers. Formerly covered by ancient Lake Maumee, a predecessor of modern Lake Erie, it is now an almost featureless, naturally poorly drained level plain. The predominant natural community in the region consisted of swamp forest dominated by American elm, black ash, and red and silver maple. Because of extensive drainage and conversion of the landscape to agriculture, this and other natural community types are now virtually nonexistent. Consequently, this small region is poor for orchids.

REGION VII—SOUTHWESTERN LOWLANDS NATURAL REGION

This region is typified by low relief and extensive, poorly drained valleys. Because of these physical characteristics most of the area's natural communities are wetlands or floodplain forests. The region is much more diverse, however, as a variety of upland community types also are present, particularly in the unglaciated section where the terrain is rather hilly and well drained. The range of diversity is apparent in the region's three sections, the Plainville Sand Section, the Glaciated Section, and the Driftless Section.

The region is average to good in terms of orchid diversity and abundance. It was certainly much higher before the destruction of its many wetlands and grassland communities. Some orchids that can still be found with consistency include *Corallorhiza wisteriana*, *Liparis liliifolia*, *Platanthera peramoena*, and *Spiranthes cernua*.

The Plainville Sand Section consists of small, scattered areas of dunes composed of windblown sand. Historically, these dunes were covered with barrens vegetation, but today the barrens are completely gone save for a few strips along railroad rights-of-way. Many species that occurred in the barrens were disjuncts, some considerably so, viz., clustered poppy-mallow (*Callirhoe triangulata*), sand hickory (*Carya pallida*), beard grass (*Gymnopogon ambiguus*), and slender marsh pink (*Sabatia campanulata*).

The Glaciated Section, the largest in area of the sections of the region, coincides with the Illinoian till plain of southwestern Indiana. This section has the least relief of the sections in the region, as the ice sheet leveled elevated landforms and filled valleys with till. In addition, the surface has been mantled with a layer of loess. Most natural communities are forest types, although several types of prairie occurred historically. Much of the landscape was wet, with swamps, marshes, wet prairie, and wet flatwoods abounding. Some of the typical lowland hardwood species still present include shellbark hickory, pin oak, shingle oak, hackberry, green ash, red maple, and silver maple. The upland forest communities generally consist of species found throughout the state.

The Driftless Section occurs south of the Illinoian glacial border, and is thus characterized by areas of greater relief than in the other sections. Most of the communities are upland forest types, occurring on slopes composed of loess and weathered sandstone and shale. Most of the upland forest tree species are the same as those throughout the region, but some more important here than elsewhere include southern red oak, post oak, blackjack oak, and, locally, chestnut oak. Flatwoods dominated by post oak are confined in Indiana to this section, as is a type of flat barrens that possesses a peculiar mix of xeric and wetland species, e.g., rushfoil (*Crotonopsis elliptica*) and blackfooted quillwort (*Isoetes melanopoda*).

REGION VIII—SOUTHERN BOTTOMLANDS NATURAL REGION

This natural region is composed of alluvial bottomlands along rivers and larger streams of southwestern Indiana. It is distinguished from other bottomland regions in the state by the high incidence of species with affinities to the lower Mississippi Valley and Gulf Coastal Plain. These species and the communities in which they are found give a distinctive southern aspect to the landscape. The strongest southern influence is reflected in the swamps and sloughs, where bald cypress, swamp cottonwood, water locust, pumpkin ash, and overcup oak occur. Southern species of the bottomland forests include pecan, sugarberry, catalpa, giant cane (*Arundinaria gigantea*), social sedge (*Carex socialis*), swamp privet (*Forestiera acuminata*), spiderlily (*Hymenocallis caroliniana*), bloodleaf (*Iresine rhizomatosa*), and catbird grape (*Vitis palmata*).

This region is only fair for orchids, since alluvial floodplain forests are not particularly good orchid habitats. Some exceptions are *Platanthera flava* var. *flava* and *Platanthera peramoena*.

REGION IX—SHAWNEE HILLS NATURAL REGION

This natural region consists of a rugged, essentially contiguous belt of hills with bedrock of Pennsylvanian and Mississippian strata (mostly sandstone and limestone) cropping out to form distinctive cliffs and rockhouses. The majority of natural communities are forest types, although a few sandstone and limestone glades, gravel washes, seep springs, and barrens are known. The two sections of the natural region are the Crawford Upland Section and the Escarpment Section.

The rugged nature of the region and its relative lack of major disturbance make it a good one for orchids. Orchids that are particularly prevalent or primarily restricted here include, among others, *Aplectrum hyemale*, *Goodyera pubescens*, *Liparis liliifolia*, *Spiranthes cernua*, *S. ovalis* var. *erostellata*, *S. tuberosa*, *S. vernalis*, and *Tipularia discolor*.

The most distinctive features of the Crawford Upland Section are the rugged hills draped with sandstone cliffs and rockhouses. These rock environments provide an environment for several species with Appalachian affinities, e.g., mountain spleenwort (*Asplenium montanum*), mountain laurel (*Kalmia latifolia*), umbrella magnolia (*Magnolia tripetala*), sourwood (*Oxydendrum arboreum*), and Allegheny spurge (*Pachysandra procumbens*). The forest communities are quite diverse, consisting of an oak-hickory assortment on the upper slopes, with the coves having a mesic component similar to the mixed mesophytic forests of the Cumberland Plateau as defined by Braun (1950).

The Escarpment Section includes the rugged hills situated along the eastern border of the region. In a way, the section is a blend of sections from two natural regions; the Crawford Upland of the Shawnee Hills, and the Mitchell Karst Plain of the Highland Rim. Sandstone caps most of the hills, creating environments similar to the Crawford Upland, while at lower elevations limestone is predominant, harboring many of the species found on the Mitchell Karst Plain. As a consequence of the section's mix of geology, it is extremely diverse in communities and species. In addition to the cliffs and many forest types, limestone glades, barrens, gravel washes, and caves also are present.

This natural region occupies, in part, the Highland Rim physiographic region of the Interior Low Plateaus. The underlying strata are predominantly Mississippian, although some Pennsylvanian rock crops out in places. The region is large and rugged, especially in the eastern sections, but cliffs are less common than in the Shawnee Hills. Most of the Highland Rim consisted of upland forest historically, but a large area of barrens occurred as well, particularly in central Harrison and Washington counties. Three distinct sections are recognized for the region: the Mitchell Karst Plain Section; the Brown County Hills Section; and the Knobstone Escarpment Section. Because of the diversity of natural communities, as well as the relative lack of disturbance, this natural region is a good one for orchids. In addition to the typical species of statewide distribution and those of the Shawnee Hills, this region has *Malaxis unifolia* and *Spiranthes ochroleuca*.

The major feature of the Mitchell Karst Plain Section is the karst (sinkhole) plain. Several natural community types are associated with this plain, including cave, sinkhole pond and swamp, flatwoods, chert barrens, limestone glade, and several upland forest types. The plain is relatively level and rolling, although in some areas, especially near the section's periphery, limestone cliffs and rugged hills are present. Soils vary in pH and nutrients, but most are acidic (except near the limestone outcrops). Possibly the largest area of chert barrens in Indiana was located in this section, but only a few acres remain. Sinkhole ponds and swamps also are present, providing contrast to the dry conditions of the barrens.

The Brown County Hills Section is characterized by deeply dissected uplands underlain by siltstone, shale, and sandstone. The bedrock is near the surface but rarely crops out. The soils are typically acid in reaction. The natural communities are rather uniform in composition; the ravines and lower slopes are dominated by mesic species; e.g., American beech, red oak, and white ash, and the upper slopes have an almost pure stand of oak, particularly chestnut oak. The chestnut oak slopes characteristically have a thick growth of green brier (*Smilax rotundifolia*), low growing shrubs (*Gaylussacia baccata* and *Vaccinium pallidum*), and a carpet of sedges, notably *Carex picta*.

The Knobstone Escarpment Section is similar in terms of substrate and topography, but is distinguished by floristic, faunistic, and compositional differences of the forest communities. Major differences are the presence of Virginia pine, as well as generally drier, harsher conditions on the upper slopes of the rugged hills. Rock outcrops are few, but glades of exposed siltstone occur locally on steep, south-facing slopes. Xeric forests of blackjack oak, chestnut oak, and scarlet oak typically border the glades. Species known from this section but not elsewhere include a species of bluegrass (*Poa cuspidata*), Harvey's buttercup (*Ranunculus harveyi*), and stout goldenrod (*Solidago squarrosa*).

This natural region is identified and named not for a predominance of bluegrass (*Poa* spp.), but for the similarities of the physiography and natural communities of the region to the Bluegrass region of Kentucky. The region's surface topography, although formerly glaciated, is influenced primarily by bedrock topography, and hence further similarity to the Kentucky Bluegrass. Limestone and calcareous shale are the principal bedrock types present. Most of the natural region was originally forested, although a few glade, cliff, and barrens communities are known, as well as non-forested aquatic communities. The three sections of the Bluegrass Natural Region are the Switzerland Hills Section, the Muscatatuck Flats and Canyons Section, and the Scottsburg Lowland Section.

Even though much of the landscape is greatly altered, this region is fairly good for orchids. Some of the more interesting and uncommon are *Isotria verticillata*, *Platanthera flava* var. *flava*, and *Spiranthes lucida*. *Corallorhiza wisteriana* and *Spiranthes ovalis* var. *erostellata* are possibly more common in this natural region than in others.

The Scottsburg Lowland Section consists primarily of wide alluvial and lacustrine plains bordering the major streams of the section, namely the Muscatatuck River, East Fork of the White River, Silver Creek, and their tributaries. Hills and bedrock outcroppings are rare. Predominant natural communities are floodplain forest and swamp, although areas of upland forest occur locally. The swamp community is characterized by the occurrence of swamp cottonwood, red maple, pin oak, river birch, and green ash. The slightly better drained floodplain forest adds sweetgum, swamp chestnut oak, swamp white oak, American elm, black gum, American beech, shellbark hickory, and, rarely, pecan. Characteristic herbs include *Carex louisianica*, *C. muskingumensis*, common wood reed (*Cinna arundinacea*), Virginia day flower (*Commelina virginica*), and lizard's tail (*Saururus cernuus*).

The Muscatatuck Flats and Canyons Section consists primarily of a broad, relatively flat west-sloping plain with steep-walled canyons entrenched by major streams. The plain is best characterized by the presence of poorly drained flatwoods with a substrate of acidic silt-loam soils. These flatwoods typically have American beech, red maple, sweetgum, pin oak, swamp chestnut oak, swamp white oak, black gum, and tulip tree. The canyons feature steep slopes and cliffs of Silurian and Devonian limestone that provide an environment quite unlike the flats. These sites are comparatively rich floristically, having a predominantly mixed mesophytic forest composition. Special species of communities within the canyons include crinkleroot (*Cardamine diphylla*), American pennywort (*Hydrocotyle americana*), *Spiranthes lucida*, and sullivantia (*Sullivantia sullivantii*).

Deeply dissected uplands composed of Ordovician calcareous shale and limestone characterize the Switzerland Hills Section. Although the region is glaciated, deposits of till are generally thin or absent. Bedrock is near the surface, but cliffs are rare. Most of the natural communities are forested, although a few barrens remnants are known. The mixed mesophytic forest type is well represented, especially in the ravines. Tree species are basically the same as for mesic forests over much of the state, but add (although local) yellow buckeye and white basswood.

This region consists of those rivers (or portions of rivers) where the average flow is 7,000 cubic feet per second or greater. This includes all of the Ohio River bordering Indiana, the White River up to the confluence of its two forks, and the Wabash River from its mouth to near Attica in Fountain County. Because this natural region is an entirely aquatic one, it is not utilized by orchids. However, these rivers have over long periods of time entrenched the adjacent landscape, providing habitat and corridors for orchids to grow and migrate.

A Partial Listing of Natural Communities of Indiana

The following are brief descriptions of the principal natural communities that occur in Indiana. The classification scheme and most community names are from White and Madany's (1978) descriptions for Illinois, with some modifications to conform to the author's interpretation of communities in the Indiana landscape. Strictly aquatic communities have been omitted, as have caves and other primary communities that have few or no orchids.

To help one understand where natural communities occur with respect to one another in the landscape, and what orchids utilize them, a profile sketch of a hypothetical landscape is illustrated in Figures 7a and 7b.

FOREST COMMUNITIES

Forests are tree-dominated communities. They occur on a variety of soil types and landforms, and formerly occupied more than three-quarters of Indiana's landscape. Except in rugged, untillable areas, most of the forest has been cleared for agriculture. Forest environments are extremely important to many of our orchids, especially those species in southern Indiana, where open wetland and prairie habitats have always been uncommon.

UPLAND FOREST

Upland forests are well-drained, tree-dominated communities, situated away from wetlands and the zone of flooding of adjacent watercourses. There are three major types.

Dry Upland Forest. This community is excessively drained, resulting in generally small tree growth and the presence of species adapted to drought. Characteristic species include black oak, scarlet oak, post oak, blackjack oak, chestnut oak, pignut hickory, poverty grass (*Danthonia spicata*), hairy

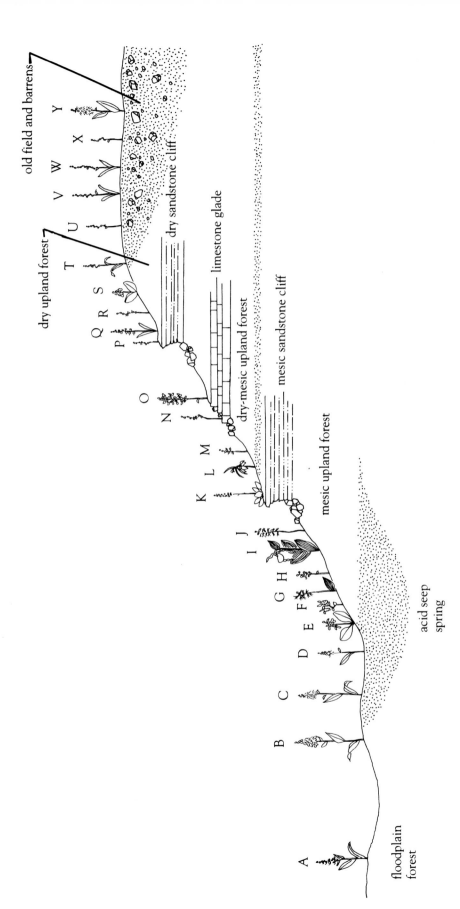

FIGURE 7a. Profile of a hypothetical natural community arrangement in southern Indiana. The orchids illustrated are placed in the natural community where they characteristically occur. A) *Platanthera flava* var. *flava*; B) *Platanthera peramoena*; C) *Platanthera lacera*; D) *Platanthera clavellata*; E) *Galearis spectabilis*; F) *Triphora trianthophora*; G) *Aplectrum hyemale*; H) *Corallorhiza wisteriana*; I) *Cypripedium calceolus* var. *pubescens*; J) *Tipularia discolor*; K) *Goodyera pubescens*; L) *Isotria verticillata*; M) *Corallorhiza odontorhiza*; N) *Spiranthes magnicamporum*; O) *Hexalectris spicata*; P) *Spiranthes tuberosa*; Q) *Spiranthes cernua*; R) *Spiranthes lacera*; S) *Liparis liliifolia*; T) *Spiranthes ovalis*; U) *Spiranthes lacera*; V) *Spiranthes ochroleuca*; W) *Spiranthes cernua*; X) *Spiranthes tuberosa*; Y) *Platanthera lacera*

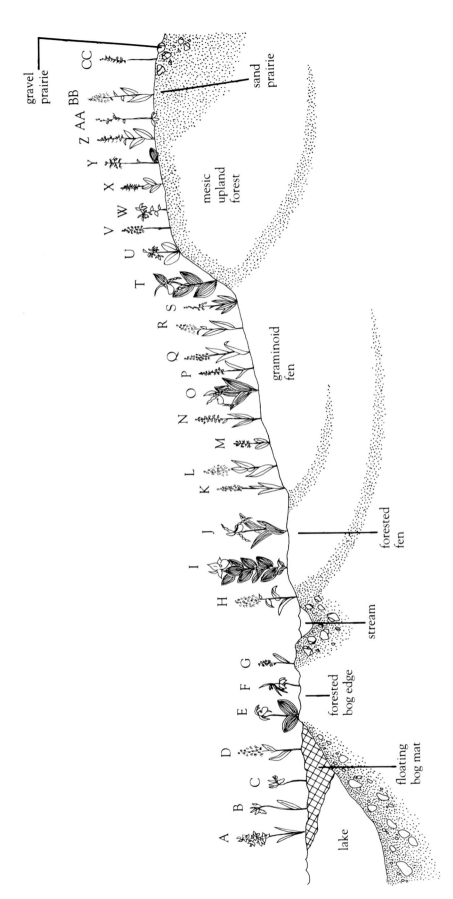

Figure 7b. Profile of a hypothetical natural community arrangement in northern Indiana. The orchids illustrated are placed in the natural community where they characteristically occur. A) *Calopogon tuberosus*; B) *Pogonia ophioglossoides*; C) *Arethusa bulbosa*; D) *Platanthera ciliaris*; E) *Cypripedium acaule*; F) *Isotria verticillata*; G) *Platanthera clavellata*; H) *Platanthera psycodes*; I) *Cypripedium calceolus* var. *parviflorum*; K) *Platanthera hyperborea*; L) *Platanthera leucophaea*; M) *Liparis loeselii*; N) *Spiranthes romanzoffiana*; O) *Cypripedium candidum*; P) *Spiranthes cernua*; Q) *Platanthera dilatata*; R) *Platanthera lacera*; S) *Spiranthes lucida*; T) *Cypripedium calceolus* var. *pubescens*; U) *Galearis spectabilis*; V) *Corallorhiza maculata*; W) *Triphora trianthophora*; X) *Coeloglossum viride*; Y) *Aplectrum hyemale*; Z) *Platanthera flava* var. *herbiola*; AA) *Spiranthes lacera*; BB) *Platanthera lacera*; CC) *Spiranthes magnicamporum*

bushclover (*Lespedeza hirta*) and late low blueberry (*Vaccinium pallidum*). Orchids include *Corallorhiza odontorhiza, Hexalectris spicata, Isotria verticillata, Spiranthes cernua, S. ochroleuca,* and *S. tuberosa.*

Dry-mesic Forest. Not as excessively drained as a dry forest, this community usually has better soil development. Characteristic species include white oak, red oak, white ash, shagbark hickory, flowering dogwood, hop hornbeam, bare-stemmed tick trefoil (*Desmodium nudiflorum*), woodland sunflower (*Helianthus divaricatus*), Christmas fern (*Polystichum acrostichoides*), and blue-stemmed goldenrod (*Solidago caesia*). Characteristic orchids are *Corallorhiza wisteriana, Cypripedium calceolus* var. *pubescens, Isotria verticillata, Liparis liliifolia,* and *Tipularia discolor.*

Mesic Upland Forest. Moist soils richly endowed with humus are characteristic in this type. American beech, sugar maple, tulip tree, red oak, American basswood, bladdernut, wild ginger (*Asarum canadense*), glade fern (*Athyrium pycnocarpon*), waterleaf (*Hydrophyllum* spp.), and trillium (*Trillium* spp.) are typical species of mesic forests. Notable orchids include *Aplectrum hyemale, Corallorhiza wisteriana, Cypripedium calceolus* var. *pubescens, Galearis spectabilis,* and *Triphora trianthophora.*

FLOODPLAIN FOREST

Floodplain forests are forest communities that are periodically inundated by overflow from streams and rivers. Three basic kinds of floodplain forests can be identified, these separated by the degree and duration of flooding. Soils may be composed of silty alluvium or outwash sand, the latter generally more favorable for orchid growth.

Wet Floodplain Forest. The most frequently flooded and closest in distance to the watercourse, wet floodplain forests are typically dominated by sycamore, cottonwood, silver maple, and box elder. Wood nettle (*Laportea canadensis*) and poison ivy (*Rhus radicans*) also are important. This community normally does not have orchids, with the exception of a few individuals of *Platanthera peramoena* or *P. flava.*

Wet-mesic Floodplain Forest. This forest normally occurs on the first terrace beyond the wet floodplain forest. Not inundated for as long as wet floodplain forest, it is better drained and hosts a greater diversity of species, including pin oak, swamp white oak, sweetgum, black gum, green ash, American elm, red elm, hackberry, spicebush, spike grass (*Chasmanthium latifolium*), common wood reed (*Cinna arundinacea*), honewort (*Cryptotaenia canadensis*), and golden ragwort (*Senecio aureus*). As in the wet floodplain, few orchids are present. For one orchid, *Platanthera peramoena*, wetmesic floodplain is the preferred habitat. *Platanthera flava* and *Spiranthes ovalis* var. *erostellata* also are known from this community.

Mesic Floodplain Forest. Mesic forest exists on the highest terraces in the floodplain. It is not greatly different from mesic upland forest, but gets flooded periodically (not necessarily every year). American beech, black walnut, tulip tree, red oak, red elm, blue beech, spicebush, white trout lily (*Ery-*

Mesic upland forest, Putnam Co. Lee Casebere.

thronium albidum), waterleaf (*Hydrophyllum* spp.), blue phlox (*Phlox divaricata*), and May apple (*Podophyllum peltatum*) are just a few of the characteristic species present. Mesic floodplains are good habitats for mesic woodland orchids, such as *Galearis spectabilis* and *Triphora trianthophora*, and are especially favorable for *Aplectrum hyemale*, as extensive colonies may be found in such environments.

Flatwoods are level or nearly level forest communities. They are typically poorly drained and commonly possess ephemeral pools during wet seasons. The poor drainage creates an environment somewhat like a floodplain forest, and in fact many floodplain species are in flatwoods as well. The slightly elevated areas between ponded areas are usually mesic, although there are local areas (in southwestern Indiana) that are exceptionally dry. Flatwoods are most common on till plains, lacustrine plains, and former floodplains long abandoned. Many orchid species occur in flatwoods environments, but none are unique to them. Basically those orchids found in mesic forests and floodplains are found in flatwoods.

PRAIRIE COMMUNITIES

Prairie communities are natural grasslands devoid of significant tree and shrub growth. They are typically diverse communities with a high percentage of forbs, particularly members of the Asteraceae. Prairie was most prevalent in northwestern Indiana but occurred throughout the state in localized areas. There are three basic types of prairie in Indiana: dry, mesic, and wet. Dry-mesic and wet-mesic types also are present, these intermediate between the aforementioned types. Substrates range from silt-loam to sand, the differences between them in places resulting in marked differences in species composition. Areas where prairie grades into forest are called savannas. Depending on the site, savannas are predominantly prairie vegetation with widely spaced trees. Bur oak was the predominant tree in the mesic savannas, whereas black oak occurred in the drier prairies. Almost all of Indiana's prairies and savannas are gone, having been converted to agriculture.

Dry Prairie. This excessively drained community occurs primarily on substrates of sand and gravel, but also may occur on silt-loam if situated on steep slopes. Little bluestem (*Andropogon scoparius*), side-oats grama (*Bouteloua curtipendula*), fall witch grass (*Leptoloma cognatum*), and porcupine grass (*Stipa spartea*) are characteristic dominants. As moisture increases additional species appear, including lead plant (*Amorpha canescens*), western sunflower (*Helianthus occidentalis*), blazing stars (*Liatris aspera* and *L. scariosa*) and Indian grass (*Sorghastrum nutans*), among others. Orchids are not common in dry and dry-mesic prairie, although some *Spiranthes* do well in them, particularly *S. magnicamporum*.

Mesic Prairie. Mesic prairie communities occur on moist but well-drained sites and possess a high diversity of species, particularly forbs. Some of the major species include big bluestem (*Andropogon gerardii*), little bluestem (*A. scoparius*), rattlesnake master (*Eryngium yuccifolium*), downy sunflower (*Helianthus mollis*), hoary puccoon (*Lithospermum canescens*), rosin weed (*Silphium integrifolium*), prairie dock (*S. terebinthinaceum*), stiff goldenrod (*Solidago rigida*), and Indian grass (*Sorghastrum nutans*). A greater diversity of orchids occurs in the mesic (and wet-mesic) prairie than in any of the other types, especially if the prairie is on sand. Some of these orchids are *Calopogon tuberosus, Cypripedium candidum, Liparis loeselii, Platanthera flava* var. *herbiola, P. lacera, P. leucophaea, Spiranthes cernua,* and *S. lacera.*

Wet Prairie. Wet prairies occur on soils saturated for most of the year. They are not particularly diverse, being dominated primarily by blue joint grass (*Calamagrostis canadensis*) and prairie cordgrass (*Spartina pectinata*). Associated forbs include New England aster (*Aster novae-angliae*), blue flag (*Iris virginica*), marsh phlox (*Phlox glaberrima*), and Culver's root (*Veronicastrum virginicum*). Wet prairies are generally not important orchid habitats, except where hummocks rise above the saturated zone to provide better drainage.

BARRENS COMMUNITIES

Barrens are excessively drained landscapes where drought is the principal factor responsible in the manifestation of vegetation present. As a consequence of drought, the vegetation is relatively sparse, and consists only of those species adapted to or tolerant of such conditions. Succulence, heavy pubescence, reduced leaf surface, thick cuticles, deep root systems, gnarled stems, and ephemeral appearance are just some of the adaptations that allow plants to occur in the harsh conditions. Characteristic barrens species include little bluestem (*Andropogon scoparius*), puccoon (*Lithospermum caroliniense*), prickly pear cactus, (*Opuntia humifusa*), bracken fern (*Pteridium aquilinum*), oak species (especially *Quercus coccinea, Q. marilandica, Q. stellata,* and *Q. velutina*), and fame flower (*Talinum rugospermum*). Barrens are typically sunny environments, but may possess some shade due to the presence of stunted trees and shrubs. Barrens occur on sites composed of sand, bedrock (commonly called glades), and gravel, and on finer soils where a fragipan occurs at or near the surface. Barrens are important environments for *Hexalectris* and *Spiranthes,* viz., *S. cernua, S. lacera, S. magnicamporum, S. ochroleuca, S. tuberosa,* and *S. vernalis.*

WETLAND COMMUNITIES

Wetlands are communities that are flooded or have saturated soils for most of the year. On a moisture scale they are the opposite of barrens, and have species that either tolerate or require excessive moisture. Wetlands may be dominated by graminoid vegetation, herbs, trees, or shrubs. This community type features extremely important habitat for orchids, particularly those with northern affinities that reach the southern limit of their range in Indiana.

Swamp. Swamps are wetlands dominated by trees and/or shrubs where surface water is present for most of the year. Species diversity is not great in Indiana swamps, but several of the species found in swamps are confined to such environments; e.g., bald cypress, swamp cottonwood, and featherfoil (*Hottonia inflata*). Other plants of swamps include pumpkin ash, overcup oak, buttonbush (*Cephalanthus occidentalis*), arrow arum (*Peltandra virginica*), and swamp rose (*Rosa palustris*). The orchid flora in swamps is not diverse; some that do occur are *Liparis loeselii* (on fallen logs), *Platanthera flava* (both varieties), and *P. peramoena.*

Fen and Seep Spring. These communities are characterized by groundwater flowing to the surface and spreading in a diffuse manner, usually through a muck soil. Where the groundwater is acid and low in mineral content, it is called an acid seep spring. Similarly, near-neutral seepage results in a circumneutral seep spring. Highly mineralized and alkaline groundwater flow results in a community called a fen. Each of these seepage community types has a distinct assemblage of plants, although many overlap. Acid seep springs have a flora characteristic of bogs, e.g., black chokeberry (*Aronia melanocarpa*), winterberry (*Ilex verticillata*), *Osmunda* ferns and *Sphagnum*, as well as the orchids *Platanthera clavellata* and *P. lacera.* Circumneutral seep springs are typically dominated by marsh marigold (*Caltha palustris*) and skunk cabbage (*Symplocarpus foetidus*), and if forested, black ash. *Cypripedium reginae, Liparis loeselii,* and *Platanthera psycodes* are characteristic orchids of circumneutral seeps. Fens are extremely diverse floristically, including several sedges such as *Carex hystericina, C. interior, C. leptalea,* and *C. sterilis,* prairie Indian plantain (*Cacalia plantaginea*), Kalm's lobelia (*Lobelia kalmii*), shrubby cinquefoil (*Potentilla fruticosa*), and Riddell's goldenrod (*Solidago riddellii*). Characteristic orchids include *Calopogon tuberosus, Cypripedium candidum, Liparis loeselii,* and *Spiranthes cernua.* In forested fens, such as those dominated by tamarack and black ash, *Cypripedium calceolus* var. *parviflorum, C. reginae, Liparis loeselii,* and *Platanthera hyperborea* may be found.

Bog. A true bog is an acidic, mineral-poor, water-filled depression with much of its surface covered by a floating mat of vegetation. A bog does not get its water from groundwater seepage or runoff, but rather from direct precipitation. There is no outflow of water. True bogs are rare in Indiana, if indeed we have any that would meet the purist's definition. We do have aquatic environments with floating *Sphagnum* mats and acid indicator plants, but these have an apparent inflow and outflow of water. Regardless of the flow, I shall call these bogs. Typical species include bog rosemary (*Andromeda glaucophylla*), leatherleaf (*Chamaedaphne calyculata*), round-leaved sundew (*Drosera rotundifolia*), buckbean (*Menyanthes trifoliata*), pitcher plant (*Sarracenia purpurea*), highbush blueberry (*Vaccinium*

corymbosum), and large cranberry (*V. macrocarpon*). Bog orchids include *Calopogon tuberosus*, *Cypripedium acaule* (usually on bog borders), *Platanthera ciliaris*, *P. lacera*, and *Pogonia ophioglossoides*.

Sand, Muck, and Marl Flats. These communities, with either a base of sand, muck, marl, or a mixture of all three, occur most commonly on the shallow borders of natural ponds or lakes, or on glacial outwash plains. They are for the most part continuously saturated or moist, but inundated only periodically. The vegetation is usually short in stature and composed of many annuals, particularly sedges and rushes. At some sites, the flats may be forested with species tolerant of poor drainage, viz., pin oak, black gum, red maple, and quaking aspen. The sand and muck flats are generally acidic, while those influenced by calcareous water are alkaline (see Panne). Marl flats are strongly alkaline. Species characteristic of marl flats include twig rush (*Cladium mariscoides*), olive sedge (*Eleocharis flavescens* var. *olivacea*), autumn sedge (*Fimbristylis autumnalis*), shrubby cinquefoil (*Potentilla fruticosa*), hair beak rush (*Rhynchospora capillacea*), and low nut rush (*Scleria verticillata*). Orchids of these communities include *Calopogon tuberosus*, *Liparis loeselii*, *Pogonia ophioglossoides*, *Spiranthes cernua*, and *S. lucida*.

Plants of the acidic flats include purple false foxglove (*Agalinis purpurea*), colic root (*Aletris farinosa*), round-leaved sundew (*Drosera rotundifolia*), grass-leaved goldenrod (*Euthamia graminifolia*), swamp dewberry (*Rubus hispidus*), and yellow-eyed grass (*Xyris torta*). Orchids of these sites include *Calopogon tuberosus*, *Platanthera ciliaris*, *P. clavellata*, *P. flava* var. *herbiola*, *Pogonia ophioglossoides*, and *Spiranthes cernua*.

Panne. A panne is an interdunal wet depression receiving groundwater from, in our case, Lake Michigan. As the water level of Lake Michigan fluctuates, so it does in the pannes. When the Lake is up, the pannes are deep pools; when the Lake is down, the pannes are exposed sand flats. Because the water in Lake Michigan is alkaline, so are the pannes. Floristically the pannes have many of the same species as alkaline marl flats and fens. Orchids that can be found in pannes include *Calopogon tuberosus, Liparis loeselii, Platanthera hyperborea, Pogonia ophioglossoides,* and *Spiranthes cernua.*

Marsh. A marsh is a community dominated by tall sedges, grasses, and an assortment of herbaceous plants adapted to soils which have water near or slightly above the surface for most of the year. Whorled loosestrife (*Decodon verticillatus*), spatterdock (*Nuphar advena*), pickerel weed (*Pontederia cordata*), common arrowhead (*Sagittaria latifolia*), bulrushes (*Scirpus acutus* and *S. validus*), and cat-tails (*Typha* spp.) are a few of the typical species that compose a marsh. Marshes are most prevalent in northern Indiana, where they occur in broad floodplains, basins, and natural lake borders. Marshes are not particularly good environments for orchids unless there are hummocks or peat flats within that can raise the orchids above the flooded soils and dense marsh vegetation. If such perches are provided, *Calopogon, Pogonia,* and other orchids of open wetlands may be found.

Sedge Meadow. A sedge meadow is a wetland community dominated by sedges (notably *Carex* spp.) that occurs slightly above the permanent water table. The erect sedge (*Carex stricta*) is a major dominant, along with *C. lasiocarpa, C. scoparia, C. stipata,* and *C. vulpinoidea.* Other sedges include twig rush (*Cladium mariscoides*), bulrushes (*Scirpus acutus* and *S. validus*), and wool grass (*Scirpus cyperinus*). Rushes are also important, especially *Juncus effusus* and *J. tenuis* var. *dudleyi.* Sedge meadows occur primarily next to natural lakes and marshes as well as fens, bogs, and other wetlands. If not too dense, they are good habitats for orchids. Likely ones include *Calopogon, Liparis loeselii, Platanthera lacera,* and *Spiranthes cernua.*

PRIMARY COMMUNITIES

Primary communities are those that are composed mostly of exposed bedrock or sand with vegetation maintained in an early stage of succession. Cliff and lakeshore are the principal types. Because lakeshore is generally not a habitat for orchids (except possibly for ephemeral occurrences of *Spiranthes lucida*), only cliffs will be discussed here.

Cliff. Cliffs are vertical expanses of exposed bedrock. In Indiana they may be composed of sandstone, limestone, shale (rarely), or conglomerate. Cliffs normally are situated within a forested setting, but some occur along open stream valleys. Different assortments of plants occur on cliffs, depending on the cliff's rock type, aspect, and exposure. Ferns are especially prevalent on cliffs, and are good indicators of cliff type. For example, on sandstone cliffs

pinnatifid spleenwort (*Asplenium pinnatifidum*), lacy wood fern (*Dryopteris intermedia*), marginal shield fern (*D. marginalis*), and rock clubmoss (*Lycopodium porophilum*) are characteristic. On limestone cliffs one may find walking fern (*Asplenium rhizophyllum*), wall rue (*A. ruta-muraria*), and cliff brake ferns (*Pellaea atropurpurea* and *P. glabella*). Shale and conglomerate cliffs are normally too unstable to have much of any development of vegetation, and consequently no characteristic species. Generally, cliffs are not good orchid habitats, although the mossy slopes immediately above many mesic sandstone cliffs are a preferred habitat of *Goodyera pubescens*. *Spiranthes cernua* and *S. tuberosa* are at home above dry south-facing sandstone cliffs. *Hexalectris spicata* may occur on dry slopes above limestone.

CULTURAL COMMUNITIES

A cultural community is created when any human disturbance modifies a natural community to the extent that it is no longer recognizable as that community. Cropland, quarries, strip mines, lawns, old fields, buildings, reservoirs, etc., all come under this category. Surprisingly, cultural communities occasionally are excellent habitats for some orchid species. Old fields, if not dominated by exotic plants, are great for many *Spiranthes*, and fields reclaimed by brush and young trees are favorite habitats for *Liparis liliifolia* and *Spiranthes ovalis* var. *erostellata*. Generally, though, most cultural areas are useless to orchids, and most human activities cause more harm than good.

Finding Orchids

Taking to the field in search of wild orchids is one of the most challenging and exciting pursuits in botany. I compare it to looking for hidden treasure, as certain species are just as precious and difficult to find. Similarly, finding orchids can take a great deal of research, looking for clues that will help in identifying specific localities to inventory. Perhaps the most important tool one can possess for finding orchids is a knowledge of orchid habitat preferences. In reality, the best way to find orchids is not to look for orchids *per se*, but to look for orchid habitat. In accomplishing this one needs not only to learn what an orchid's specific preferences are, but also how to recognize and locate the natural communities in which the preferred conditions occur. This is not a particularly easy task, as it requires knowledge of geology, soils, hydrology, floristics, and other related disciplines. Such knowledge is invaluable in finding orchids.

A good start to determining habitat preferences is to consult the appropriate section in the species accounts in this work, as well as works pertaining to surrounding states, especially Sheviak (1974) for Illinois and Case (1987) for Michigan and other Great Lakes states. The information above on natural communities of Indiana should be helpful in identifying communities, and aerial photos, topographic maps, soil survey maps, geologic maps, and appropriate published literature are all good initial sources for locating them.

If one cares not to do all the homework mentioned above, the next best option is simply to explore as much of the natural landscape as possible, thereby improving the chances of encountering orchids. Many of the species may not be found using this method, however, especially if certain rather inhospitable communities are avoided.

Other considerations to take into account for finding orchids are season of year and geographic location. To observe a particular species in bloom it is critical that the search be made during the appropriate range of dates (see Table 1). Even skilled planning does not guarantee success in finding a plant in good flower, however; on more than one occasion I have tracked down an orchid to discover only wilted blossoms. See Phenology, above, for a discussion of the variables controlling blooming.

Searching for a given species in the appropriate part of the state is also important. For example, the Indiana collections of *Platanthera orbiculata* were taken from mesic upland forest communities in the northern part of the state. For a variety of reasons, most notably climate, there is virtually no chance for finding this orchid in southern Indiana, even though more area of mesic upland forest occurs there than in northern Indiana. However, discoveries of amazing disjunct occurrences do happen—e.g., *Tipularia discolor* in La Porte County—making the pursuit all the more fun.

Orchid Conservation

In presettlement times and for much of the nineteenth century, orchids were evidently common in Indiana, presenting little need to espouse their conservation. An 1880 price list of native plants sold by W. C. Steele of La Porte illustrates this well. His list includes thirteen species of orchids for sale, many for as little as one penny each. They were offered in increments of one dozen, 100, or 1,000! And all were collected within ten miles of his home!

Today we clearly have fewer orchids in the state, and although most of our native orchids are not in immediate danger of being extirpated, it is certainly conceivable that there will be fewer to observe as more and more of our landscape is developed. To insure that the orchids of Indiana do not approach critically low numbers we must, first and foremost, keep and maintain as much of the landscape as possible in a relatively undisturbed condition. Without suitable habitat our orchids will not survive. Unlike many other plants, terrestrial orchids generally do poorly in cultivation, and thus without protecting orchids in their wild state there is little hope for their continued existence here. Take a long look at these photographs, of the last Indiana individuals of *Arethusa bulbosa* and *Platanthera hookeri*, and hope that the same fate does not befall other native orchids.

Although protection of habitat can offer at least some degree of assurance that there will continue to be orchids in Indiana, it is not a guarantee, nor is it the final answer. Unscrupulous collecting, either for gardening purposes or for building a herbarium collection, can and has hurt certain populations of orchids, sometimes to the point of local extirpation (see discussion under *Cypripedium reginae*). Thus, readers are urged to refrain from collecting or digging. If one must collect for scientific purposes, take as few specimens as possible, and then only if the population is large enough to sustain a reduction in numbers (I would suggest leaving at least ten individuals if in proximity to one another—more if the plants are widely scattered). Leaving the orchid's roots may also help, in that the individual plant may survive on existing reserves until the following season (albeit in a weakened condition). This is not true for all orchids, however; certain species of *Platanthera* collected in such a manner rarely survive (Sheviak, 1990). Although one might argue the need for taking a plant for scientific purposes, it is rarely justifiable to dig plants for horticulture, as very few orchids survive transplantation, and those that do rarely live more than a few years. Similarly, do not purchase native orchids from garden centers or mail-order nurseries, regardless of claims that their plants are nursery-grown and suitable for home gardens. No nursery is currently capable of large-scale commercial propagation of North American terrestrial orchids. Unscrupulous nurseries collect orchids in the wild, maintain them temporarily under nursery conditions, and then ship them as "nursery-grown" to unsuspecting patrons. Their plants will likely succumb just as would any taken directly from the wild. Unless you are able to salvage plants from a site marked for imminent destruction, it is best to leave orchids in their preferred haunts and resist the desire to bring them home.

Arethusa bulbosa (dragon's mouth). Photo of last known individual of *Arethusa* in Indiana. May 1983, Kosciusko Co. Jim Aldrich.

Platanthera hookeri (Hooker's orchid). Photo of one of the last known individuals of this species in Indiana. June 1961, Porter Co. Valdemar Schwarz.

There are several native orchids listed on the state's official list of rare, threatened, and endangered plants (Aldrich, Bacone, and Homoya, 1986). Orchids on this list are in such low numbers in the state that they should never be disturbed (again, unless the site is in immediate threat of destruction). Those on the list (updated to reflect current information) are:

Arethusa bulbosa	—extirpated
Coeloglossum viride	—threatened
Corallorhiza trifida	—extirpated
Cypripedium calceolus var. *parviflorum*	—rare
Cypripedium candidum	—rare
Hexalectris spicata	—rare
Malaxis unifolia	—endangered
Platanthera ciliaris	—endangered
Platanthera clavellata	—rare
Platanthera dilatata	—endangered
Platanthera flava var. *flava*	—endangered
Platanthera hookeri	—extirpated
Platanthera hyperborea	—threatened
Platanthera leucophaea	—extirpated
Platanthera orbiculata	—extirpated
Platanthera psycodes	—rare
Spiranthes lucida	—rare
Spiranthes magnicamporum	—endangered
Spiranthes ochroleuca	—threatened
Spiranthes romanzoffiana	—endangered
Spiranthes vernalis	—rare

For the categories used above, endangered equals 1 to 5 extant occurrences in the state; threatened equals 6 to 10 extant occurrences; and rare equals 11 to 20 extant occurrences.

Guide to the
——— Species Accounts ———

KEYS

A botanical key is simply a tool used to identify an unknown plant. A dichotomous key, such as the type used in this work, consists of couplets (contrasting pairs of descriptive statements) that contain information about a plant's features. Because couplet halves contain contrasting information, only one-half of the couplet should match the unknown plant at hand (assuming that the plant is considered in the key!). After carefully reading the couplet, and choosing the best fit, the reader is then directed further into the key to make more choices until ultimately a determination is reached. Using the key to orchid genera, for example, the key begins with couplet "A" and "AA." Entry "A" identifies a genus with a whorl of leaves, whereas entry "AA" identifies genera with leaves arranged otherwise. If the orchid in question has whorled leaves, *voilà*, a determination has already been reached! If the plant does not have whorled leaves, then entry "AA" is the correct choice. At the end of entry "AA" is letter "B." This means that you must continue through the key by next looking at couplet "B" and "BB."

Continue the process of elimination until you have reached a satisfactory determination. If, in comparing your determination with a morphological description, photograph or illustration, you find that you have made a mistake, return to the key and begin again. One might be able to reduce the amount of time in the keying process by going to the incorrect determination and working backwards. This is not recommended for beginners however, as backward keying may cause more confusion and delay. And unless one has some familiarity with the orchid family, it is best to start with the key to genera before proceeding to the key to species. With experience one can bypass much of the keying process and go directly to the key to species or even to specific couplets involving just two taxa.

ARRANGEMENT OF TAXA

In this work the order of orchid taxa is alphabetical. The genus name is listed first, followed by an alphabetical arrangement of species within the genus (and then varieties if applicable). Traditionally most botanists have arranged taxa phylogenetically, but such an arrangement almost always necessitates constant use of an index, a task that can get cumbersome. For those interested in a phylogenetic arrangement, see Introduction under Classification, or refer to other botanical works such as Luer (1975) or Dressler (1981).

SCIENTIFIC AND COMMON NAMES

Although both scientific and common names are given for each orchid taxon, scientific names have priority, and thus are used most frequently in this text. The principal reasons for this are that scientific names are standardized and are superior at showing relationships between taxa. Common names are not standardized (what I learned as pink lady's-slipper may be moccasin flower to you), and most do not show relationships (the crested coral-root orchid is not a "true" coral-root, in that it isn't a *Corallorhiza*). Thus, for scientific accuracy and improvement of communication, one should learn scientific names.

Scientific names are not difficult. It is simply a matter of familiarity. Not many people are intimidated by the names *Iris, Magnolia, Vanilla, Poinsettia, Hydrangea*, and the like, yet these are all scientific names of familiar genera. With usage, the scientific names of our native orchids will become familiar as well. To encourage usage, phonetic spellings of the Indiana orchid taxa are provided (Appendix A).

The genus (plural: genera) name, in combination with a specific epithet (or name), yields a binomial that is referred to as a species, the basic unit in the classification of living organisms. The binomial, each one unique for each species, is somewhat like the parts of speech. Think of the genus name as the noun, and the specific epithet as the adjective describing some trait that a group of individuals within the genus have in common. Although this analogy is not always workable (some epithets, such as those that commemorate people, places, etc., do not provide descriptive information), it does help in understanding the species concept. For example, the species name for white lady's-slipper is *Cypripedium candidum. Cypripedium* identifies the group (lady's-slippers), and *candidum* (= white) refers to those lady's-slipper plants that have a white lip (among other characters). To aid in the understanding and use of scientific names the derivations of the generic and specific names are given. The nomenclature and derivations are from Luer (1975) unless otherwise noted. The scientific names of the non-orchids listed follow Gleason and Cronquist (1991), with a few exceptions. Where an exception occurs the equivalent name in Gleason and Cronquist is provided in Appendix B, with the name followed by "GC." Common names for those species identified in the text by scientific name only are listed in Appendix B. In general, common names only are used for trees, simply because their names are well established and understood.

PHOTOGRAPHS AND ILLUSTRATIONS

An attempt was made to use photographs taken in Indiana only, and all are with but one exception. The photograph not taken in Indiana was from nearby Lake County, Illinois. For each plate the species, county and state location, date of photograph, photographer, and scale are identified.

For those species not extant in Indiana a line drawing is used to illustrate the appearance of the plant. These are used to alert the reader quickly to the species' status in the state. In a way the line drawings are symbolic, in that they appear as "ghostly" images of plants of a former time.

SIZE MEASUREMENTS

Although the keys, plates, and pertinent discussion should be sufficient for one to identify correctly a given Indiana orchid, descriptions are also provided to confirm a determination. The size measurements included may be of special interest to the beginner, as several of the orchids are smaller (or rarely larger) than what many people expect. The two measurements that are particularly useful in this respect are height of plant (including the inflorescence), and length of lip. Because measurements are somewhat variable from plant to plant, a measurement range taken from what I consider typical Indiana specimens is provided. For species with numerous flowers, floral measurements are taken from the lower half of the inflorescence.

Readers interested in additional measurements of native orchids can find them in the excellent descriptions provided by Luer (1975), Correll (1978), and Case (1987).

BLOOMING PERIOD

A range of dates is provided, denoting when the orchid has been observed in bloom in Indiana. For a more detailed discussion, the reader is referred to the section on Phenology in the Introduction.

DISTRIBUTION MAPS

Orchid distribution within Indiana is depicted by the documented presence of an orchid species within a given county (see map, Fig. 8, for names and locations of Indiana counties). The solid circle represents a herbarium specimen that was collected in the county denoted. Photographs suitable for identification also were accepted as vouchers. Most of the herbarium specimens observed were from Indiana University (IND), Butler University (BUT), University of Notre Dame (ND), and Purdue University (PUL), but other substantial collections checked included those from the University of Illinois (ILL), Field Museum of Natural History (F), United States National Museum, Smithsonian Institution (US), New York Botanical Garden (NY), which includes the recently acquired collections from DePauw University (DPU) and Wabash College (WAB), Missouri Botanical Garden (MO), and Orchid Herbarium of Oakes Ames (AMES). Smaller but nonetheless important collections of Indiana orchids observed included those from Indiana State University (TER), Ball State University (BSUH), Han-

FIGURE 8. **Counties of Indiana**

over College, Miami University (MU), University of Michigan (MICH), Michigan State University (MSC), Ohio State University (OS), The Morton Arboretum (MOR), Eastern Illinois University (EIU), University of Cincinnati (CINC), University of Wisconsin (WIS), Philadelphia Academy of Natural Sciences (PH), Milwaukee Public Museum (MIL), Hayes Regional Arboretum, and Earlham College (EAR).

The open circles represent observations I have made in the field since the initiation of this project in 1982. In these cases voucher specimens were not made primarily because the populations observed had low numbers of individuals, and I did not feel it worth endangering the population for a county record. I recognize that such reports cannot be verified, but I include them to provide a picture of the distribution of the species as I know it.

Conversely, I have not included map symbols for reports of species by other authors. Although many reports are certainly valid, some are not, and I have no good way of distinguishing between them. This is especially true when I do not have personal knowledge of the taxonomic skills, especially for orchids, of the various reporters. I do however discuss reports that represent significant regional occurrences, or the occurrence of a rare species.

The absence of a symbol within a county boundary does not necessarily signify that the orchid does not occur in that county. It may be that the county has not been thoroughly botanized, and that no one has seen the orchid even though it is there. It also may be that people have seen the orchid in the county, but because a voucher specimen or documented photo was not made, I am unaware of their observation.

On the other hand, the presence of a symbol for a county does not necessarily represent a current occurrence of the orchid. The vast majority of the symbols represent very old collections (fifty years and older), and it is quite possible that the orchid no longer occurs in the county. This is especially true in regions that have had considerable habitat loss in recent years, such as in urban areas and highly agricultural areas.

The continental range maps were drawn using a variety of sources, primarily state and provincial floras and atlases, and specific works on state and regional orchid floras. Other sources included range maps of specific species found in the scientific literature, and information (based on vouchered occurrences and a few field observations) provided by contemporary botanists through personal communication; the states and persons are cited in the Acknowledgments. For each orchid species I added the locality information to a single map, and then "connected the dots," shading areas between adjacent occurrences to generate the species' range. Where there were gaps in information, I determined an orchid's range by extrapolation, shading areas between known occurrences that appeared to have likely habitat, especially if the areas were located in the same physiographic region as the occurrences. I had to do this for many of the western states, as well as Canada, Mexico, and Central America. I tried to avoid taking too much liberty in extrapolation, however, because "painting with a broad brush" can result in an inaccurate and misleading map with little utility.

RANGE

This is a discussion of the orchid's range in Indiana. Information other than what can be gleaned from the county distribution map is included here, such as comments about the orchid's occurrence within specific natural regions, and reports of disjunct occurrences.

HABITAT

This section includes information about the environment in which the orchid grows. For persons interested in locating orchids in the field it is perhaps the most important section of the book. In general, the habitat information comes from my experience with the species in the Indiana landscape. Additional information was gathered from herbarium specimen labels, published literature, and correspondence and discussions with knowledgeable individuals.

Much of the habitat information is presented in the context of natural communities (see Introduction, Indiana as Orchid Habitat), but specifics about pH requirements, soil moisture needs, species associates, etc., are also provided when known. Species associates are those plants observed growing in proximity to the orchid in an Indiana habitat. Species that occur together generally have the same growing requirements; thus, knowing the associates of an orchid is helpful in identifying appropriate orchid habitat. The occurrence of associates will not guarantee an orchid's presence, however; it is more common to find the associates, and not the orchid.

DISCUSSION

A smorgasbord of information may be found here, ranging from a discussion on population trends, to identifying a particular Indiana specimen illustrated in a classic botanical work. Other topics include details on identifying difficult taxa, life history information, observation accounts, collection history, search technique suggestions, and folklore.

Key to Indiana
Orchid Genera

A.   Leaves clustered in a terminal whorl .... *Isotria*

AA.   Leaves otherwise, either basal, alternate, a single leaf,
or absent .... B.

     B.   Lip petal slipper-, cup-, or sac-shaped .... C.

          C.   Lip 1.8 cm long or greater; anthers two, one each
positioned on the sides of a large shield-like staminode;
flowers 1–2 (3) per inflorescence .... *Cypripedium*

         CC.   Lip 1.3 cm long or less; anther one, no staminode
present; flowers 5 or more per inflorescence .... D.

             D.   Plants with basal leaves only, these dark green
with white venation; flowers white, lip cleft
above, occurring on a tight, wand-like
raceme .... *Goodyera*

            DD.   Plants without basal leaves (but several stem
leaves present); flowers pale green, greenish-pink,
to purplish-brown, scattered loosely on a terminal
raceme; lip constricted near middle, with basal
(upper) portion cup-shaped and commonly
filled with nectar .... *Epipactis*

      BB.   Lip not slipper-, cup-, or sac-shaped .... E.

          E.   Leaves absent or senescing at anthesis;
(*Arethusa* keyed here due to late leaf
development) .... F.

             F.   Flower solitary, petals and sepals
pink; single green leaf developing
after flowering; plant of sunny
bogs .... *Arethusa*

            FF.   Flowers several, petals and sepals
variously colored but not pink
(except possibly for localized spots,
striping, or shading); leaves absent
at anthesis, or reduced to nonphotosynthetic sheaths, or present
as faded or withered overwintering
leaves .... G.

G.   Petals and sepals predominantly white or cream .... *Spiranthes*

GG. Petals and sepals other than white or cream.................................H.

    H.   Plants with a single, overwintering photosynthetic leaf, it present but withered and dying at anthesis (spring), or if absent at anthesis (summer), then flowers with a conspicuous lip spur...I.

        I.   Flowers with a conspicuous spur, blooming in late July and August; upper surface of overwintering leaf green (rarely purple), undersurface dark purple; leaf absent at anthesis...*Tipularia*

        II. Flowers spurless, blooming in early May to mid-June; upper surface of over-wintering leaf pleated with green and white parallel venation, undersurface light purplish-green; leaf normally present but in a senescing condition at anthesis ....*Aplectrum*

    HH. Plants without photosynthetic leaves at any season; no lip spur present...J.

        J.   Lip greater than 1 cm long; petals and sepals yellowish-purple to tan with purple striping; plants restricted to southern Indiana hills with limestone outcrops................................. *Hexalectris*

        JJ. Lip less than 1 cm long; petals and sepals greenish, greenish-purple, to yellowish-brown, without bold striping, but lip may possess purple spots; plants of various woodland habitats throughout the state...........................*Corallorhiza*

EE. Leaves present at anthesis (*Aplectrum*, with a senescing leaf, also keyed here) ....K.

    K.   Flowers with a spur...L.

        L.   Leaves basal, two (rarely one) in number ....M.

            M.   Petals and sepals pink (rarely white), all coming together to form a hood over the white (rarely pink) lip; leaves elliptic, fleshy; floral bracts commonly surpassing flowers .... *Galearis*

            MM. Petals and sepals green, greenish-white, or white, all not joined together to form a hood; leaves mostly orbicular; floral bracts not surpassing flowers ... *Platanthera* (*P. orbiculata* and *P. hookeri*)

        LL. Leaves not basal, but occurring alternately on the stem... N.

            N.   Spur less than 3 mm long, bag-shaped (scrotiform); opening to spur obscure......... ....*Coeloglossum*

            NN. Spur 3 mm long or greater, commonly much more so, and cylindrical; opening to spur evident............................... *Platanthera*

    KK. Flowers without a spur ....O.

O. Flowers pink (rarely white); plants of open wetlands and/or prairie habitats .... P.

    P. Flowers normally one per stem; flower resupinate (lip lowermost) .... Q.

        Q. Floral bract conspicuous, leaf-like; a single ovate leaf present at middle of stem during anthesis .... *Pogonia*

        QQ. Floral bract small, seemingly absent; no leaves apparent on stem during anthesis .... *Arethusa*

    PP. Flowers commonly three or more; flowers non-resupinate (lip uppermost) .... *Calopogon*

OO. Flowers not pink, or only slightly so; if pinkish, then plants not of open, sunny wetlands and/or prairies .... R.

        R. Inflorescence of numerous (normally greater than 10), white or cream-colored flowers commonly arranged in a spiral or ranks of flowers .... *Spiranthes*

        RR. Inflorescence not as above; flowers green, purplish, or whitish-pink; if all white, then less than 5 in number and not arranged in an evident spiral or ranks of flowers .... S.

        S. Leaf one .... T.

            T. Leaf ovate; lip less than 3 mm long, green .... *Malaxis*

            TT. Leaf elliptic; lip greater than 8 mm long, white with purple markings .... *Aplectrum*

        SS. Leaves two or more .... U.

            U. Leaves two (may be one in sterile condition), basal; flowers green or purplish .... *Liparis*

            UU. Leaves commonly three or more on a zigzag stem; no basal leaves; flowers white to whitish-pink .... *Triphora*

Species Accounts

APLECTRUM
Nuttall

Aplectrum is derived from the Greek words *a*, meaning "without," and *plektron*, "spur," in reference to its spurless flowers. Although there are other orchids that have spurless flowers, this name may have been used to distinguish *Aplectrum* from *Tipularia* and *Calypso*—the other orchid genera with a single overwintering leaf (Luer, 1975). *Aplectrum* has only two species ascribed to it, the North American species, *A. hyemale*, and an additional one in Japan (Luer, 1975).

Aplectrum hyemale (Muhlenberg *ex* Willdenow) Nuttall

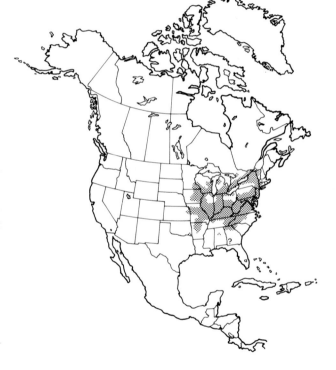

COMMON NAMES: puttyroot, Adam-and-Eve.

SPECIFIC EPITHET DERIVATION: *hyemale* = "winter," in reference to the winter leaf of the species.

DESCRIPTION: Plant glabrous throughout, 30–35 cm tall. Roots slender, attached to a bulbous corm. **Leaf solitary,** elliptic, **plicate, basal,** 12–15 cm long x 6–7 cm wide, **upper surface light green with white veins,** lower surface lightly tinted with purple. **Inflorescence** a loose raceme, **scapose,** with 8–15 flowers, each subtended by an inconspicuous floral bract 2–4 mm long. **Lip** 10–12 mm long x 5–7 mm wide, generally **obovate, 3–lobed, white with purple markings. Petals oblanceolate,** 6–8 mm long x 2–2.5 mm wide, **greenish-white, tinted with purple, especially at the tips.** Sepals 8–10 mm long x 2–3 mm wide, otherwise like petals.

BLOOMING PERIOD: early May to mid-June.

RANGE: Occurs throughout the state, but it is by far most common in the southern half of the state, particularly in the Shawnee Hills and Highland Rim natural regions. It becomes quite rare in the northwestern Indiana natural regions, viz., Grand Prairie and Northwestern Morainal. In the Lake Michigan Dunes region Pepoon (1927) cited an 1888 observation (collection?) by Babcock at Berry Lake (now Whiting) Indiana, and an undated discovery by Hill at Wheeler, Indiana. These populations have been destroyed. A population is extant in the Indiana Dunes State Park in Porter County (Valdemar Schwarz, Marlin Bowles, personal communication).

HABITAT: The favored habitat of *Aplectrum* is rich mesic forest, espe-

OPPOSITE: *Aplectrum hyemale* (puttyroot). May 1988, Shelby Co. Perry Scott. x1.

ABOVE, LEFT: *A. hyemale*. May 1988, Tippecanoe Co. Lee Casebere. x1⅓.

ABOVE, RIGHT: *A. hyemale* f. *pallidum*, May 1988, Noble Co. Lee Casebere. x3.

BOTTOM: *A. hyemale*, winter leaf. November 1990, Hamilton Co. Lee Casebere. x⅓.

Aplectrum hyemale   65

cially in ravines or along high terraces of streams or rivers; however, almost any forest community may have a few of these plants. Typical overstory dominants in preferred sites include American beech, red elm, black walnut, white ash, Ohio buckeye, sugar maple, red oak, white oak, and shagbark hickory. Understory plants commonly associated with *Aplectrum* include *Asimina triloba*, *Botrychium dissectum*, *Carex jamesii*, *C. plantaginea*, *Cystopteris protrusa*, *Delphinium tricorne*, *Hydrangea arborescens*, *Hydrophyllum appendiculatum*, *H. canadense*, *Impatiens capensis*, *Lindera benzoin*, *Phlox divaricata*, *Podophyllum peltatum*, *Polystichum acrostichoides*, *Solidago flexicaulis*, and *Stylophorum diphyllum*.

DISCUSSION: *Aplectrum*, like *Tipularia*, has the curious trait of having an alternative vegetative lifecycle; i.e., instead of having a growing season from spring to autumn, as do most plants, its season is autumn to spring. Because *Aplectrum* is completely capable of conducting photosynthesis during the winter (although much less so during very cold weather—Auclair, 1972), it avoids the competition for light with which other plants struggle in the normal growing season, which may explain *Aplectrum*'s "role reversal." Although *Aplectrum*'s leaf remains virtually unscathed through the rigors of winter, it begins to wither and fade shortly before the emergence of the flowering stalk in early to mid-May, and completely deteriorates soon after flowering. Typically, most *Aplectrum* individuals do not flower, and those that do are often hidden by companion vegetation, and thus hard to find. Sometimes, however, impressive displays occur when seemingly every plant in a dense population blooms. After flowering, and throughout the summer, all signs of the puttyroot are gone until a new leaf emerges in mid to late September. The possible exception to the summer absence is the presence of capsules. Hogan (1983) has shown *Aplectrum* to be autogamous, and possibly agamospermous, and thus the percentage of fruit-set is consistently high.

The puttyroot, so named because of the putty-like, mucilaginous consistency of its corms, is also known as the Adam-and-Eve orchid. This name alludes to the presence of two underground corms on each plant. The newest developed corm (Eve) is attached to the leaf of the current year, and is an offshoot of the previous year's corm (Adam). Gibson (1905) attributed the origin of the name Adam-and-Eve to the "Negroes and poor whites in Georgia and the Southern States, where the orchids grow freely. They wear them [the corms] as amulets, and tell each other's fortunes by placing the separated bulbs in water, and according as 'Adam or Eve pops up calculate the chances of retaining a friend's affection, getting work, or living in peace with neighbours.'"

The corms are said to have been used by the early settlers to glue together broken pieces of china, and by the Indians for topical treatment of sores (Correll, 1978). In the past the corms also were eaten, possibly for medicinal reasons. According to Evermann and Clark (1920), "The mealy mucilaginous corm is one of the queer things that boys pretend to like the flavor of."

Aplectrum flowers are quite pleasing to the eye, but one must have good timing to catch them in their best display. The flowers have a tendency to droop, with the sepals only partially spreading. Only in their most perfect bloom are the flowers fully open. A most attractive form of puttyroot (*forma pallidum* House), with its clear green color, is known from one colony in Noble County.

ARETHUSA
Linnaeus

Named for the mythical Greek character Arethusa, a nymph transformed into a spring, our *Arethusa* is also a water creature, as it grows in wetland habitats. Most botanical texts (Fernald, 1950; Gleason, 1952) indicate that there are two species within the genus *Arethusa,* one from North America and one from Japan. The Japanese species has since been relegated to the genus *Eleorchis.* Wiggins (1980) lists *Arethusa rosea* Benth., a Baja California endemic, in his *Flora of Baja California.* This taxon is now treated as *Bletia rosea* (Lindl.) Dressler (DeAda Mally, personal communication).

Arethusa bulbosa Linnaeus

COMMON NAMES: dragon's mouth, arethusa.

SPECIFIC EPITHET DERIVATION: *bulbosa* = "bulbed," in reference to its bulbous corms.

DESCRIPTION: Plant glabrous, 15–20 cm tall. Roots slender, attached to a small bulbous corm, 10 mm long x 5 mm wide. **Leaf solitary,** lanceolate, **emerging after flowering,** 4–6 cm long x 6–10 mm wide. **Inflorescence with 1** (rarely 2) **flower**(s) atop a solitary stem, each **with a small floral bract** 2–4 mm long. Lip 20–25 mm long x 12–15 mm wide, obovate, with short lateral lobes and wavy margins. **Central portion of lip fringed with yellow bristles.** Remainder of **lip** smooth and **pink, with pinkish-purple markings throughout. Petals** oblong to oblanceolate, **pink,** 2–2.5 cm long x 3–4 mm wide. Sepals similar to petals, 3–4 cm long x 8–10 mm wide.

BLOOMING PERIOD: mid-May to mid-June.

RANGE: *Arethusa* has been documented only from Kosciusko, Lake,

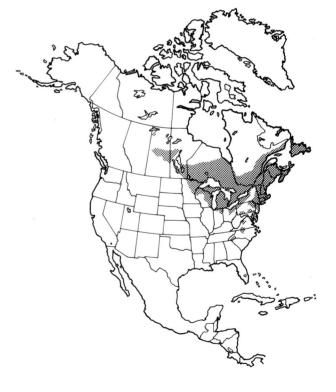

Arethusa bulbosa
(dragon's mouth)
full plant x1, flower x2-½

Steuben, and Wells counties. With the exception of Wells County, habitat still exists in the other counties, as well as in others of the Northern Lakes and Northwestern Morainal natural regions. The photograph in Luer (1975) portraying *Arethusa* in Steuben County is in error; the plants shown are actually in Hillsdale County, Michigan. Thompson's report (1892) of *Arethusa* for Carroll County cannot be verified nor trusted, as Thompson appears to have been somewhat careless in his botanical work (see discussion under *Malaxis monophyllos* in Excluded Species). However, Carroll County possibly did have suitable *Arethusa* habitat prior to the extensive draining of its wetlands, so his report is not absurd.

HABITAT: *Arethusa* is primarily a denizen of sphagnum bogs. All of the herbarium specimen labels denote that the plants were taken from bogs or swamps, but provide little other habitat information. Peattie (1930) reported it growing in wet swales (possibly prairie-like?) in the Indiana Dunes. Hull (1935) noted it growing with *Rhus vernix* in a sphagnum bog in the vicinity of Gary. W. N. Clute's note about Hull (1935) described the *Arethusa* site as a deep shaded bog with *Menyanthes, Sarracenia,* and *Pogonia.* At the Kosciusko County station it was growing in a sphagnum moss hummock at the base of a poison sumac shrub. Species that grew with *Arethusa* included *Drosera rotundifolia, Isotria verticillata, Sarracenia purpurea, Thelypteris palustris,* and *Vaccinium macrocarpon.* Future efforts to locate *Arethusa* should be directed to areas with sphagnum hummocks, although Case (1987) reports *Arethusa* growing in fen habitats (as well as bogs) in Michigan.

DISCUSSION: There is no question that *Arethusa* is one of the most attractive of Indiana's native orchids. Observing *Arethusa* in Indiana has been the privilege of few, however, for this bog jewel has never been common here, and there are currently no sites known to harbor it.

The majority of *Arethusa* collections date back to the late 1800s and early 1900s. The earliest ones were taken in the Miller (now Gary) area of Lake County in 1879 by E. Bastin. One of the last collections also came from Lake County, it taken in 1933 by E. D. Hull. At the site where Hull collected *Arethusa,* he noted only two plants the following year (Hull, 1935). The reason for the decline, as pointed out in an editor's footnote of Hull's article by Indianapolis botanist Willard Clute, was the site being converted to a pasture of coarse grasses that was "sufficient to bring extirpation to *Arethusa.*"

For almost fifty years following Hull's observation *Arethusa* was thought to have been extirpated from the state. Although botanists continued to search for the elusive orchid, it was always to no avail. Then, during a 1983 inventory of a small, overgrown sphagnum bog in Kosciusko County, IDNR biologists Jim Aldrich and Virgil Brach came upon a single, flowering stem of *Arethusa.* They knew the importance of their find, and took great care not to disturb the plant while photographing it. Unfortunately, their care was for naught, as the lone stem they were observing appears to have been Indiana's last known individual of *Arethusa.* Repeated visits to the bog have failed to find any sign of the orchid. See a photograph of this last known individual of *Arethusa* in Indiana in the Introduction, Orchid Conservation section.

The challenge now is to find more *Arethusa,* hoping that it won't take another fifty years to achieve success! Areas of seemingly suitable habitat exist, albeit small in total acreage, so the hope is not without foundation.

CALOPOGON

R. Brown in Aiton

The name *Calopogon,* derived from the Greek words *kalos* and *pogon,* means "beautiful beard," in reference to the bristled labellum of the flowers. *Limodorum* was a common early name for the group—in fact it was its first name—but *Calopogon* is the currently accepted name. There are four recognized species, all occurring within the borders of the United States. Three are restricted entirely to the southeastern states, whereas one, *C. tuberosus,* is found throughout most of the eastern U.S., eastern Canada, and portions of the West Indies.

Calopogon is easily distinguished from the other genera occurring in Indiana by its grass-like leaves and pink, non-resupinate flowers.

Calopogon tuberosus (Linnaeus) Britton

[Syn: *Calopogon pulchellus* (Salisbury) R. Brown]

COMMON NAMES: grass-pink, grass-pink orchid.

SPECIFIC EPITHET DERIVATION: *tuberosus* = "tuberous," in reference to the orchid's tuberous corm.

DESCRIPTION: Plant glabrous, 40–45 cm tall. Roots slender, fibrous, attached to corm. **Leaf typically one, basal, grass-like,** linear-lanceolate, 17–22 cm long x 10–18 mm wide. **Inflorescence** a loosely flowered raceme, of **3–10 non-resupinate pink flowers,** with floral bracts 5–6 mm long. **Lip** 15 mm long x 8 mm wide, appearing entire, **with obscure lateral lobes near base, and apex dilated into a triangular lobe. Club-shaped bristles, yellow to orange-tipped, on veins of upper surface between lateral and terminal lobes of lip.** Petals pink, ovate-lanceolate to oblong, 14–16 mm long x 4–5 mm wide. Sepals pink, ovate, 18–20 mm long x 6–8 mm wide. **Column winged and petal-like.**

BLOOMING PERIOD: mid-May to late July.

RANGE: Occurs almost exclusively in the northern half of the state. There is a report for southwestern Indiana by Schneck (1876), and a specimen collected in 1836 from the "Knobs" of Floyd County by Dr. A. Clapp. The Floyd County specimen is made somewhat suspect by the fact that there is no listing of *Calopogon* in Clapp's collection ledger. However, Clapp listed *Calypso americana* R. Brown (= *C. bulbosa*), a species that could not possibly have occurred near New Albany. It is conceivable that he confused names, calling his plant *Calypso* instead of *Calopogon*. The use of the name *Calopogon* on the specimen label can be explained by the fact that after Clapp's death most of his specimens were remounted and relabeled (and possibly in some cases renamed) by J. M. Coulter (1876). The occurrence of *Calopogon* in the New Albany area is certainly within reason, but not from the Knobstone region. Rather, the orchid was most likely collected in the limestone or chert barrens located west of the Knobs. Many grassland species are known from that area, and it could have harbored *Calopogon* quite suitably.

PRECEDING PAGE: *Calopogon tuberosus* (grass-pink). June 1990, Steuben Co. Lee Casebere. x³/₄.

ABOVE: *C. tuberosus*, with crab spider. June 1988, La Grange Co. Lee Casebere. x1.

HABITAT: *Calopogon* is a sun-loving species that occurs in many of the same habitats that harbor *Pogonia*; i.e., sphagnum bogs, fens, moist sand flats, and marly lake borders. It also grows in mesic and wet-mesic sand prairie. In fens *Calopogon* grows with *Cladium mariscoides, Eupatorium perfoliatum, Liparis loeselii, Pogonia ophioglossoides, Potentilla fruticosa, Scirpus acutus, Smilacina stellata, Solidago patula, Sorghastrum nutans, Spiraea tomentosa, Thelypteris palustris, Typha angustifolia,* and *Zizia aurea.*

Calopogon appears to reach its greatest vigor in sphagnum bogs, where it grows with *Carex lasiocarpa, Decodon verticillatus, Drosera rotundifolia, Pogonia ophioglossoides, Potentilla palustris, Rhus vernix, Salix petiolaris, Scirpus validus,* and *Thelypteris palustris.* In wet sand/peat flats, *Calopogon* grows with *Aletris farinosa, Drosera rotundifolia, Euthamia graminifolia, Lycopodium inundatum, Osmunda regalis, Platanthera flava* var. *herbiola, Pogonia ophioglossoides, Polygala cruciata, Scleria triglomerata, Spiranthes cernua,* and *Xyris torta.*

Marly lake border is an especially favored habitat of *Calopogon*, as it is here that sometimes hundreds of plants occur. Characteristic associates include *Eleocharis rostellata, Carex sterilis, C. viridula, Cicuta bulbifera, Hypericum kalmianum, Liatris spicata, Lythrum alatum, Panicum implicatum, Potentilla fruticosa, Rhynchospora capillacea, Senecio pauperculus, Scirpus acutus, S. lineatus, Solidago ohioensis,* and *Thalictrum revolutum.*

DISCUSSION: Like its companion the rose pogonia, *Calopogon tuberosus* is also a pink "bearded" orchid of the wetlands found in Indiana's northern counties. As well, both have similar flowering seasons, and both can occur in great numbers at a given site, either in the same year or in alternating years. *Calopogon* is the only Indiana orchid with flowers that are non-resupinate. As indicated in the Introduction, the lip is lowermost in most orchid species, but in *Calopogon,* because of the lack of a 180–degree twist of the ovary and flower pedicel (stalk), the lip is uppermost.

Because a major function of an orchid lip is to provide a landing platform and nectar guide for would-be pollinators, the question arises how *Calopogon* gets pollinated, as its lip appears unsuitable for such purposes. The answer is one of deception. The orchid lures passing insects into landing on its bearded lip by creating an illusion of pollen and nectar. Instead of pollen and nectar, however, the insect discovers only pseudopollen. To add insult to injury, the lip is typically unable to support the weight of the visiting insect, such as a honeybee, and it comes crashing down onto the column with the bee attached. True pollen grains from the column attach to the bee's backside and are carried along to another flower for another exercise of deceit. There the same ritual is repeated, but this time pollen grains from the previous flower may be deposited onto the stigma of the new flower, and cross-fertilization ensues. It appears awkward, but it works nevertheless.

COELOGLOSSUM
Hartman

Coeloglossum is a monotypic genus that occurs throughout the temperate regions of the northern hemisphere. Few native Indiana orchid species can boast such a worldwide distribution.

Coeloglossum means literally "hollow tongue," from the Greek *koilos,* for "hollow," and *glossa,* for "tongue." The "hollow tongue" is in reference to the short, saccate nectary extending below the base of the labellum.

Historically, the species we now place in *Coeloglossum* has been placed among several different genera. In this century most authors have placed it in the genus *Habenaria,* usually as *H. viridis* var. *bracteata.* Luer (1975) pointed out several features of the plant that justify its separation from *Habenaria* and *Platanthera,* such as the presence of forked fleshy tuberoids and a microscopic membrane over the viscidium. Although these distinctions may seem slight, they serve to justify observations that *Coeloglossum* does not seem to "fit" in *Habenaria* or *Platanthera*.

Coeloglossum viride (Linnaeus) Hartman

[Syn: *Habenaria viridis* (Linnaeus) R. Brown var. *bracteata* (Muhlenberg) A. Gray]

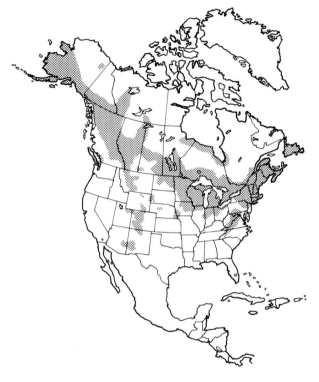

COMMON NAMES: long-bracted orchid, frog orchid, satyr orchid.

SPECIFIC EPITHET DERIVATION: *viride* = "green," in refererence to the overall greenish color of the species.

DESCRIPTION: Plant glabrous, 20–25 cm tall. Roots fleshy, forking from a thickened rootstock. **Leaves** 2–3, **obovate to oblanceolate,** 6–7 cm long x 2–2.5 cm wide. **Inflorescence** a tight raceme of 8–15 flowers, **with conspicuous leafy bracts,** these lanceolate, 15–20 mm long x 3–4 mm wide. **Lip** 4–6 mm long x 2–3 mm wide, **green,** oblong, **with 2 lateral lobes and an inconspicuous central lobe at the apex. Spur** at base of lip **scrotiform,** 1–2 mm long. Petals linear-lanceolate, green, 3–4 mm long x 1–1.5 mm wide. Sepals ovate, green, 4–5 mm long x 2 mm wide. **Petals and sepals converge to form a hood over the column.**

BLOOMING PERIOD: early May to mid-June.

RANGE: Generally confined to the northern one-third of Indiana. A major southern extension extends into west-central Indiana, with scattered populations as far south as Vigo County.

HABITAT: *Coeloglossum viride* is most often found in rich, mesic forests, but it also has been collected, although rarely, from swamps, tamarack bogs, and, according to Peattie (1930), pine woods. The wet borders of vernal pools, a habitat type described by Case (1987) as harboring the orchid in southern Michigan, have yielded a few specimens in northeastern Indiana. Deam (1940) wrote about two large colonies growing on the low border of Crooked Lake in Noble County, but those orchids are a different species (see Discussion).

In the mesic forest environment, *Coeloglossum viride* occurs in a variety of aspects, from the tops of slopes in hilly situations to stream terraces in ravine valleys and floodplain forests. In west-central Indiana most populations occur on the forested hills and ravines bordering the

Coeloglossum viride (long-bracted orchid). June 1990, Wabash Co. Lee Casebere. x1.

Wabash River valley. Typical overstory trees of these forests include American basswood, sugar maple, tulip tree, American beech, American elm, black walnut, blue beech, red oak, and white ash. A multitude of herbaceous associates occurs with *Coeloglossum*; at one site in Tippecanoe County I noted *Actaea alba*, *Asarum canadense*, *Botrychium virginianum*, *Cryptotaenia canadensis*, *Geranium maculatum*, *Lindera benzoin*, *Osmorhiza claytonii*, *Polymnia canadensis*, *Rhus radicans*, and *Smilacina racemosa*.

Sheviak (1974) states that *Coeloglossum* occurs in xeric, disturbed bluff-top habitats just west of Indiana in Champaign and Vermilion counties, Illinois. The proximity of the Illinois sites indicates a good likelihood of such habitat usage by *Coeloglossum* in Indiana.

C. *viride* (long-bracted orchid). June 1990, Wabash Co. Lee Casebere. x1½.

DISCUSSION: *Coeloglossum viride* is not a spectacular orchid; certainly many people have passed by it without a second glance. It is an uncommon, "unsociable" orchid, rarely occurring with more than one or two others of its own kind. I have searched acre upon acre of seemingly suitable habitat only to encounter a few individuals in less than a handful of localities. My experience in this is consistent with that of others, including Deam (1940). One exception is noted by Cunningham (1896): "Dr. Stanley Coulter says that it [*Coeloglossum*] is fairly abundant in Tippecanoe [County]." Interestingly, most of the currently known populations in Indiana are in Tippecanoe County.

In his *Flora of Indiana*, Deam (1940) claimed to have found two large colonies on the low border of Crooked Lake in Noble County. He said: "This is the only place I have seen two specimens or more in a place." However, his voucher (*Deam 54449*, IND) from that population is *Platanthera flava* var. *herbiola*, and not *Coeloglossum*. It should be noted that his plants are atypical for *P. flava*, as the flowering spikes are shorter than normal, and in fruit only. However, the overall habit of the plant, its floral remnants, its lanceolate leaves, and its colonial growth clearly point to *P. flava*.

Coeloglossum and *Platanthera flava* are commonly confused, especially as dried specimens. The main reason for the confusion is the presence of long floral bracts in both orchids. Regardless of the bracts, when blooming there should be no confusion, as the flowers are quite different. Sterile plants can be determined by a number of characters, best used in combination. *Platanthera flava* typically has relatively narrow, acute, lanceolate leaves, and is a colonial orchid of swamps and wet prairie. *Coeloglossum* is primarily a plant of upland sites, occurring singularly, with leaves (especially the lower ones) somewhat obovate to oblanceolate (broadest toward the tip) and rather blunt. In addition, the bracts are leafier in *Coeloglossum* than in *P. flava*.

All individuals of *Coeloglossum viride* in Indiana belong to variety *virescens* (Muhlenberg) Luer. Plants of var. *virescens* are taller and possess longer floral bracts than the typical variety (var. *viride*).

CORALLORHIZA
(Haller) Chatelain

Corallorhiza, from the Greek *korallion*, for "coral," and *rhiza*, for "root," is a genus of leafless, fleshy, saprophytic and/or hemi-parasitic orchids composed of approximately ten species. Most are native to the Americas, with only one, *C. trifida*, occurring in both the Old and New World. There are four species indigenous to Indiana.

Like *Hexalectris*, the coral-roots essentially live their lives underground, deriving their nutrition (via mycorrhizae) from decaying organic matter, and breaking the surface of the soil only briefly for the purpose of reproduction. They have been reported to become dormant for several years between flowerings, but because of their saprophytic, subterranean existence, an absence above ground does not necessarily indicate dormancy.

Members of *Corallorhiza* do not have roots, instead having toothed, multi-branched rhizomes resembling coral, hence the common and botanical names.

CORALLORHIZA
A.   Plants blooming in spring, from mid-April to mid-June .... B.
      B.   Stems and flowers greenish to greenish-white overall; lip three-lobed and unspotted (in southern Great Lakes populations, including Indiana); sepals spreading; rare plant, apparently extirpated, known only from the Lake Michigan Dunes region .... *Corallorhiza trifida*
      BB.   Stems and flowers light brown, purplish, to orange brown; lip purple spotted, not three-lobed; sepals closely joined (but not fused) with petals; relatively common in the southern half of state, extremely rare elsewhere ....
.... *Corallorhiza wisteriana*
AA. Plants blooming in late July to late October .... C.
      C.   Lip three-lobed; flowers commonly with widely spreading perianth parts, giving the flower an "open" look ....
.... *Corallorhiza maculata*

CC. Lip unlobed; flowers commonly with perianth parts tightly appressed to one another, giving the flower a "closed" look (or if "open" the sepals and petals still convergent, but separated from the lip) .... *Corallorhiza odontorhiza*

Corallorhiza maculata (Rafinesque) Rafinesque

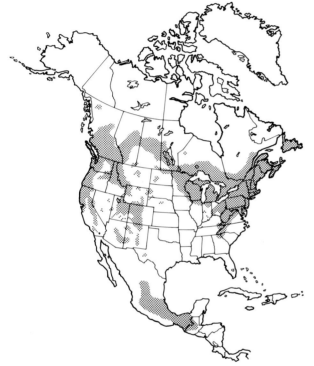

Corallorhiza maculata (spotted coral-root). August 1989, La Grange Co. Lee Casebere. x1.

COMMON NAME: spotted coral-root.

SPECIFIC EPITHET DERIVATION: *maculata* = "spotted," in reference to the purplish spots on the flowers.

DESCRIPTION: Plant glabrous, leafless, with a yellowish to purplish, fleshy stem, 20–30 cm tall. **Roots absent. Rhizome multi-branched, coralloid.** Inflorescence avg. 10–15 flowers, each subtended by a minute floral bract. **Lip** 4–6 mm long x 3–4 mm wide, ovate, **three-lobed, white with purple spots.** Petals yellowish-purple, oblanceolate, 4–5 mm long x 1–2 mm wide. Sepals similar to petals, but slightly larger. **Perianth parts spreading, giving the flower an "open" look.**

BLOOMING PERIOD: late July to mid-September.

RANGE: *Corallorhiza maculata* is found predominantly in the northern one-third of the state, and from a few collections in southern Indiana as far south as Floyd County. Most collections have been made in the Northern Lakes Natural Region, followed by the Northwestern Morainal Natural Region and the Entrenched Valley Section of the Central Till Plain Natural Region. South of the Wisconsinan glacial limit collections have been made only in the Highland Rim Natural Region, specifically the Knobstone Escarpment and Brown County Hills sections.

HABITAT: Most occurrences of *Corallorhiza maculata* are in mesic to dry-mesic upland forest communities composed of white oak, red oak, black oak, sugar maple, American beech, and white ash. It grows with an array of plants typical of such environments, including *Amelanchier arborea, Aster shortii, Brachyelytrum erectum, Cornus florida, Desmodium nudiflorum, D. glutinosum, Hepatica americana, Osmorhiza claytonii, Os-*

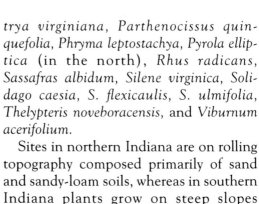

trya virginiana, Parthenocissus quinquefolia, Phryma leptostachya, Pyrola elliptica (in the north), *Rhus radicans, Sassafras albidum, Silene virginica, Solidago caesia, S. flexicaulis, S. ulmifolia, Thelypteris noveboracensis,* and *Viburnum acerifolium.*

Sites in northern Indiana are on rolling topography composed primarily of sand and sandy-loam soils, whereas in southern Indiana plants grow on steep slopes within a rugged landscape of thin, silt-loam soils over sandstone, siltstone, and shale.

Like the other coral-roots, *C. maculata* is not particularly adverse to disturbance; in fact, minor disturbances apparently enhance habitat, as relatively few plants are found in densely shaded, mature forest sites. For example, at one site in Brown County I found *C. maculata* growing along the edge of a hiking trail, but could find no plants in the undisturbed forest beyond.

C. maculata (spotted coral-root). August 1978, Porter Co. Don Kurz. x3.

DISCUSSION: The spotted coral-root is clearly one of Indiana's most attractive coral-roots. Unlike *Corallorhiza wisteriana* and *C. odontorhiza*, which seem hesitant to open their flowers, *C. maculata* boldly spreads its vividly colored petals and sepals to all incoming pollinators. Yet not many people take the opportunity to enjoy it, probably because blooming is normally during the hottest time of the year. *Corallorhiza maculata* also is not particularly easy to find, partly because of its rarity and also because it is a small plant that is camouflaged in the backdrop of foliage and leaf litter.

Indiana has the distinction of having the southernmost occurrences of the *Corallorhiza maculata* in the Midwest. Although I was aware of this fact during the research for this book, I was somewhat doubtful that the species was extant in southern Indiana today. Thus, it was a great surprise to encounter a few plants of the orchid on July 30, 1985, just north of Nashville in Brown County. I am unaware of additional current southern Indiana observations of the orchid, but given the great amount of potential habitat available, certainly more plants await discovery. The Floyd County collection (*Friesner s.n.*, BUT) is especially interesting, as it occurs just across the Ohio River from Kentucky, where only one site for the orchid is known, that in distant Harlan County (Marc Evans, personal communication). Perhaps a significant Kentucky record occurs in suitable habitat adjacent to Floyd County.

Several taxa variously treated as varieties and forms have been de-

scribed for *Corallorhiza maculata*, but much remains to be discovered before the complex taxonomic problem can be resolved. The *C. maculata* that occurs in Indiana correlates with the "late-flowering" taxon described by Freudenstein (1987). An "early-flowering" taxon also occurs in the Great Lakes region, but apparently is not found in Indiana. In general, the late-flowering taxon has smaller and fewer flowers than the early-flowering one.

Corallorhiza odontorhiza (Willdenow) Nuttall

COMMON NAMES: autumn coral-root, late coral-root, fall coral-root.

SPECIFIC NAME DERIVATION: *odontorhiza* = "toothed root," in reference to the tooth-like swelling of the stem above the rhizome.

DESCRIPTION: Plant glabrous, leafless, with a brownish to purplish fleshy stem, 12–20 cm tall. **Roots absent. Rhizome multi-branched, coralloid, attached to a swollen stem base.** Inflorescence a loose raceme of 8–15 flowers, each subtended by a minute floral bract. **Lip 2–4 mm long x 2–4 mm wide,** ovate to obovate, **entire, white with purple spots.** Petals lanceolate, greenish-purple, 3–4 mm long x 1 mm wide. Sepals similar to petals. Petals and sepals converge to form a hood over the lip. **Flowers commonly cleistogamous.**

BLOOMING PERIOD: mid-August to late October.

RANGE: *Corallorhiza odontorhiza* occurs virtually statewide, although it is rare to absent in the northeast and east-central parts of the state. Bradner (1892) reported it for Steuben County, but no specimens have been seen. It is by far most common in the Shawnee Hills and Highland Rim natural regions, followed closely by the Bluegrass Natural Region and the Entrenched Valley Section of the Central Till Plain Natural Region. In the northwest it is very local, but common in suitable habitats. Schneck (1876) reported it from Gibson and Posey counties, but I have seen no specimens to support this claim.

ABOVE: *Corallorhiza odontorhiza* (autumn coral-root), showing chasmogamous flowers. September 1968, Porter Co. Valdemar Schwarz. x1½.

OPPOSITE: *C. odontorhiza*, showing cleistogamous flowers. August 1992, Morgan Co. Mike Homoya. x1.

HABITAT: *Corallorhiza odontorhiza* occurs primarily in dry-mesic and dry upland forest communities. Other habitats include flatwoods (especially in the southeastern and far northwestern parts of the state), mesic upland forests, forested ravine bottoms, and pine plantations. The orchid is the most disturbance tolerant of the Indiana coral-roots. In fact, it is more often found in young regrowth forest and along and on forest trails and other openings than in mature forests. Deam (1940) reported it growing even "in bare places in fallow fields." Like *C. wisteriana*, it occurs on both acidic and basic substrates—till, sandy outwash, loess, and sandstone and limestone derived silt-loams.

In upland sites, typical overstory trees associated with the orchid include white oak, black oak, chinquapin oak, American beech, sugar maple, tulip tree, shagbark hickory, and flowering dogwood. Understory associates include *Aster shortii*, *Cimicifuga racemosa*, *Conopholis americana*, *Desmodium nudiflorum*, *Eupatorium rugosum*, *Geranium maculatum*, *Osmorhiza longistylis*, *Parthenocissus quinquefolia*, *Potentilla simplex*, *Smilax rotundifolia*, and *Solidago caesia*.

In the flatwoods communities overstory trees are typically sweetgum, American beech, tulip tree, red maple, black gum, and pin oak. Understory species include *Botrychium dissectum*, *Eupatorium rugosum*, *Gaultheria procumbens*, *Maianthemum canadense* (northern Indiana only), *Mitchella repens*, and *Potentilla simplex*.

DISCUSSION: *Corallorhiza odontorhiza* is less spectacular than the other orchids native to Indiana, but not because it is small or has uncolorful flowers; on the contrary, the flowers are no smaller than some species of *Spiranthes*, and its petals possess that impressive "jewelaceous" texture. The problem is that the vast majority of individuals possess flowers that never open (a condition called cleistogamy). Because the flowers are apparently autogamous (and possibly agamospermous), as evidenced by the nearly 100 percent of the ovaries swollen with seed even before the flowering stalk attains full size, there is no need for pollinators, and consequently, no need for flowers to attract them.

Case (1987) indicates two forms of *Corallorhiza odontorhiza* occurring in the Great Lakes region; cleistogamous (self-fertilizing, flower closed) and chasmogamous (flower open, with the potential for cross-pollination). He indicates that populations of the two forms are

uniformly segregated. Such is not true in Indiana. Plants with chasmogamous flowers are rarely found, and are usually interspersed with cleistogamous plants.

Corallorhiza odontorhiza is reported to be rare in the Midwest (Deam, 1940; Mohlenbrock, 1970; Sheviak, 1974; Case, 1987), but I have found it to be one of the more regularly encountered native orchids, and easily the most common coral-root in Indiana. In fact, it is one of the few orchids that I have seen within the city limits of Indianapolis!

The historic records of *Corallorhiza odontorhiza* give a different account of its abundance. There are few reports and collections of this species by the early botanists, suggesting that it was either a rare plant, or simply overlooked. I suspect the former, as our early botanists had no trouble in finding other inconspicuous species. Why then is this orchid relatively common now compared to earlier times? One answer may be a greater ability to colonize disturbed sites. Many but not all of the very early collections of *C. odontorhiza* were taken from relatively undisturbed forest environments, whereas today plants primarily occur in disturbed sites. Why this is so I do not know. Perhaps an examination of a plant with a parallel history may produce some insight. Trailing ground pine, *Lycopodium digitatum,* is also a formerly rare plant that now is quite common. Compare the comments by Deam (1940) about the ground pine's occurrence prior to 1940 ("Extremely local. Found on moist, rocky slopes"), with what we know about the species today (very common and even invasive, especially in old-field and mid-successional habitats). Sheviak (personal communication) suggests that the reason for the ground pine's change in abundance and range may be attributed to an opportunistic ecotype that invaded from the eastern United States. The ecotype possesses a gene combination favorable to occupying disturbed habitats—habitats apparently unfavorable to "indigenous" ecotypes of *L. digitatum*—and now a "rare" species is seemingly everywhere. Whether the greater frequency and range expansion of *C. odontorhiza* can be attributed to the invasion of a disturbance-adapted ecotype is in need of further study. See the discussion of *Spiranthes ovalis* var. *erostellata* for an example of another autogamous orchid that has spread similarly in recent years.

Corallorhiza trifida Chatelain

COMMON NAMES: early coral-root, northern coral-root.

SPECIFIC EPITHET DERIVATION: *trifida* = "three-parted cleft," in reference to the three-lobed lip of the species.

DESCRIPTION: **Plant glabrous, leafless, with a yellowish-green fleshy stem, 10–20 cm tall. Roots absent. Rhizome multi-branched, coralloid.** Inflorescence a loose raceme of 5–8 flowers, each subtended by a minute floral bract. **Lip 3–4 mm long x 2 mm wide, white, obovate, three-lobed, the terminal lobe much larger than the laterals and rounded at the apex.** Petals oblanceolate, yellowish-green, 3 mm long x 1 mm wide. Dorsal sepal similar to petals, 3–4 mm long x 1 mm wide. Lateral sepals oblanceolate, falcate, yellowish-green, 3–4 mm long x 1 mm wide.

BLOOMING PERIOD: mid-May to mid-June.

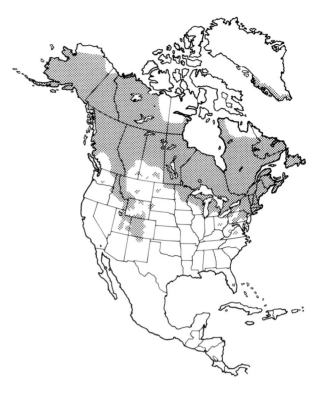

RANGE: This northern orchid is known with certainty only from Lake County, where a total of five plants were taken: three by E. J. Hill in 1887 (*Hill 211888*, ILL), and two by L. M. Umbach in 1897 (*Umbach 2812*, WIS). An additional specimen(s) may have been taken by Hill, as Higley and Raddin (1891) and Pepoon (1927) cite a collection (report?) by Hill from "Sand ridges, east of Berry Lake, Ind., Hill!" If the information reported is printed verbatim from the specimen label, the collection must be of one other than *Hill 211888*, as the latter's label information is worded "damp woods, Whiting, Ind." Regardless, the location is generally the same, as Berry Lake, when it existed, was within the city limits of Whiting.

Millers, Indiana, is the location given on the Umbach specimen (*Umbach s.n.*, WIS). However, Pepoon (1927) stated Clarke Junction was the site of the (an) Umbach collection. Because Clarke Junction and Millers are not one and the same, there were either two Umbach collections (no Clarke Junction specimen was found), or Pepoon incorrectly reported the locality.

Pepoon (1927) and Peattie (1930) reported that *Corallorhiza trifida* was abundant near Dune Park, in Porter County, but no specimens exist to verify the reports. Dune Park (not Indiana Dunes State Park) has been destroyed by industrial development, so there is no hope of verification by locating additional living specimens.

The reports of *Corallorhiza trifida* for Floyd County by Coulter, Coul-

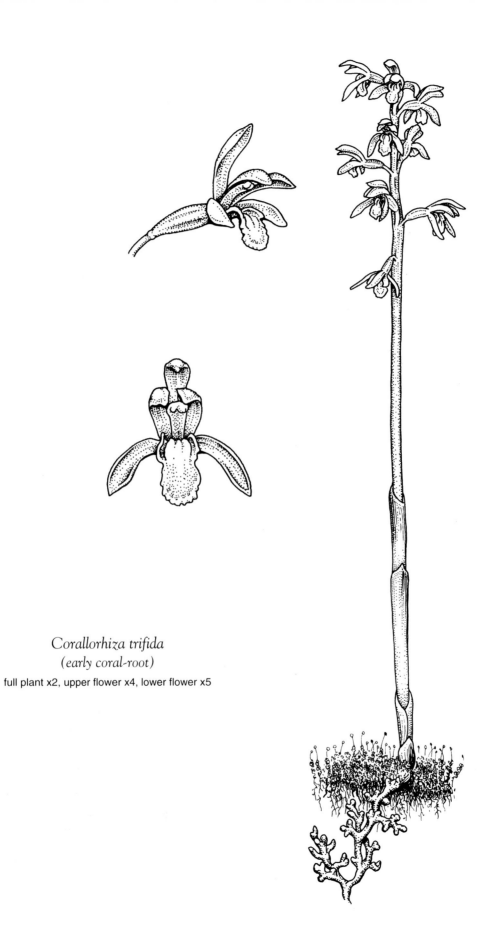

Corallorhiza trifida
(early coral-root)

full plant x2, upper flower x4, lower flower x5

ter, and Barnes (1881), Cunningham (1896), and Coulter (1900) are obviously in error. The records are attributed to Dr. A. Clapp of New Albany, who did indeed denote a collection of *C. trifida* (as *C. innata*, a synonym) from the New Albany area in his collection log. However, neither he nor any of the authors mentioned above reported *C. wisteriana*, a relatively common spring blooming coral-root in southern Indiana. It is clear that they applied the incorrect name to *C. wisteriana*.

Because of the orchid's northern affinities, the likelihood of its occurrence outside of the Lake Michigan dunes region is doubtful. The only possible exception for discovery is in the Northern Lakes Natural Region.

HABITAT: Very little is known about the habitat of *Corallorhiza trifida* in Indiana. What meager information we do have is from labels of specimens collected by Umbach and Hill (see above), and reports by Pepoon (1927) and Peattie (1930). Umbach's collection was from a "tamarack swamp," and Hill's from "damp woods." Pepoon and Peattie reported it from low, wet dune swale woods.

Case (1987) reports that the orchid's primary habitats in the southern edge of its Great Lakes range are mucky, brushy borders of cedar-balsam-spruce swamps and dark, white cedar thickets. White cedar (*Thuja occidentalis*), formerly common in the Indiana Dunes, is now extant only in Cowles Bog, and balsam (*Abies balsamea*) and spruce (*Picea mariana*) never occurred here in recorded history, thus limiting good potential habitat.

DISCUSSION: *Corallorhiza trifida* easily qualifies as Indiana's rarest coral-root, and also has the most restricted range of all the coral-roots in the state. Elsewhere in its range it is locally abundant, but like many species that are on the edge of their range, as *C. trifida* is here, numbers decrease and habitat requirements become more specific (and in some cases different from the typical). That makes for an all the more interesting search to relocate this dainty, yellow-green orchid. Even with the failed attempts by botanists in recent years to locate this orchid, there is still hope that it still resides somewhere in the Lake Michigan Dunes area, tucked away in some remote, mosquito-infested swampy woods where few have ventured.

Indiana plants of *Corallorhiza trifida* are referable to what some authors recognize as var. *verna* (Nuttall) Fernald. This variety, or form, as most currently designate it, occurs in the southern portion of the species' range, and differs from the typical form in being pale yellow-green (compared to brown-tinged), and having a white, unspotted lip (purple-spotted in the northern forms).

The presence of chlorophyll in *Corallorhiza trifida* indicates that it has, at least to some degree, the property of photosynthesis. It is primarily saprophytic, however, and in some cases, may actually be hemiparasitic. Campbell (1970) has shown that via mycorrhizae there is a connection between the rhizome of the orchid to the roots of cedar (*Thuja*) or spruce (*Picea*), whereby nourishment is transferred from the tree roots to the orchid. This partial parasitism is apparently not species specific, because in the far north the orchid occurs in areas locally devoid of cedar and spruce. Its close association with cedar and spruce in the southern part of its range provides for interesting speculation regarding its occurrence in Indiana. It is not known if *C. trifida* was intimately associated with cedar in Indiana, but the orchid did occur in areas generally known to have the tree. Thus, the the orchid's absence here may be a consequence of the decline and near-absence of cedar.

Corallorhiza wisteriana Conrad

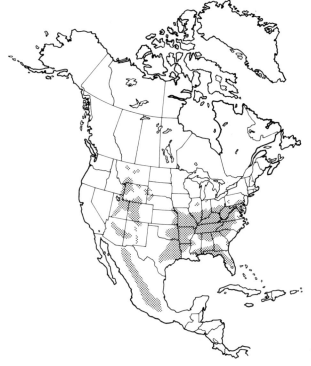

Corallorhiza wisteriana (spring coral-root). May 1989, Ripley Co. Lee Casebere. x1⅓.

COMMON NAMES: spring coral-root, Wister's coral-root.

SPECIFIC EPITHET DERIVATION: *wisteriana*, in honor of American botanist Charles Wister.

DESCRIPTION: Plant glabrous, leafless, with reddish to yellowish, fleshy stem 20–30 cm tall. **Roots absent. Rhizome multi-branched, coralloid.** Inflorescence a loose raceme of 8–14 flowers, each subtended by a minute floral bract. **Lip 5–6 mm long x 3–4 mm wide,** ovate, **entire, white with purple spots.** Petals lanceolate, yellowish to purplish-brown, 4–5 mm long x 1 mm wide. Sepals similar to petals, 5–6 mm long x 1–1.3 mm wide. Petals and sepals converge to form a hood over the lip. **Flowers normally chasmogamous.**

BLOOMING PERIOD: mid-April to early June.

RANGE: *Corallorhiza wisteriana* is generally restricted to the southern half of Indiana, with one remarkable exception occurring in St. Joseph County. Its current distribution pattern is generally the same as that given by Deam (1940), thus indicating that the factors controlling distribution in the past are still in effect.

HABITAT: This coral-root occurs primarily in moist but well-drained upland forest communities. Some sites where it occurs are surprisingly dry, but even there ample leaf litter is present to retain soil moisture. The orchid typically occurs at mid-slope in ravine situations where moderate moisture conditions prevail. Soil pH is apparently not critical (except for extremes), as *C. wisteriana* occurs in both sandstone and limestone derived substrates. The orchid's tolerance of various soil con-

ditions thus explains its occurrence across all natural regions in southern Indiana.

Where *Corallorhiza wisteriana* is typically found, sugar maple, white oak, chinquapin oak, red oak, blue beech, American beech, white ash, and shagbark hickory are characteristic overstory dominants. Some of the associated herbaceous and shrub species include *Asarum canadense, Cornus alternifolia, Dirca palustris, Festuca subverticillata, Hepatica acutiloba, Iris cristata, Mitella diphylla, Osmorhiza claytonii, Poa sylvestris, Senecio obovatus, Silene virginica, Viburnum rufidulum,* and *Viola rostrata.*

DISCUSSION: *Corallorhiza wisteriana* is one of the earliest orchids to bloom in Indiana. Although most plants of *C. wisteriana* bloom in May, some individuals in the southern counties open their flowers as early as mid-April. The orchid is commonly overlooked, as its leafless, reddish to yellow-brown stems and tiny flowers have little chance competing for attention when trilliums, fire pinks, and larkspurs are at their full glory.

C. wisteriana (spring coral-root). May 1989, Ripley Co. Lee Casebere. x1½.

Corallorhiza wisteriana is the only orchid occurring predominantly in the southeastern U.S. and having an additional range in the Rocky Mountains. This distribution pattern is interesting because other orchids occurring in both the eastern and western U.S. have more or less contiguous distributions through boreal Canada. Although eastern and western plants of *C. wisteriana* are essentially the same morphologically, one characteristic that separates the two is an apparent difference in minimum temperature tolerances. While conclusive proof has not been presented, the inability of plants to become established in northern Indiana and elsewhere in the northeastern U.S. appears to be due to an intolerance of cold. The western plants seem better adapted to low temperatures, as they can occur at relatively high elevations in the Rocky Mountains as far north as Montana and Idaho.

East of the Rockies, there are few examples of *Corallorhiza wisteriana* extending into more northern latitudes. Two in the Midwest include a population in La Salle County, Illinois (specimen cited in Sheviak, 1974), and another in St. Joseph County, Indiana (*Mottier and Pickett* 1473, IND). Both collections were taken from sites approximately 100 miles distant from the nearest stations to the south. Case (1987), although acknowledging and accepting the voucher for St. Joseph County, expresses the possibility that the location may be in error, as "Ind" was penciled on the label by someone other than the collectors, and apparently at a later date. However, Mottier and Pickett were known to have collected in northern Indiana, so the orchid most likely did come from St. Joseph County, Indiana. That plus the fact that the specimen is in relatively good flowering condition for a collection from such a late date (June 1914) suggests that it was taken from a northern site.

The significance of these northern populations is unclear. Either they are products of long-distance seed dispersal, or they are relics of a former time when the orchid's normal range extended into more northern latitudes than today. A third hypothesis suggests that the populations are not disjunct, but are outliers of an existing contiguous range (with the "missing links" not yet discovered). In Indiana the latter hypothesis is very unlikely, as almost 80 years have passed since the orchid's discovery in St. Joseph County, and a great deal of botanizing has taken place in northern Indiana in the interim without other populations being discovered.

I suspect long-range seed dispersal is responsible for the establishment of the northern Indiana population, especially considering that orchid seeds are capable of traveling great distances via wind currents. However, Sheviak (1974) presents a plausible scenario for relict status in Illinois, suggesting that historic changes in climate may have allowed for the introduction, and subsequent extirpation, of the orchid in northern latitudes, leaving in recent times only isolated populations existing in suitable microclimatic refugia.

Deam 40366 (NY), collected in Dearborn County, was used as a model for the *Corallorhiza wisteriana* illustration in *The New Britton and Brown Illustrated Flora of the Northeastern United States and Adjacent Canada* (Gleason, 1952).

—— CYPRIPEDIUM ——
Linnaeus

The name *Cypripedium* was created by combining the Greek word *Kypris,* for Cypris, goddess of love and beauty, and, according to Luer (1975), the Latin *pedis,* for "foot." Schultes and Pease (1963), however, indicate that *Kypris* and *ped(i)lon,* for "sandal," combine to form *Cypripedium.*

Known in England as Lady's-slipper as early as 1616 (Niles, 1904), the common name of *Cypripedium* was a contraction of the Latin *Marianus,* referring to "Our Lady," the Virgin Mary, and *calceolus,* the Latin word for shoe or slipper. According to Niles (1904), Linnaeus, when naming the orchid for his Species Plantarum, objected to dedicating the genus to the mother of Christ (he was a devout Lutheran), and instead chose to name it after Cypris (Aphrodite), the Greek goddess of love. Linnaeus may have chosen Cypris because she was the Greek equivalent to Venus, the latter also known as "Our Lady" to the early Romans.

Cypripedium differs from the rest of Indiana's orchids in having two fertile anthers (instead of one). It also differs in possessing loose, granular pollen (as opposed to typical pollinia of other genera). The anthers are located on both sides of a large staminode or "shield" situated behind and above the opening to the pouch (see Introduction, Fig. 3). The presence of the two anthers has led some botanists to consider assigning *Cypripedium* to a separate family, but such a treatment would likely not be acceptable to most orchidologists.

Depending on treatment, there are between thirty and fifty species of *Cypripedium* in the world. Most occur in the temperate regions, but a few occur in the Arctic, as well as the subtropics. There are eleven species in North America, four of which occur in Indiana.

CYPRIPEDIUM

A.   Lip yellow.. B.

    B.   Flowers small, lip averaging 2 cm long; lateral petals dark purple; leaves commonly 3 (4), elliptic to ovate-lanceolate; plants primarily of organic soils with calcareous seepage .... *Cypripedium calceolus* var. *parviflorum*

    BB.   Flowers relatively large, lip 3 cm or more long; lateral petals greenish to yellowish brown; leaves commonly 4 (5), ovate to ovate-lanceolate; plants primarily of well-drained sandy-loam or silt-loam soils (uncommonly in muck soils) .... *Cypripedium calceolus* var. *pubescens*

AA.   Lip white or pink.. C.

    C.   Leaves basal, in pairs (single leaf common in sterile plants); lip mostly pink to pinkish-purple, with a frontal longitudinal fold .... *Cypripedium acaule*

    CC.   Leaves not basal, 3 or more in number, alternating on the stem; lip mostly white, or white with a "wash" of pink on the front and extending around the sides; lip with a rounded opening above..D.

        D.   Petals greenish-yellow with purple streaks, undulate to slightly twisted; lip white, commonly suffused with pinkish-purple streaks underneath....................
.... *Cypripedium candidum*

        DD.   Petals white, broad and untwisted; lip white and normally with a "wash" of pink on the front and sides...*Cypripedium reginae*

Cypripedium acaule Aiton

COMMON NAMES: pink lady's-slipper, pink moccasin flower.

SPECIFIC EPITHET DERIVATION: *acaule* = "without a stem," in allusion to the leafless flowering stalk arising from the seemingly "stemless" pair of basal leaves.

DESCRIPTION: Plant mostly short-pubescent throughout, 25–35 cm tall. **Leaves basal, normally 2** (1 in some sterile plants), elliptic, ribbed, 15–18 cm long x 8–10 cm wide. Roots fibrous. **Inflorescence** consisting of **a single flower**, it **subtended by a** green, lanceolate, **foliaceous bract**, 3–4 cm long x 1–1.2 cm wide. **Flowering stem a scape.** Lip 4–6 cm long x 3–4 cm wide, **pink, obovoid, with a longitudinal cleft in front.** Petals ovate-lanceolate, **purplish, slightly twisted**, 4 cm long x 1 cm wide. Dorsal sepal lanceolate to elliptic-lanceolate, purplish, 3–4 cm long x 1.2–1.5 cm wide. **Lateral sepals united** behind the lip, ovate-lanceolate, purplish, 3.5–4 cm long x 1.6–1.8 cm wide. Staminode ovate, purplish.

BLOOMING PERIOD: mid-May to mid-June.

RANGE: Confined to the northern one-fourth of the state, principally in the Northern Lakes and Northwestern Morainal natural regions. The report for Monroe County (Andrews, 1927) is certainly in error, as the county is beyond the range for the species, and suitable habitat is apparently lacking.

HABITAT: In Indiana *Cypripedium acaule* is a bog plant, although elsewhere in its range it can occur in dry, acid soils in upland conifer and oak woodlands. Most Indiana plants grow on sphagnum moss hummocks in the shaded borders of bogs and natural lakes. At some sites, the orchid does grow for short periods in full sun, but normally it is shaded during the heat of day by nearby tall shrubs and trees. Interestingly, W. C. Steele, in writing about orchids of northern Indiana (1881), stated that *C. acaule* does well in swamps with full sunlight. He goes on to state that the removal of tamarack trees in a given swamp will be little if any detriment to *C. acaule*, whereas *C. reginae*, in the same swamp under the same conditions, will decline. Given my experience, I suspect he may have crossed the two species in his writing, as *C. reginae* is the one more likely to thrive in full sun.

FOLLOWING PAGE: *Cypripedium acaule* (pink lady's-slipper). June 1983, Steuben Co. Lee Casebere. x1½.

Tamarack, red maple, and poison sumac are the principal woody plants that provide shade for *Cypripedium acaule*. Also commonly in close association are *Aronia prunifolia*, *Ilex verticillata*, and *Vaccinium corymbosum*. Smaller associates include *Chamaedaphne calyculata*, *Dryopteris cristata*, *Menyanthes trifoliata*, *Osmunda cinnamomea*, *O. regalis*, *Platanthera ciliaris*, *P. clavellata*, *Rhynchospora alba*, *Sarracenia purpurea*, and *Vaccinium oxycoccos*. In a Steuben County bog the orchid grows with *Aralia nudicaulis*, *Cornus alternifolia*, *Cypripedium calceolus pubescens*, *Gaylussacia baccata*, *Maianthemum canadense*, *Osmunda cinnamomea*, *Trientalis borealis*, *Trillium grandiflorum*, and *Vaccinium atrococcum*.

DISCUSSION: The pink lady's-slipper is one of the more common and familiar wildflowers in the northeastern U.S. and Canada, but in Indiana this attractive orchid is very uncommon. This is because most of Indiana's bogs (the orchid's principal habitat) have been drained or otherwise altered. Unless the remaining bogs are protected, further enjoyment of this lady's-slipper in Indiana is clearly in jeopardy.

Cypripedium acaule is sometimes referred to as the stemless lady's-slipper. This name has caused confusion for some, as the flower of this orchid is obviously not "stemless." The name is referring to the flowering stalk and basal leaves attached directly to an underground rhizome, giving the impression that the plant is without a stem. Another interesting common name of *Cypripedium acaule* is Noah's Ark. Although Correll (1978) listed it as one of the orchid's many common names, Clapp (1852) listed only that name. Some texts use Noah's Ark for a common

Cypripedium acaule   95

name of *C. calceolus* as well. I've yet to determine the meaning of the name, but I wonder if it's in allusion to the many insects that sometimes occur in the orchid's lip, as if passengers in a boat. Another possibility is that pioneer children used the lip as a boat, and floated them in water (Marlin Bowles, personal communication).

In a sterile condition other orchid species with paired basal leaves are sometimes confused with *Cypripedium acaule*. *Cypripedium acaule* has basal leaves that are deeply ribbed and hairy; the others (*Galearis, Liparis, Platanthera hookeri, P. orbiculata*) are glabrous and, with the exception of a midrib, virtually ribless.

Elsewhere in its range albino color forms of *Cypripedium acaule* (*forma albiflorum* Rand and Redfield) are not uncommon, particularly in the northeastern U.S. and Canada (Brackley, 1985). I have not encountered any *albiflorum* in Indiana, either in the field or herbarium. However, color forms tend to appear sporadically within normal populations, and thus the white form could occur here.

Cypripedium calceolus Linnaeus var. *parviflorum* (Salisbury) Fernald

[Syn: *Cypripedium parviflorum* Salisbury]

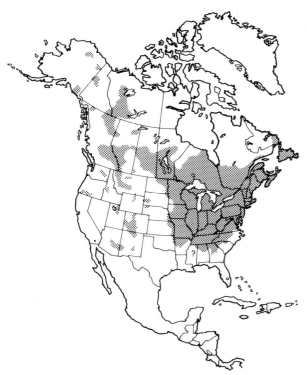

Map shows combined ranges for all varieties.

COMMON NAME: small yellow lady's-slipper.

SPECIFIC EPITHET DERIVATION: *calceolus* = "little shoe," in reference to the shoe-like shape of the lip; *parviflorum* = "small flower," in reference to the small flowers of the variety.

DESCRIPTION: **Plant mostly short-pubescent** throughout, 35–40 cm tall. Roots fibrous, 7–12 cm long. **Leaves 3–4, elliptic** to ovate-lanceolate, ribbed, **plicate (especially during anthesis)**, 14–18 cm long x 5–6 cm wide. **Inflorescence** consisting of **1 or 2 flowers** terminating the stem. **Floral bract foliaceous**, ovate-lanceolate, 5–6 cm long x 1.5–2 cm wide. **Lip 2 cm long x 1.5 cm wide, yellow, glossy, obovoid, commonly spotted with purple about the inner surface and edges of dorsal opening. Petals** linear-lanceolate, **deep reddish-purple to purplish-brown, twisted,** 3–4 cm long x 5 mm wide. Dorsal sepal ovate-lanceolate, colored like the petals, 3–4 cm long x 1.5 cm wide. **Lateral sepals**

united (except for a small apical separation) behind and below lip, colored like the petals, 3–3.5 cm long x 1.5 cm wide. Staminode triangular, yellow, and spotted with purple.

BLOOMING PERIOD: mid-May to early June.

RANGE: Occurs only in the northern half of the state, principally in the Northern Lakes and Northwestern Morainal natural regions, with a few outlying populations in the Central Till Plain Natural Region. Reports of this variety from southern Indiana, especially of plants from upland habitats, are undoubtedly variety *pubescens*.

HABITAT: *Cypripedium calceolus* var. *parviflorum* is a wetland plant occurring most commonly in habitats very similar to those of *C. reginae*, and indeed the two are typically found in association with one another. Preferred habitats are seepage communities composed of calcareous muck or peat saturated with cool, slowly moving ground water. The orchid usually is found growing in light shade provided by black ash, tamarack, poison sumac, and selected shrubby species of willow and dogwood. At a few fens and mesic sand prairie sites the orchid grows in full sunlight, at places in association with another of its congeners, *C. candidum*. Normally *C. candidum* grows in the most open areas of the site (where shorter stature vegetation and full exposure to the sun prevail), while *C. calceolus parviflorum* occurs on the edge where vegetation is coarser and lightly shaded by scattered trees and tall shrubs. The two species do intermingle, however, and may produce the hybrid *C. X andrewsii*.

In shaded sites, *Cypripedium calceolus parviflorum* occurs with *Caltha palustris, Cardamine bulbosa, Carex stipata, C. stricta, Cypripedium reginae, Equisetum fluviatile, Glyceria striata, Impatiens capensis, Lindera benzoin, Pedicularis lanceolata, Poa paludigena, Saxifraga pensylvanica, Senecio aureus, Symplocarpus foetidus,* and *Thelypteris palustris.*

In open wetlands, such as fens, the small yellow lady's-slipper grows with sun-loving species such as *Carex hystericina, C. leptalea, C. sterilis, Hypoxis hirsuta, Cypripedium candidum, Liparis loeselii, Parnassia glauca, Potentilla fruticosa,* and *Zizia aurea.*

Formerly an important habitat for *Cypripedium calceolus parviflorum* in northwest Indiana, the moist prairie swale community is now restricted to a narrow zone of dune and swale along Lake Michigan. Other areas of prairie habitat are now virtually gone due to agriculture and industrialization. Pepoon (1927) lamented that *C. calceolus parviflorum*, once abundant in Lake County swales, was declining and would soon disappear because of habitat destruction. Remarkably, the orchid was, according to Swink (1966), "Still fairly frequent" in the proper habitat in at least parts of Lake County. Today it is common only in a few small localized sand areas. Some of the associates occurring with *C. calceolus parviflorum* in prairie swales include *Carex richardsonii*, *Castilleja coccinea*, *Cornus sericea*, *Cypripedium candidum*, *Erigeron pulchellus*, *Fragaria virginiana*, *Hypoxis hirsuta*, *Pedicularis canadensis*, *Phlox pilosa*, *Rhus typhina*, *Senecio pauperculus balsamitae*, and *Smilacina stellata*. Additional species in similar habitat in Illinois include *Betula pumila*, *Calopogon tuberosus*, *Platanthera hyperborea*, *Salix discolor*, and *Spiranthes cernua* (Sheviak, 1974).

DISCUSSION: The small yellow lady's-slipper is generally considered the more handsome of the two varieties of *Cypripedium calceolus*. Its small waxy lip, framed by mahogany-colored sepals and petals, is normally a deeper yellow and of greater substance than var. *pubescens* , and more sweetly scented as well. In addition, var. *parviflorum* tends to produce more stems per clump, and more flowers per stem (most populations have some stems with two flowers) than does var. *pubescens*, thus adding to its appeal.

These differences are so pronounced that one might ask why the two taxa are not considered separate species. In fact, they have been so treated historically, and still are by some authors (Strausbaugh and Core, 1970; Crovello, Keller, and Kartesz, 1983; Brackley, 1985), but the general consensus is that they belong to one species (Sheviak, 1974; Luer, 1975; Correll, 1978; Whiting and Catling, 1986; Case, 1987). Part of the reason for the single species concept is the relatively high frequency of intergradation between the two varieties. I have seen populations where it was impossible to determine an individual's varietal status (yet I also have seen perfect examples of both varieties growing within meters of one another, but segregated by habitat and showing no signs of genetic mixing). Luer (1975) suggests that the intergrades are not products of hybridization between two species, but rather part of a single species complex (of *C. calceolus*) undergoing active speciation. The bottom line is that one might get frustrated in attempts to sort out the two in some populations. Generally, though, they conform to the typical characteristics and can be recognized.

Because *Cypripedium calceolus* var. *parviflorum* is exclusively a wetland plant (at least in Indiana), reports of this variety from non-wetland habitats, especially in southern Indiana, are doubtless var. *pubescens*. Many of these reports can be explained by an over-emphasis of a singular trait, such as size. Although the lip of var. *parviflorum* averages smaller than var. *pubescens*, there are rare individuals of the latter that have an equally small lip. In these cases one should consider several traits, including size, color (especially of sepals and lateral petals), and habitat before making a determination.

Cypripedium calceolus Linnaeus var. *pubescens* (Willdenow) Correll

[Syn: *Cypripedium parviflorum* Salisbury var. *pubescens* (Willdenow) Knight; *Cypripedium pubescens* Willdenow]

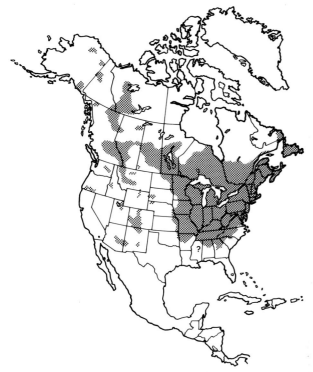

Map shows combined ranges for all varieties.

COMMON NAMES: large yellow lady's-slipper, yellow moccasin flower.

SPECIFIC EPITHET DERIVATION: *calceolus* = "little shoe," in reference to the shoe-like shape of the lip; *pubescens* = "downy" or "hairy," in reference to the hairs which cover the stem and leaves of the variety.

DESCRIPTION: Plant normally densely pubescent throughout, 40–50 cm tall. Roots fibrous. **Leaves 4–5, ovate,** ovate-lanceolate, or elliptic, ribbed, 13–17 cm long x 7–11 cm wide. **Inflorescence consisting of 1** (rarely 2) flower(s) terminating the stem. **Floral bract foliaceous,** ovate-lanceolate, 7–10 cm long x 3–4 cm wide. **Lip 3–4 cm long x 3 cm wide, yellow, obovoid, purple-spotted within. Petals linear-lanceolate, yellowish-green, twisted,** 7–8 cm long x 0.5 mm wide. Dorsal sepal ovate-lanceolate, color of the petals, 5–6 cm long x 2 cm wide. **Lateral sepals united** (except for small apical separation) behind and below lip, color of the petals, 4–5 cm long x 1.5–2 cm wide. Staminode triangular, yellow with a few red spots.

BLOOMING PERIOD: late April to mid-June.

RANGE: Occurs statewide, being absent today in certain regions of the state primarily because of habitat destruction.

HABITAT: The large yellow lady's-slipper typically is found in mesic and dry-mesic upland forests, particularly those situated on east and west-facing slopes. South-facing slopes are normally too dry, and north-facing slopes too shaded. Exceptions to this generality depend on such factors as soil type, degree of slope, width of valley between slopes, and location in the state.

Because of the wide geographic range of *Cypripedium calceolus* var. *pubescens* in the state, it is difficult to identify a specific set of forest canopy species that one may encounter at any given site. However, some of those that I have observed with regularity include white oak, red oak, black oak, chinquapin oak, tulip tree, sugar maple, American basswood,

Cypripedium calceolus var. *pubescens* (large yellow lady's-slipper). May 1982, Fountain Co. Mike Homoya. x½.

hop hornbeam, bigtooth aspen, and sassafras. Similarly, a variety of understory species and ground flora occurs with *Cypripedium calceolus* var. *pubescens*. Some of those noted include *Adiantum pedatum, Arisaema triphyllum, Aster macrophyllus, Botrychium virginianum, Brachyelytrum erectum, Carex careyana, C. hirtifolia, C. jamesii, C. laxiculmis, C. pensylvanica, Caulophyllum thalictroides, Desmodium nudiflorum, Dryopteris marginalis, Euonymus obovatus, Fragaria virginiana, Geranium maculatum, Hamamelis virginiana, Hepatica acutiloba, Osmorhiza longistylis, Parthenocissus quinquefolia, Podophyllum peltatum, Polystichum acrostichoides, Smilacina racemosa, Solidago caesia, S. flexicaulis, Staphylea trifolia, Thaspium barbinode, Uvularia grandiflora,* and *Zizia aurea.*

Although the vast majority of large yellow lady's-slippers are encountered in woodland habitats, the variety also is found in other habitats, including hill prairies, and wetlands with organic and sandy soils saturated with ground water. In these habitats the orchids can tolerate a surprising amount of exposure, especially those growing in full sunlight on treeless gravel slopes and in hill prairies.

Moreover, while *Cypripedium calceolus* var. *pubescens* can occur in mildly acidic soils, it most frequently occurs in areas of neutral and calcareous substrates. Thus, one is more likely to encounter the orchid at or north of the terminus of the Shelbyville Moraine (= terminus of Wisconsinan glaciation), where most of the neutral and basic soils occur, than in the rest of the state. Soil pH preference of *Cypripedium calceolus* var. *pubescens* is particularly evident in areas where soils are derived principally from parent bedrock material (and strong pH reactions exhibited depending on rock type). Because most of Indiana (and the Midwest) was glaciated and/or covered with loess, leaving substrates that are primarily circumneutral, this feature is best observed elsewhere. In the Black Hills of South Dakota, where geology and soils contrast greatly within a relatively small area, *Cypripedium calceolus* is virtually absent in the granitic and sandstone (and thus mostly acidic) parts of the Hills, but is locally abundant in the limestone region there (personal observation; Kravig, 1969). The virtual absence of the orchid in soils with low pH in New Hampshire, the "granite state," and its apparent restriction to neutral soils there, also illustrates the general avoidance of acidic substrates (Brackley, 1985)

C. calceolus var. *pubescens* (large yellow lady's-slipper) May 1989, Porter Co. Lee Casebere. x³/₄.

Contrary to what many believe, *Cypripedium calceolus* var. *pubescens* does not require pristine conditions for growth. In fact, most large populations are found in areas that have a history of disturbance: selective tree harvest and/or light grazing and/or fire. Sites with dense shade, such as occurs in forests without the above history, typically do not have the orchid, or possess only a few non-vigorous individuals.

DISCUSSION: Because of its size, showiness, and relative abundance, *Cypripedium calceolus* var. *pubescens* is the most familiar of all Indiana lady's-slippers. The orchid is not commonly seen, however, which makes finding one a special occasion. In almost every instance finding yellow lady's-slippers involves getting off the well-worn path (unfortunately, most plants that ever occurred near trails have long since been removed by unscrupulous collectors) and searching the more remote parts of a forested tract. Do not expect to find them easily, as many an hour and day can be spent searching without success. A reminder—one should not venture off a path in areas where it is prohibited; hiking is restricted to trails at many public properties.

If you have the good fortune to find the yellow lady's-slipper, keep in mind that the orchid is extremely variable and that your plants may not appear exactly like those depicted in the photographs. I have seen a range of flower shapes and sizes, from plants so small that the entire flowering plant could fit into the palm of one's hand (in the Black Hills of South Dakota), to plants over two feet in height (in southern Illinois) that possessed triangular, pointed slippers. Most of our Indiana populations do not display such a range of forms, but some might. This is especially true in northern Indiana, where plants have features approaching those of *C. calceolus* var. *parviflorum*.

Cypripediums have long been considered to have medicinal properties, and were used by the early Indiana physicians as sedatives and antispasmodics. Dr. A. Clapp, an Indiana pioneer physician and botanist from New Albany, wrote about the yellow lady's-slipper: ". . . a hypochondriacal patient, who could not sleep, and was not benefited by any preparation of opium, never failed of sound rest after taking twelve grains of the powdered root" (Clapp, 1852). To my knowledge, *Cypripedium* roots are no longer used as a pharmaceutical, but are still sold by some herb companies. I strongly recommend against buying them, as the practice creates a market that could severely deplete wild populations.

Cypripedium X andrewsii Fuller

COMMON NAME: Andrews' lady's-slipper.

SPECIFIC EPITHET DERIVATION: *andrewsii*, in honor of botanist Edward Andrews, the discoverer of the hybrid.

DESCRIPTION: Generally intermediate in form between *Cypripedium calceolus* (either more like var. *pubescens* or var. *parviflorum*) **and *C. candidum*.** Considerable variation in lip and sepal color exists, but in most Indiana plants the lip is white (as in *C. candidum*) or cream, with maroon sepals and petals (as in *C. calceolus* var. *parviflorum*).

BLOOMING PERIOD: mid-May to early June.

RANGE: Known only from Lake and Steuben counties, although it could conceivably occur wherever *Cypripedium candidum* and *C. calceolus* exist together.

HABITAT: This hybrid occurs in habitats suitable for either *Cypripedium calceolus* or *C. candidum*. The known population in Lake County (from *C. candidum* and *C. calceolus* var. *parviflorum* parentage) occurs in a habitat typical of *C. calceolus* var. *parviflorum*, viz., saturated, partially shaded dunal swales. Associates there include *Cornus sericea*, *Cypripedium calceolus* var. *parviflorum*, *C. candidum*, *Equisetum arvense*, *Fragaria virginiana*, *Maianthemum canadense* var. *interius*, *Pedicularis canadensis*, *Prunus virginiana*, *Rhus aromatica*, *R. radicans*, *R. typhina*, *Salix myricoides*, *Senecio pauperculus*, and *Smilacina stellata*.

Because of the similar habitat preferences of *C. candidum* and *C. calceolus* var. *parviflorum*, and the usual proximity of one to the other, the crossing between them is more likely to occur than is the crossing between *C. candidum* and *C. calceolus* var. *pubescens* (the latter normally occurs in upland forest habitats separated from *C. candidum* habitat). Plants of *C. calceolus* var. *pubescens* and *C. candidum* do cross, however, and their progeny can occur in either wetland or upland habitats.

DISCUSSION: *Cypripedium X andrewsii* is the name given to plants produced by what is believed to be the crossing of *C. candidum* and *C. calceolus* (remember that the hybrid is putative—no one has successfully reared progeny to maturity to verify the cross). The name applies regardless if the cross is between *C. candidum* and *C. calceolus* var. *pubescens*, or *C. candidum* and *C. calceolus* var. *parviflorum*, as Voss (1966) and Sheviak (1974) have shown that, according to the International Code of Botanical Nomenclature, these can be only one nothospecies name for a cross between two species, regardless of whether more than one variety is involved. Many references have given separate names to the crosses, using *C. X andrewsii* Fuller for the *C. candidum/C. calceolus* var. *parviflorum* cross, and *C. X favillianum* Curtis for the *C. candidum/C. calceolus* var. *pubescens* cross, but only *C. X andrewsii* is valid. As provided for in the International Code of Botanical Nomenclature, these different crosses are here treated as varieties of the notho-

Cypripedium X *andrewsii* (Andrews' lady's-slipper). May 1981, Lake Co. Marlin Bowles. x$^{1}/_{2}$.

species *C.* X *andrewsii*. The cross between *C. candidum* and *C. calceolus parviflorum* is *C.* X *andrewsii* var. *andrewsii*, and the *C. candidum/C. calceolus* var. *pubescens* cross is *C.* X *andrewsii* var. *favillianum* (Curtis) Boivin.

The variety *andrewsii* is a very attractive plant, possessing the maroon sepals and petals of *C. calceolus* var. *parviflorum* and the white slipper of *C. candidum*. The variety *favillianum* is less spectacular, the lip commonly being yellowish, and the sepals and petals greenish-brown. To my knowledge the latter cross has not been observed in Indiana.

At one *Cypripedium* X *andrewsii* population in Lake County, apparent backcrossing between the hybrid and one or both parent taxa has taken place. Known as a "hybrid swarm," the population contains a variety of intermediate forms, leaving one only to guess at the possible genetic combinations expressed in each clump of plants.

Cypripedium candidum Muhlenberg *ex* Willdenow

COMMON NAMES: white lady's-slipper, small white lady's-slipper.

SPECIFIC EPITHET DERIVATION: *candidum* = "white," in reference to the white lip of the species.

DESCRIPTION: **Plant normally pubescent** throughout, 25–30 cm tall. Roots fibrous. **Leaves** 3–4, elliptic-lanceolate, **plicate and ascending (especially during anthesis)**, ribbed, 10–13 cm long x 3–5 cm wide. **Inflorescence** typically of **1 flower** terminating the stem. **Floral bract foliaceous**, lanceolate, 5–7 cm long x 1.5–2 cm wide. **Lip** 1.5–2 cm long x 1–1.3 cm wide, **white, obovoid, commonly spotted with purple about the orifice, and streaked with purple within, outer veins at the back of the lip various shades of purple. Petals linear-lanceolate, greenish with some streaking of brown, slightly twisted**, 3–3.5 cm long x 3–4 mm wide. Dorsal sepal ovate to ovate-lanceolate, color of the petals, 2.5–3 cm long x 1–1.2 cm wide. **Lateral sepals united** (except for a small apical separation) behind and below lip, color of the petals, 2–2.5 cm long x 6–8 mm wide. Staminode ovate, yellow, and spotted with purple.

BLOOMING PERIOD: mid-May to late June.

RANGE: Occurs in the northern half of the state, with most occurrences in the Northern Lakes and the Northwestern Morainal natural regions. Schneck (1876) reported *Cypripedium candidum* for the counties along the lower Wabash River. Although his reports are not substantiated with specimens, they are probably correct, as considerable areas of suitable habitat (prairie) existed in the lower Wabash River area prior to European settlement.

Clapp indicated the presence of *C. candidum* in the barrens near the New Albany, Indiana area in his personal copy of *A Synopsis of the Flora of the Western States* (Riddell, 1835), in which he kept notes on plants he encountered in the vicinity of New Albany from the 1830s to 1862 (see Introduction, History of Indiana Orchidology). Knowing of the many prairie species that occurred (and still occur sporadically) in the remnant barrens in Floyd, Harrison, and Washington counties, I can easily believe that he observed *C. candidum*. Why Deam (1940) did not mention Clapp's note in his *Flora of Indiana* is not known. Deam had Clapp's book, so he either overlooked the listing or ignored it in disbe-

Cypripedium candidum (white lady's-slipper). May 1988, Wabash Co. Lee Casebere. x³/₄.

C. candidum (white lady's-slipper). May 1986, La Grange Co. Lee Casebere. x1.

lief. Clapp's note is particularly credible in light of the fact that *C. candidum* currently exists in a barrens community not far from southern Indiana in Hardin County, Kentucky (Ettman and McAdoo, 1979).

HABITAT: *Cypripedium candidum* is primarily a species of moist, organic, calcareous soils found in prairie, fen, sedge meadow, and marsh communities. Most of the extant populations in Indiana are in fens, but the orchid was probably most common here in prairie prior to its destruction. Indiana populations are on muck substrates or calcareous sand, but elsewhere the orchid occurs also in dry, low organic soils (in Kentucky—see above), and clayey-loam soils (in Missouri—Steyermark, 1963). In brief, the principal habitat requirements of *C. candidum* include a relative lack of disturbance, a calcareous substrate, and considerable sunlight (although in extremely rare cases the orchid occurs on wooded slopes—Bowles, 1983).

Because *Cypripedium candidum* is the most shade-intolerant of Indiana's lady's-slippers, it declines and eventually disappears at sites where shade-producing trees and shrubs invade. Thus, at sites where invasion of woody species occurs, diligent management must be undertaken for the orchid to survive. This is not only true for *C. candidum*, but for most of the species that typically occur with it. Some of these include *Cacalia plantaginea, Carex cryptolepis, C. leptalea, C. meadii, C. sterilis, C. stricta, Cypripedium calceolus* var. *parviflorum, Deschampsia cespitosa, Parnassia glauca, Potentilla fruticosa, Selaginella eclipes, Silphium terebinthinaceum, Smilacina stellata, Thelypteris palustris, Typha latifolia* (locally), and *Zizia aurea*. These species are so indicative of good *C. candidum* habitat that wherever they are found (in combination) one should always be alert for the orchid's occurrence.

DISCUSSION: As *Cypripedium reginae* is the behemoth of lady's-slippers, *C. candidum* is the minikin. Although tiny by comparison, it is exceedingly charming, with its dainty, waxy white slipper shining like a fine Limoges porcelain figurine. And were that not enough, its flowers have an intoxicating though delicate fragrance.

Like most treasured art, the small white lady's-slipper is a rare find indeed. This was not the case 150 years ago, however, before Indiana's prairies were subjected to the steel plow. *Cypripedium candidum* was a common orchid then, probably occurring by the millions in mile after mile of the Grand Prairie of northwestern Indiana. It apparently was common even in far southwestern Indiana, as Schneck (1876) wrote of it: "rapidly disappearing, once common here." Today only a dozen or so sites in all of Indiana are known to harbor this aristocrat of orchids.

One reason is the orchid's intolerance of disturbance. Although it occurs in sites that have had some past disturbance, and in fact may require minor disturbances for reproduction (Bowles, 1983), excessive or long-term disturbances are usually not tolerated. This intolerance impedes its ability to disperse, as suitable sites of undisturbed habitat, being small and separated by long distances, are generally beyond the normal range of seed dispersal. Thus, adequate protection of sites with existing populations is essential for the continued occurrence of *C. candidum* in Indiana.

Deam 20008 (NY), collected in Porter County, was used as a model for the *Cypripedium candidum* illustration in *The New Britton and Brown Illustrated Flora of the Northeastern United States and Adjacent Canada* (Gleason, 1952).

Cypripedium reginae Walter

[Syn: *Cypripedium spectabile* Salisbury]

COMMON NAMES: showy lady's-slipper, queen lady's-slipper.

SPECIFIC EPITHET DERIVATION: *reginae* = "queen," in reference to the majesty of this spectacular species.

DESCRIPTION: **Plant densely pubescent** throughout, **50–70 cm tall**. Roots fibrous. Leaves 4–6, ovate-lanceolate, ribbed, 15–20 cm long x 9–12 cm wide. **Inflorescence of 1 or 2** (rarely 3) **flowers** terminating the stem. **Floral bract foliaceous**, elliptic to ovate-lanceolate, 8–10 cm long x 3–3.5 cm wide. **Lip** 3.5–4.5 cm long x 3 cm wide, **obovoid, white, with a "wash" of rose-pink on front and sides.** **Petals** ovate-lanceolate to oblong-elliptic, **white, not twisted**, 3 cm long x 1.2–1.5 cm wide. Dorsal sepal ovate-orbicular, white, 3.5–4 cm long x 3 cm wide. **Lateral sepals united** behind and below lip, ovate-orbicular, white, 3–3.5 cm long x 2–2.3 cm wide. Staminode ovate, white with lateral bars of yellow, and purple spots.

BLOOMING PERIOD: early June to early July.

RANGE: Known primarily from the northern one-third of the state, *Cypripedium reginae* occurs as far south as Putnam and Randolph counties. Its occurrence further south is quite limited, this due to the rarity of suitable seepage communities south of the Wisconsinan glacial border. I have encountered only one reference to an occurrence from the far south, and it is over 150 years old. In his *Travels in the Interior of North America in the Years 1832–1834*, Prince Maximilian wrote: "The area on the opposite shore [White River, between Owensville and Vincennes] differs significantly and at this point, as before, there appears some sandy soil suitable for the plants mentioned earlier from sandy ground and the prairies of St. Louis, but here a few others occur: a flame-colored lily (*Lilium catesbaei*), the large-flowered lady's-slipper (*Cypripedium spectabile*), a species of *Yucca* and several others" (Maximilian, 1841).

Additional places for possible occurrence of *C. reginae* in southern Indiana are the moist limestone cliffs along some of the drainages in southeastern and south-central Indiana. It occurs on limestone cliffs in the Ozarks of Missouri (Steyermark, 1963; Summers, 1987), as well as in the driftless area of northwestern Illinois (Sheviak, 1974).

HABITAT: The principal habitat of *Cypripedium reginae* in Indiana is best defined by the effect it has on one visiting it: "up to your knees (maybe higher!) in muck." Saturated muck, such as occurs in fens, circumneutral seep springs, and glacial depressions, is the principal substrate of the orchid. In those fens and seep springs that are particularly springy, walking can be rather precarious. Seepage of, or contact with, ground water is apparently critical, as no population I am aware of occurs without it. The constant supply of groundwater keeps soil temperatures cool and consistently moist, thereby allowing this northern orchid to survive at Indiana latitudes.

Of the seepage communities, those with scattered trees and shrubs harbor the largest populations of showy lady's-slipper. Fens with scattered tamarack are especially good habitats, as are seep springs lightly shaded by poison sumac and black ash. At sites where trees are absent, the orchid is normally situated around opening edges or around shrub "islands" composed of willow and dogwood. Although light shade may be somewhat beneficial to *C. reginae*, dense shade is deleterious. Sites that develop closed canopies generally have a concomitant decline in *C. reginae* numbers.

Although many different species occur with showy lady's-slipper, there is a rather consistent set of species common to most sites, including *Aster puniceus*, *Caltha palustris*, *Carex bromoides*, *Filipendula rubra*, *Glyceria striata*, *Impatiens capensis*, *Pedicularis lanceolata*, *Poa paludigena*, *Rhus vernix*, *Solidago patula*, *Symplocarpus foetidus*, and *Thelypteris palustris*. Other species noted include *Cacalia plantaginea*, *Carex stricta*, *Equisetum arvense*, *E. fluviatile*, *Liatris spicata*, *Parnassia glauca*, *Potentilla fruticosa*, *Smilacina stellata*, and *Zizia aurea*.

DISCUSSION: Most of Indiana's native orchids are rather diminutive

Cypripedium reginae (showy lady's-slipper). June 1990. La Porte Co. Lee Casebere. x¹/₅.

C. *reginae* (showy lady's-slipper). June 1988. La Grange Co. Lee Casebere. x½.

and easily overlooked. Not so *Cypripedium reginae*. It is clearly the largest Indiana orchid, and plants two feet or more in height are not out of the ordinary. Observing a clump of this magnificent orchid is certainly one of the most unforgettable experiences of any orchidologist or wildflower enthusiast.

Because of its beauty, however, *Cypripedium reginae* merits the greatest plea for conservation. Aside from the common threat of habitat destruction, *C. reginae* has been popular among plant collectors. As early as the late 1800s large populations were being seriously depleted. Higley and Raddin (1891) stated: "It is said to have been abundant, a few years since, near Calumet, Ind., from which locality it has been nearly exterminated by florists." Pepoon (1927) reiterates their claim. Unfortunately, collecting lady's-slippers for the florist trade continues even into recent times; one person was observed in 1981 taking flowers of *C. calceolus* var. *pubescens* in a Lake County nature preserve to sell to Chicago florists!

The florist industry is not solely responsible for the collecting pressure on *Cypripedium reginae*. Some of the pioneer botanists were not exactly conservative in their collecting practices either. For example, in my research I discovered a tradition of preferential collecting of *C. reginae* for herbarium specimens. Many of these came from the same site where they were collected over a period of several years. Deam (1940) said of one population: "I found it [*C. reginae*] to be a common plant in a large springy area at the base of the high bank along Sugar Creek in Montgomery County." After having had multiple specimens removed from it by at least four different collectors over a period of two decades, there are only three clumps of the orchid present at the site. There are easily more herbarium specimens in existence that were taken from the site, than plants present there today!

One of the most unusual forms of the showy lady's-slipper in Indiana was reported by noted Chicago botanist E. J. Hill: an unusual double-flowered plant, given to him by an unidentified collector, whereby "one sac (lip) is contained in the other, but entirely free, and readily drawn out." He continued, "Though contained in the outer, it is really larger when inflated, being crumpled as it is packed away." One would think this a novelty, and indeed I have never encountered such a form, but Hill stated, "I have since been told that it is not unusual to find these double-flowered Lady's-slippers]in the Lake Michigan Dunes region of Indiana]" (Hill, 1878).

Cypripedium reginae is the only lady's-slipper in Indiana that regularly has two (sometimes three) flowers per flowering stalk. Individuals with completely white flowers (*forma albolabium* Fernald and Schubert) have been found in La Grange County, and may occur elsewhere in the state.

Cypripedium reginae is also unique among Indiana lady's slippers in its use of flies and beetles as principal pollinators. Vogt (1990) found that over ninety percent of the pollination of a Vermont population of *C. reginae* was performed by syrphid flies and, to a lesser degree, flower beetles. Apparently all other eastern North American *Cypripedium* are pollinated by bees.

Cypripedium reginae, more than any other Indiana lady's-slipper, has been charged with causing contact dermatitis. I am unaware of any documented cases of this, but the frequent mention of it in the literature should caution people with sensitive skin to avoid touching the orchid's leaves and stem.

EPIPACTIS

Swartz

Epipactis is a genus of approximately twenty species found primarily in temperate Eurasia. Two are found in North America: *Epipactis gigantea*, a native of our western states; and *E. helleborine*, a species introduced from Europe now known from the northeastern United States, southeastern Canada, and scattered regions throughout the continent.

Epipactis, from the Greek word of the same spelling, is a name given by Theophrastus (a Greek philosopher and botanist of the late fourth and early third centuries B.C.) to some unknown plant capable of curdling milk. The plant for which *Epipactis* is a namesake may have been a hellebore, of the genus *Helleborus*. Although they are dissimilar in appearance, both *Helleborus* and *Epipactis* were used for centuries as medicinal herbs, thus the possible connection. The one species of *Epipactis* found in Indiana has been placed previously in the genera *Amesia, Helleborine, Peramium,* and *Serapias;* most older manuals use one of these names.

Epipactis helleborine (Linnaeus) Crantz

[Syn: *Epipactis latifolia* (Linnaeus) Allioni]

COMMON NAME: broad-leaved helleborine.

SPECIFIC EPITHET DERIVATION: *helleborine* = "like a hellebore," in reference to the resemblance of this species to some species of *Helleborus.*

DESCRIPTION: Plant variously pubescent throughout, 25–40 cm tall. Roots slender, fibrous. **Leaves** 4–6, elliptic-lanceolate, **ribbed,** 5–8 cm long x 2–3 cm wide. **Inflorescence** a loose to dense raceme, **commonly secund,** of 6–15 flowers, each subtended by a **foliaceous, lanceolate bract** 1–2 cm long x 5 mm wide. **Lip divided by a constriction in the middle, the upper part cup-shaped, nectar-filled, and purplish-brown, the lower triangular-ovate, with a fleshy protuberance at its base, pinkish to green.** The complete lip is 6–10 mm long x 3–5 mm wide. Petals ovate-lanceolate, pinkish to green, 6–10 mm long x 3–5 mm wide. Sepals ovate, the lateral ones somewhat falcate, pinkish to green, 6–10 mm long x 4–5 mm wide.

BLOOMING PERIOD: late June to early August.

RANGE: Currently known only from counties bordering Lake Michigan, plus St. Joseph and Crawford counties. I have heard verbal accounts of its occurrence in Allen County, but these accounts are unverified.

HABITAT: A variety of habitats has been reported for *Epipactis* in other states (Luer, 1975; Swink and Wilhelm, 1979; Case, 1987), but in Indiana the orchid is restricted primarily to dune forests bordering Lake Michigan. Other Indiana habitats for *Epipactis* include a residential yard (planted?) in South Bend (*Lyon s.n.,* MICH), and a large hillside bordering the Ohio River near Alton in Crawford County (*Homoya* et al. 89-06-09-89, IND). In the latter habitat *Epipactis* was growing on a small, rocky terrace situated between a series of large limestone cliffs.

LEFT: *Epipactis helleborine* (broad-leaved helleborine), showing normal pigmentation. August 1978, Porter Co. Don Kurz. x1½.

RIGHT: *E. helleborine*, green color form. July 1989, La Porte Co. Mike Homoya. x1½.

Vegetation at the site is characterized by a canopy of chinquapin oak, blue ash, and sugar maple, and a sparse understory of *Arisaema triphyllum, Dioscorea quaternata, Hybanthus concolor, Polygonatum biflorum,* and *Rhus radicans.*

The principal substrate for the dune forest habitat is sand. At sites I have observed the sand appears to be acidic, as determined by the associated vegetation. Low pH is apparently not a requirement, as *Epipactis helleborine* occurs commonly in strongly alkaline areas in parts of the eastern U.S. and Canada. In the Dunes region the orchid grows in high quality natural communities, as well as in disturbed areas along foot trails and roads. Sites where I have observed it are dominated by black oak, sassafras, and black cherry, with *Amelanchier arborea, Hamamelis virginiana, Maianthemum canadense, Parthenocissus quinquefolia, Pteridium aquilinum, Rhus radicans, Rubus occidentalis, Smilacina racemosa, Smilax rotundifolia, Solidago caesia,* and *Vaccinium pallidum* as understory associates.

DISCUSSION: *Epipactis helleborine* apparently is a relative newcomer to the flora of Indiana. Unknown from the state until 1928 (Nieuwland and Just, 1931), its discovery represented the first record of establishment of an exotic orchid in Indiana. *Epipactis helleborine* is a species of European origin, having been first found naturalized in this country in

1879 near Syracuse, New York (Correll, 1978). Early opinions were that the orchid was indigenous, as it was found growing in a natural setting with other native orchids. Even the venerable Asa Gray considered it native, stating: "Orchids are the least introducible of plants, and I should have no doubt that this [*E. helleborine*] is truly indigenous in this only known American station" (Gray, 1879). Few botanists today would agree with Gray's statement; the orchid was probably planted in the Syracuse area by European immigrants (for medicinal purposes), and subsequently behaved like many of the Eurasian weeds introduced in North America; i.e., rapid range expansion from the point of initial introduction. Today it occurs over extensive areas of northeastern North America, and continues to spread.

Interestingly, the orchid appears to have been introduced into Indiana in a similar manner: i.e., human transport and cultivation. There is strong evidence that Indiana populations are the progeny of an intentional planting and dispersal of seed that took place in 1895 in nearby Berrien County, Michigan. Near the town of Niles, Ralph Ballard cultivated *Epipactis* and scattered its seed in a small wooded ravine on his property (Drew and Giles, 1951). By 1919 the orchid was well established and spreading. It could have easily dispersed seed and established plants in our lakeshore area by 1928.

In contrast to the introduction of *Epipactis* to the Dunes area, the Crawford County plant may have established "naturally." The Ohio River valley is a pathway of western migration for several eastern U.S. plants, and it may have similarly provided for *Epipactis* as well. If true, additional populations should occur in the Ohio River valley, and indeed such is the case. In 1986 Brainard Palmer-Ball of the Kentucky Nature Preserves Commission discovered several plants of *Epipactis* growing on an island in the Ohio River near Louisville (Marc Evans, personal communication). One cannot rule out the possibility that these plants originated from plants intentionally grown in Louisville, but such will likely remain unknown. Nevertheless, his discovery, and the record from Crawford County, Indiana, suggest that *E. helleborine* may already be established in the Ohio River valley, and that new populations will be discovered in upcoming years.

Although many recent authors report that *Epipactis* is an aggressive weed (Brackley, 1985; Soper and Murray, 1985; Case, 1987), it has yet to show such behavior here. A testament of this is the fact that its current range in Indiana, with the exception of the recently discovered Crawford County specimen, is essentially the same as it was during its discovery over fifty years ago. That is not to say that *Epipactis* won't rapidly expand in Indiana someday. Yet, at this point, it does not appear poised to threaten our native flora.

If *Epipactis* is a "weed," it nonetheless has appeal. Its foliage is rather attractive, reminiscent of *Cypripedium* leaves, and its flowers are structurally interesting. The orchid is said to have been used for centuries in Europe as a remedy for gout and a variety of other illnesses (Luer, 1975; Correll, 1978).

GALEARIS

Rafinesque

Galearis is a recently applied yet old name for the showy orchis. Placed in the genus *Orchis* over two hundred years ago by Linnaeus, the orchid was given a new name in 1833 by Rafinesque in order to distinguish it from the Old World *Orchis*. The name was not widely accepted, however, and to this day many botanists continue to place showy orchis in the genus *Orchis*. Luer (1975) was the first to utilize *Galearis* in a major publication on North American orchids, and many botanists have followed suit (Brackley, 1985; Whiting and Catling, 1986; Case, 1987). The recent shift in name acknowledges the differences between *Orchis* and *Galearis*, viz., number and position of leaves, presence or absence of tubers, and technical differences in column structure. For a complete comparison of *Orchis* and *Galearis*, see Luer (1975).

Galearis is derived from the Greek *galea*, for "hood," in reference to the cover formed over the column and upper lip by the convergence of sepals and lateral petals. Only two species have been placed in the genus: *G. spectabilis*, which ranges over much of eastern North America, including Indiana, and *G. cyclochila*, from Asia.

Galearis spectabilis (Linnaeus) Rafinesque

[Syn: *Orchis spectabilis* Linnaeus]

COMMON NAME: showy orchis.
SPECIFIC EPITHET DERIVATION: *spectabilis* = "remarkable or showy," in reference to the showy flowers.
DESCRIPTION: **Plant glabrous** throughout, 17–20 cm tall. Roots fleshy. **Leaves 2** (commonly 1 in sterile plants), **basal, oblong-obovate to elliptic, fleshy,** smooth, 10–15 cm long x 6–8 cm wide. **Inflorescence** racemose, **with 5–8 flowers, each subtended by a conspicuous floral bract** 3–4 cm long x 0.5–1.2 cm wide. **Lip** 13–17 mm long x 8–12 mm wide, **white,** rarely pink, ovate, wavy margined, **with a club-shaped spur** at its base, 10–12 mm long. **Petals linear, pinkish-purple,** 10–13 mm long x 2 mm wide. **Sepals** ovate-lanceolate, **pinkish-purple,** 10–15 mm long x 5–6 mm wide. **Petals and sepals converge to form a hood over the column.**
BLOOMING PERIOD: early April to early June.

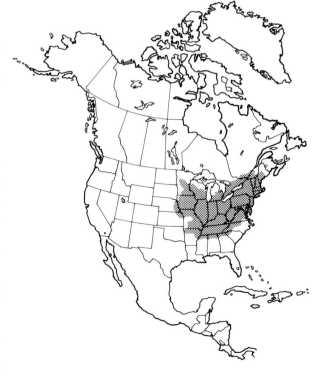

ABOVE: *Galearis spectabilis* (showy orchis). May 1988, Noble Co. Lee Casebere. x1/2.

RIGHT: *G. spectabilis*. May 1988, Noble Co. Lee Casebere. x1 1/4.

RANGE: Occurs statewide, although apparently absent in most of the Grand Prairie Natural Region.

HABITAT: *Galearis spectabilis* is a characteristic plant of mesic forests, especially of those situated on north-facing slopes and in ravine bottoms. The better drained portions of mesic flatwoods and floodplain forests also are *Galearis* habitats, but are not as commonly utilized as the upland sites. Deam (1940) indicated that black and white oak–dominated forests are a major habitat for the orchid, but I rarely encounter it in such communities.

Some authors (Sheviak, 1974; Case, 1987) report that *Galearis* responds favorably to disturbance, even colonizing early successional habitats, while others (Luer, 1975; Brackley, 1985) confine the plant to climax, unspoiled forests. Most plants in Indiana occur in mature forest communities with some minor disturbance, such as caused by selective tree removal or natural tree fall. *Galearis* is uncommon in forests with dense shade, as it is in forests where the entire canopy has been removed.

Generally a good habitat for *Galearis* is one replete with spring wildflowers, especially *Dicentra* spp., *Erythronium* spp., *Hydrophyllum* spp., and *Trillium* spp. *Aplectrum* is a rather consistent companion of *Galearis*, as are *Actaea alba*, *Allium tricoccum*, *Arisaema triphyllum*, *Asarum canadense*, *Botrychium virginianum*, *Caulophyllum thalictroides*, *Circaea lutetiana*, *Claytonia virginica*, *Delphinium tricorne*, *Lindera benzoin*, *Podophyllum peltatum*, *Polygonatum pubescens*, *Polygonum virginianum*, *Polystichum acrostichoides*, *Sanguinaria canadensis*, *Smilacina racemosa*, *Uvularia grandiflora*, and *Viola pubescens*.

DISCUSSION: The showy orchis is one of our most cherished spring wildflowers. Although not particularly showy (despite its name, its flowers are neither large nor prolific), its pastel colors and delicate fragrance make it a favorite. The fact that it blossoms in early spring enhances its reputation and familiarity, for wildflower enthusiasts ritualistically take to the woods to observe the mass blooming of spring ephemerals. Consequently, *Galearis* has probably been noticed by more people than any other woodland orchid species (with the possible exception of the more common but less colorful *Liparis liliifolia*). *Galearis* has the distinction of being our earliest flowering orchid; one specimen examined was collected in bloom on April 10.

Sterile plants of *Galearis* are sometimes difficult to distinguish from plants of *Liparis liliifolia* in similar condition. Although both have one or two basal leaves of similar size, the leaves of *Galearis* are a dull deep green, fleshier than *Liparis*, and are generally broadest in the middle to upper half of the leaf (elliptic to obovate) and somewhat rounded at the apex. The yellow-green leaves of *Liparis* are relatively thin, glossy, and broadest in the middle to slightly toward the base.

During my inspection of herbarium specimens of *Galearis* a noticeable difference in overall size became evident between plants of northern and central Indiana and those from the south. In general the southern

Indiana plants, especially those from the Shawnee Hills and the Highland Rim, are smaller than those from the glaciated areas to the north. I am not aware of any explanation for this regional difference; it may be genetically derived, or, more likely, is due to nutrition, as the older leached soils of southern Indiana are less fertile.

Two color forms of *Galearis spectabilis* have been described. Plants with the lip and all petals and sepals white are *forma gordinierii* (House) Whiting and Catling, and those with lip and all petals and sepals pink are *forma willeyi* Seymour. I have seen a slide of *forma gordinierii* taken in Montgomery County by Roger Hedge in 1982, but I am unaware of any documented evidence of *forma willeyi* in Indiana. I have recently observed the form in nearby southern Illinois, and thus its occurrence here is likely.

GOODYERA
R. Brown in Aiton

Goodyera was named in 1813 for the English botanist John Goodyer. Although the genus was known historically by various names, mostly as *Peramium* and *Epipactis*, *Goodyera* is the current legitimate name. Approximately 25 *Goodyera* species occur in various regions and climates throughout the world. There are four species in the U.S. and Canada, of which only G. *pubescens* occurs in Indiana. The remaining three, G. *tesselata*, G. *oblongifolia*, and G. *repens*, are found in Michigan; of these G. *repens* occurs closest to Indiana, but its discovery here is a remote possibility at best (see Excluded Species).

As a rule, the North American *Goodyera*s have basal, evergreen leaves terminating a creeping rhizome. The rhizome may spread in several directions from the parent plant, resulting in the formation of dense clonal colonies. In some cases the creeping rhizome results in rather unusual growth situations. At one place in southern Illinois, I observed a plant of G. *pubescens* terminating a rhizome that had extended up the deep fissure of a tree trunk. The plant, although obviously getting its nutrition from the ground below through the connecting rhizome, was growing well above the soil surface, like an epiphyte on the living tree.

Using Raunkiaer's life form classification of plants, only *Goodyera*, *Spiranthes*, and *Liparis* are hemicryptophytes among the Indiana orchids (McDonald, 1937). All others are cryptophytes (geophytes).

Goodyera pubescens (Willdenow) R. Brown

COMMON NAMES: downy rattlesnake plantain, rattlesnake orchid.

SPECIFIC EPITHET DERIVATION: *pubescens* = "hairy," in reference to the pubescent inflorescence.

DESCRIPTION: Plant pubescent on flowering stalk, and within inflorescence, glabrous elsewhere, 25–30 cm tall. **Roots** fibrous, pubescent, **from a creeping rhizome. Leaves 5–7, in a basal rosette,** ovate to oblong-elliptic, **green with prominent white veins,** 4–5 cm long x 2.5–3 cm wide. Inflorescence a tightly flowered raceme of 20–40 flowers, each subtended by a floral bract 6–8 mm long x 1–2 mm wide. Lip 3–4 mm long x 2.5–3 mm wide, **white, scrotiform, cleft above and minutely warty outside.** Petals oblong, white, 4–6 mm long x 2–3 mm wide. Sepals ovate, white with a green mid-vein and apex, 4–5 mm long x 3–4 mm wide. Petals and dorsal sepals converge to form a hood over the column.

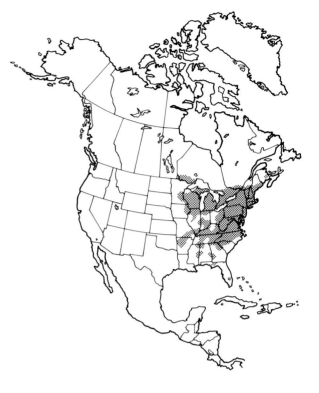

BLOOMING PERIOD: early July to mid-August.

RANGE: Although present throughout much of Indiana, *Goodyera pubescens* occurs with regularity only in the Shawnee Hills and Highland Rim natural regions. It is essentially absent from much of east-central and far southwestern Indiana.

HABITAT: Habitats of *Goodyera pubescens* include mesic flatwoods, various upland forest types, sandstone ledges, pine plantations, and, rarely, forested fens, and regrowth woodland in old-field succession. All sites are more or less acidic, somewhat sterile, and shaded. Preferred habitat requirements are apparently best met in the Shawnee Hills Natural Region, viz., mossy ledges and rims of sandstone cliffs. In these habitats dense colonies may develop, even to the exclusion of all other vegetation. Where vegetation does occur associates include *Antennaria plantaginifolia, Brachyelytrum erectum, Dryopteris marginalis, Mitchella repens, Parthenocissus quinquefolia, Pedicularis canadensis, Potentilla simplex, Senecio aureus, Viburnum prunifolium,* and commonly an abundance of bryophytes and lichens.

In mesic and dry-mesic upland forests composed of red oak, white oak, chestnut oak, black oak, tulip tree, American beech, sassafras, and red maple, associates of *Goodyera* include flowering dogwood, *Amelanchier arborea, Dioscorea quaternata, Polystichum acrostichoides, Rhus radicans, Solidago caesia,* and *Vaccinium pallidum.*

In northern Indiana *Goodyera* prefers sandy substrates dominated by white oak, red oak, black oak, red maple, bigtooth aspen, sassafras, and flowering dogwood. Some of the associates noted include *Hamamelis virginiana, Lycopodium digitatum, Maianthemum canadense, Mitchella repens*, and *Platanthera clavellata*. An unusual population occurs on a moist sphagnum hummock in a La Grange County fen (*fide* Lee Casebere). There the orchid grows under a canopy of tamarack with *Maianthemum canadense, Parthenocissus quinquefolia, Rhus vernix, R. radicans, Senecio aureus*, and *Symplocarpus foetidus*.

DISCUSSION: The foliage of most of our native orchids is not particularly noteworthy, but such cannot be said of *Goodyera pubescens*. Its white-veined leaves are quite attractive, especially when viewed against the drab grays and browns of winter. Even more visually appealing is the combination of several rattlesnake plantains growing in company with partridge berry and the Kelly green of the windswept moss, *Dicranum scoparium*. Unfortunately, that combination is possibly too attractive, as these species are commonly included in "berry bowls" and terrarium kits offered for sale through various outlets. Thousands of *Goodyera*s are removed from the wild for that purpose each year, bringing about serious population declines (or extirpation) in some areas.

The leaves of *Goodyera* are the source of its common name, rattlesnake orchid—"rattlesnake" for the similarity of leaf shape and venation pattern to the head of a snake, and "plantain" for the vague likeness of the leaves to that of the common plantain, *Plantago*. Correll (1978) states that the name "rattlesnake" is derived from the early belief that the leaves, when chewed and applied to a rattlesnake bite, would provide antidotal powers.

Although leaves of *Goodyera* can be found in any season, one must be willing to venture into the heat of summer to observe flowering. During such an occasion I had the opportunity to observe several tiny bees as they moved from flower to flower. Entomologist Dr. Leland Chandler, noted insect authority and former Hoosier, determined they were *Augochlorella striata*, a type of "mining bee." Interestingly, this species of bee is one of the pollinators of *Cypripedium candidum* (Catling and Knerer, 1980) and *Spiranthes lucida* (Catling, 1983a).

ABOVE: *Goodyera pubescens* (downy rattlesnake plantain). July 1989, Martin Co. Lee Casebere. x1½.

OPPOSITE: G. *pubescens*. July 1989, Martin Co. Lee Casebere. x1.

Hexalectris is a genus of seven species, most of which are restricted to Texas and adjacent Mexico. Only one species extends northward and eastward from Texas, that being *H. spicata*. The name *Hexalectris* is a combination of the Greek *hex,* for six, and *alectryon* , for cock. Interestingly, although the name refers to the six fleshy ridges on the upper surface of the lip, all of the plants that Luer (1975) examined had five rather than six ridges. The Indiana plants possess only five ridges as well.

Hexalectris and *Corallorhiza* are similar in that both are leafless, saprophytic and/or hemiparasitic herbs. However, they have different column structures; thus even though *H. spicata* is commonly called a "coralroot," technically it is not. Additionally, the rhizomes of *Hexalectris* are comparatively thick and unbranched next to those of *Corallorhiza*, looking more like segmented worms than the coralloid rhizomes of the latter.

Hexalectris spicata (Walter) Barnhart

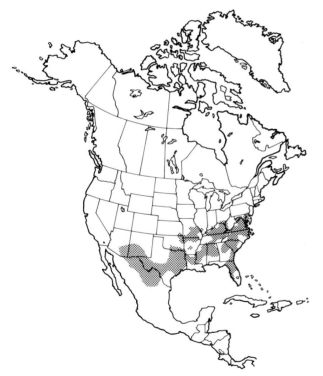

COMMON NAME: crested coral-root.

SPECIFIC EPITHET DERIVATION: *spicata* = "spiked," in reference to the spicate inflorescence.

DESCRIPTION: Plant glabrous throughout, **leafless with a tan to yellowish-purplish, fleshy stem, 25–35 cm tall. Roots absent. Rhizome thick with concentric rings, as if jointed.** Inflorescence a raceme of 8–15 flowers, each subtended by an ovate to ovate-lanceolate floral bract 5–7 mm long x 3–4 mm wide. **Lip** 13–16 mm long x 8–11 mm wide, **shallowly 3–lobed,** ovate to obovate, **white to yellowish-white with purple ridges. Petals** oblong to oblanceolate, **yellowish-purple to tan, with purple veins,** 15–17 mm long x 4–6 mm wide. Dorsal sepal is like petals, 18–20 mm long x 5–6 mm wide. Lateral sepals ovate to oblanceolate, oblique, 15–16 mm long x 6–8 mm wide.

BLOOMING PERIOD: early July to late August.

RANGE: Known only from Clark, Floyd, Harrison, and Washington counties. Blatchley's report (1897) for Crawford County ("two miles south of Wyandotte Cave . . . ") is most likely correct, but no voucher

was found. Most populations are located within five miles of the Ohio River, the sole exception in Washington County. *Hexalectris* is expected to occur in limestone areas of Lawrence and Orange counties, as well as along the Ohio River from Perry County to Jefferson County. The limestone districts of the Switzerland Hills Section of the Bluegrass Natural Region, as well as limestone outcrops farther north in the Highland Rim, offer seemingly suitable habitat, but no specimens have been documented from these areas.

HABITAT: The crested coral-root is restricted to dry, rocky slopes where limestone bedrock is evident. The presence of limestone is evidently critical, although Ettman and McAdoo (1979) report that the orchid occurs in acidic as well as calcareous (limestone-derived) soils in Kentucky. Typically, the most productive sites are slopes bordering limestone glades, where heat and drought are at their extreme. Because of the harsh, almost desert-like conditions, these slopes are sparsely vegetated, with only a few gnarled trees and some drought-tolerant herbs present. Chinquapin oak, post oak, winged elm, red cedar, redbud, blue ash, and rusty blackhaw are the most consistent overstory dominants, with *Allium cernuum, Dioscorea quaternata, Dodecatheon meadia, Euphorbia corollata, Helianthus hirsutus, Lithospermum canescens, Parthe-*

nocissus quinquefolia, *Swertia caroliniensis*, *Thaspium barbinode*, *T. trifoliatum*, and *Viola sororia* being the common herb associates.

On a few occasions I have encountered *Hexalectris* growing in full sun in a grassy limestone glade. In such an environment it grows with *Agave virginica*, *Allium cernuum*, *Andropogon scoparius*, *Blephilia ciliata*, *Liatris squarrosa*, *Lobelia spicata*, *Scleria oligantha*, and *Silphium trifoliatum*.

DISCUSSION: *Hexalectris spicata* is without question the largest and most attractive of the local saprophytic orchids. Many people, botanists included, have not seen this orchid. Those who have are impressed by its size and beauty, especially when compared to the *Corallorhiza* coral-roots.

The crested coral-root is subterranean (other than its flowering stalk) and nonphotosynthetic; by not photosynthesizing it has no need, other that to produce seed, to appear above ground. Because of this trait, it is erratic in appearing in a given locality from one year to the next. Flowering stems can be found at a site one year, not the next year (or years), and then again (perhaps different individuals) at some later date. What controls this behavior is unknown, and likely will remain so until controlled life history studies can be conducted (which will be extremely difficult to do because of the orchid's peculiar life history and the difficulty in propagating and cultivating terrestrial orchids).

ISOTRIA
Rafinesque

This genus is characterized by the whorled arrangement of its leaves positioned atop an herbaceous stem. This character is apparently unique among orchids (although see Homoya, 1977), yet the name *Isotria* does not reflect this, rather the floral features that are common to many of our other native orchids. *Isotria* is from *isos*, for "equal," and *tria*, for "three," in reference to the orchid's three sepals of equal length.

The principal common name for *Isotria*, whorled pogonia, alludes to its whorl of leaves and its similarity to *Pogonia*, a genus where the species of *Isotria* were formerly placed. *Isotria* consists of only two species: *I. verticillata* and *I. medeoloides*. Both are restricted to the eastern U.S. and Canada; only *I. verticillata* occurs in Indiana. *Isotria medeoloides* is the rare, smaller relative of *I. verticillata*, and is currently listed as federally endangered by the U.S. Fish and Wildlife Service. There is a distinct possibility that *I. medeoloides* may occur in Indiana, as it is known from southwestern Michigan (Case with Schwab, 1971), southern Illinois (Sheviak, 1974; Homoya, 1977), and southern Ohio (Case, 1987). The Michigan population is no more than ten miles from the La Porte County line. Considering the locations and habitats of these sites, the areas in Indiana that appear to offer the greatest likelihood of having *I.*

medeoloides are found in the Northwestern Morainal, Shawnee Hills, and Highland Rim natural regions.

Because of the possibility of finding *Isotria medeoloides* in Indiana, a key listing characters used for separating it from *I. verticillata* is given below. For an excellent account of the life history and pollination biology of the genus, see Mehrhoff (1983).

ISOTRIA

A. Sepals purplish, at least twice as long as petals; flowers normally one per plant; pedicel of capsule over 2 cm long; stem purple .... *Isotria verticillata*

AA. Sepals greenish-yellow, scarcely exceeding petals in length; flowers one or two per plant; pedicel of capsule less than 1.5 cm long; stem green .... *Isotria medeoloides*

Isotria verticillata (Muhlenberg *ex* Willdenow) Rafinesque

COMMON NAME: large whorled pogonia.

SPECIFIC EPITHET DERIVATION: *verticillata* = "whorled," in reference to the whorled arrangement of its leaves.

DESCRIPTION: Plant glabrous throughout, 15–25 cm tall. **Roots very long,** to several dm, **from which new plants arise. Leaves 5–6 in an apparent whorl atop a hollow, purplish stem** (rarely a "stray" leaf present at midstem), oblong-lanceolate to obovate, 3–5 cm long x 1.5–2 cm wide. **Inflorescence a single flower** positioned atop the stem on a pedicel 2–4 cm long. **Lip** 13–18 mm long x 7–9 mm wide, oblong to obovate, **3–lobed, yellowish-green, with the lateral lobes purplish, the middle lobe with a green, longitudinal fleshy ridge.** Petals yellow-green, obovate, 14–17 mm long x 4–5 mm wide. **Sepals widely spreading, dark purple, 4–6 cm long x 1–3 mm wide.**

BLOOMING PERIOD: early May to mid-June.

RANGE: Currently known in Indiana from five natural regions: Northern Lakes, Northwestern Morainal, Bluegrass, Shawnee Hills, and Highland Rim. Without doubt, the greatest number of occurrences are in the Highland Rim, particularly in the Brown County Hills Section. Oddly,

it is extremely rare in the large tracts of seemingly suitable habitat of the adjacent Shawnee Hills Natural Region.

HABITAT: *Isotria verticillata* occurs in three distinct habitat types in Indiana: steep, dry to dry-mesic forested slopes, sphagnum bogs, and mesic flatwoods. These habitats appear to have little in common, other than being decidedly acid in reaction. The upland forested sites are typically situated on steep west-facing slopes of deep ravines, at the sharp breaks where dry and dry-mesic forest grades into mesic forest on the lower slopes. Here the soil is quite shallow, only a few inches above Mississippian-aged siltstone, shale, and sandstone bedrock. Some of the typical overstory species in this environment include white oak, black oak, chestnut oak, American beech, black gum, and red maple. Understory associates of *I. verticillata* include *Carex picta, Cornus florida, Cunila origanoides, Desmodium nudiflorum, Gaylussacia baccata, Malaxis unifolia, Medeola virginiana, Mitchella repens, Sassafras albidum, Smilax rotundifolia, Vaccinium pallidum,* and *Viburnum acerifolium. Carex picta* is an especially good indicator of *Isotria* habitat.

Bog habitat of the whorled pogonia is restricted to the northern natural regions. Here this orchid grows on moist hummocks of sphagnum, an environment quite different from that in southern Indiana. Aside from red maple, the two habitats have few species in common. Compare those species associated with *Isotria* in dry-mesic upland forests with a Kosciusko County bog habitat for the orchid where *Acer rubrum, Aronia melanocarpa, Larix laricina, Menyanthes trifoliata, Osmunda cinnamomea, O. regalis, Rhus vernix, Salix pedicellaris, Sarracenia purpurea, Thelypteris palustris, Vaccinium corymbosum,* and *V. macrocarpon* occur.

The mesic flatwoods habitat of *Isotria verticillata* is not well known. Only a few collections have ever come from the habitat, all these occurring in the Bluegrass Natural Region. I have observed one small population growing in a flatwood dominated by black gum, pin oak, white oak, southern red oak, swamp chestnut oak, red maple, and sassafras. Understory associates include *Carex albolutescens, C. annectens, C. debilis, C. swanii, Rhus radicans,* and *Vitis labrusca.*

DISCUSSION: The large whorled pogonia has a mysterious and foreign appearance seemingly more typical of tropical jungles than of the dry hills, flatwoods, and bogs of Indiana. This exotic quality is clearly seen

in the flower, which, with its long spreading sepals, resembles the threatening pose of some weirdly shaped spider.

To find and see the flowers of *Isotria* is no easy task, for in addition to the overall rarity of the species, only a small percentage of a population blooms in any given year. In some years a population, which may be as dense as 60 stems per square meter (Homoya, 1977), may have no blooms at all. Thus, even knowledge of an exact location of this uncommon orchid provides no guarantee that a visit during the appropriate blooming time will yield a view of the flower.

When not in flower or fruit, plants of *Isotria* bear a remarkable resemblance to sterile plants of Indian cucumber-root (*Medeola virginiana*). Even experienced botanists may need a second look to confirm an identification. Both species have a whorl of similar-looking leaves at the top of a solitary stem, both form colonies composed of many clonal individuals, and both commonly occur side by side in mixed populations! Upon close examination, *Isotria* leaves are generally broadest toward the tip (oblong-obovate), whereas those of *Medeola* are slightly more tapering and pointed (oblong-oblanceolate). However, variation in leaf shape in individuals of both taxa necessitates use of other diagnostic features. One can easily separate sterile plants of the two by inspecting their stems. *Medeola* has a solid, wiry stem covered (at least in the early part of the growing season) with a "coat" of woolly hairs. *Isotria* has a thick, hollow stem completely devoid of pubescence. One can determine the nature of the stem without cutting simply by lightly squeezing it between thumb and forefinger. A "give" in the stem will indicate that it is hollow.

The extreme rarity of *Isotria* in the Shawnee Hills Natural Region is one of the great puzzles in Indiana orchidology. Seemingly ideal habitat is abundant there, and in proximity to numerous populations in the Highland Rim. Yet only one population is known. Given that extensive botanizing in the area has failed to reveal many plants, it may be that some quality of the environment there—e.g., substrate—is not favorable for *Isotria* growth. Other species with a similar pattern of distribution include *Carex picta*, *Epigaea repens*, and *Malaxis unifolia*.

LIPARIS

L. C. Richard

By North American standards, *Liparis* is a large genus. Of the orchid genera found in Indiana, *Liparis*, with over 250 species worldwide, is second only to *Spiranthes* in total number of species through its range. In the United States and Canada, however, there exist but four species, two of which occur in Indiana. A third (*L. elata*) is restricted to Florida and a fourth, *L. hawaiensis*, occurs in Hawaii. The latter, similar to our *L. loeselii*, is one of only three orchid species native to the state of Hawaii.

The name *Liparis* is well chosen. Derived from the Greek *liparos*, for "fat" or "greasy," it alludes to the oily look of the leaves that is characteristic of the group. The name *Liparis* is easily recalled by remembering that both *Liparis* and lipid (another word for fat), are derived from the same basic root.

Both *Liparis loeselii* and *L. liliifolia* possess a pair of shining leaves positioned atop a hardened corm (pseudobulb). *Liparis, Spiranthes,* and *Goodyera* are the only Indiana orchids identified by McDonald (1937) as being hemicryptophytes. All other are cryptophytes (geophytes).

LIPARIS

A.   Flowers purplish; lip 10 mm long or longer, strongly obovate; pedicels equal to or longer than capsules; leaves elliptic to ovate; plants of upland woodlands ....*Liparis liliifolia*

AA. Flowers green or yellowish-green; lip averaging 5 mm long, obovate to mostly oblong; pedicels short, less than length of capsules; leaves elliptic-lanceolate; plants mostly of wetland habitats..*Liparis loeselii*

Liparis liliifolia (Linnaeus) L. C. Richard *ex* Lindley

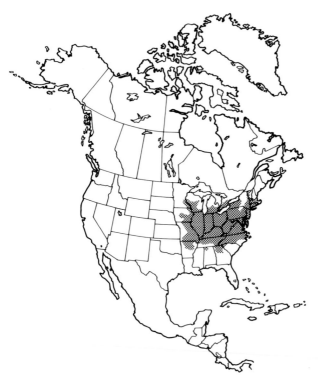

COMMON NAME: lily-leaved twayblade, large twayblade.

SPECIFIC EPITHET DERIVATION: liliifolia = "lily-leaved," in reference to similarity to the leaves of *Lilia*, an old group including *Erythronium* (trout lily) and *Convallaria* (lily-of-the-valley).

DESCRIPTION: Plant glabrous throughout, 15–18 cm tall. **Roots** fibrous, **attached to a pseudobulb. Leaves 2** (or 1 in some sterile plants), **shiny,** light green, **elliptic to ovate, 8–10 cm long x 5–6 cm wide.** Inflorescence a loose raceme of 15–25 flowers, each subtended by a minute bract. **Lip** 10–12 mm long x 7–9 mm wide, **translucent purple, obovate,** with a central pointed tip. **Petals filiform, purple ,** 10–13 mm long x 0.25–0.5 mm wide. Sepals light green, oblong-lanceolate, with revolute margins, 9–12 mm long x 1–1.5 mm wide. **Column winged,** exposed and arching above lip, 3–4 mm long.

BLOOMING PERIOD: early May to late June.

RANGE: There is probably not a county in Indiana that does not have

this orchid, with the possible exception of a few counties in the Grand Prairie and the Central Till Plain natural regions. This is one of the few orchids documented for Marion County (Indianapolis), with a voucher taken even from the historic Crown Hill Cemetery (*Buser 1033*, IND)!

HABITAT: Of the native Indiana orchids, *Liparis liliifolia* has possibly the greatest ecological amplitude. It occurs in both dry and moist sites, rocky sites and those with deep soil, and forested sites as well as old-fields. Although generally considered a woodland species, *Liparis liliifolia* is uncommon in forests with a dense canopy. Rather, most plants occur in the lightly shaded areas of the forest, such as occur at the crests of steep ravine slopes, or in openings formed by natural tree fall or human activity—e.g., light selective timber harvest, construction of forest trails and roads, and creation of edge by clearing. In addition to preferences for canopy gaps, *L. liliifolia* most commonly occurs in substrates consisting of well-drained, mildly acidic soils.

Perhaps the premier habitat for *Liparis liliifolia* is young regrowth forest (trees from 5 to 30 years old, depending on the site) on land previously cleared and utilized for pasture and crops. I have seen hundreds of plants in such habitats, as have others (Sheviak, 1974; Case, 1987). Deam (1940) reported finding hundreds of plants in a 19–year-old catalpa plantation on ground formerly cultivated in strawberries! Some examples of mid-successional sites where large populations have been observed include a regrowth forest of tulip tree, sassafras, and flowering dogwood on a flat atop a large hill; a sycamore plantation; a pine plantation; a former pasture dominated by red cedar and flowering dogwood; the border of a dirt road through a regrowth forest of black maple; and a young oak forest situated on a south-facing slope. Species associated with *L. liliifolia* at such sites include *Botrychium dissectum*, *Celastrus scandens*, *Eupatorium rugosum*, *Parthenocissus quinquefolia*, *Poa compressa*, *P. pratensis*, *Potentilla simplex*, *Prunella vulgaris*, *Rhus radicans*, *Rubus occidentalis*, and many others.

Although *Liparis liliifolia* does best in partial shade, it is capable of tolerating full sun and intense heat. I have observed plants growing in full sun in an old field in Tippecanoe County with *Antennaria plantaginifolia*, *Carex hirsutella*, *Fragaria virginiana*, *Pedicularis canadensis*, and *Potentilla simplex*. Interestingly, that same old field harbored *L.*

PRECEDING PAGE: *Liparis liliifolia* (lily-leaved twayblade). June 1990, Wabash Co. Lee Casebere. x1.

ABOVE: *L. liliifolia*. June 1989, Montgomery Co. Lee Casebere. x1¾.

loeselii (see discussion for that species). I have also observed plants growing in a limestone glade, one of the harshest environments in Indiana. There, however, some shade was provided by a nearby red cedar.

DISCUSSION: *Liparis liliifolia* is perhaps the most common woodland orchid in Indiana, thanks to its ability to colonize and occupy several habitat types. Like other orchids utilizing successional habitats, *L. liliifolia* may be more common now than historically. For example, compare Pepoon's statement (1927) regarding *L. liliifolia* in the Chicago region ("very rare. Only an occasional isolated plant") with that of Swink and Wilhelm (1979) for generally the same area ("This is the most adaptable native orchid of the Chicago region, and apparently on the increase under the disturbed environmental conditions of the present day"). Today's more or less regular occurrence of *L. liliifolia* elsewhere in northern Indiana and its apparent rarity there decades ago (as indicated by the literature and its poor representation in herbaria) suggest a population change as well. Such a phenomenon also evidently occurred in Illinois (Sheviak, 1974). As far as can be determined, there has been no apparent change over the years in population numbers or size in southern Indiana.

Populations of *Liparis liliifolia* are well known for their fluctuations (Sheviak, 1974; Luer, 1975; Whiting and Catling, 1986; Case, 1987). This is particularly evident in the successional communities, where *L. liliifolia* populations of several hundred plants have been known to decline dramatically in a matter of a few years. There appears to be a specific window of time in which the orchid finds its most suitable growth, before and after which it is absent at a site. Competition from pioneer weeds may prevent establishment of *L. liliifolia* in the early successional stages of a site, and dense shade along with thick layers of leaf litter may cause the orchid to wane as the developing forest matures.

A specimen of *Liparis liliifolia* collected by C. C. Deam (*Deam 23401*, NY) from Harrison County was used as a model for the *L. liliifolia* illustration in *The New Britton and Brown Illustrated Flora of the Northeastern United States and Adjacent Canada* (Gleason, 1952).

The green-flowered form (*forma viridiflora* Wadmond) of this species has been reported from a closed canopy mesic savanna in Lake County (Marlin Bowles, personal communication).

Liparis loeselii (Linnaeus) L. C. Richard

COMMON NAME: Loesel's twayblade.

SPECIFIC EPITHET DERIVATION: *loeselii*, a name in honor of Johann Loesel, an early German botanist.

DESCRIPTION: **Plants glabrous** throughout, 11–17 cm tall. **Roots** fibrous, **attached to a pseudobulb. Leaves 2** (or 1 in some sterile plants), **shiny,** light green, **elliptic-lanceolate, 8–12 cm long x 2.5–3.5 cm wide.** Inflorescence a loose raceme of 10–15 flowers, each subtended by a minute bract. **Lip** 5–6 mm long x 2–3 mm wide, **yellowish-green, translucent, obovate to oblong,** arched near the middle, with a pointed tip. **Petals filiform, greenish-yellow,** 4–5 mm long x 0.25 mm wide. Sepals greenish-yellow, with revolute margins, 5–6 mm long x 1 mm wide. Column arching above lip, 3 mm long.

BLOOMING PERIOD: mid-May to late June.

RANGE: Occurs primarily in the northern one-third of the state, especially in the Northern Lakes Natural Region. However, collections in recent years have shown its range to extend as far south as Jackson and Sullivan counties. Small, sterile plants of what were believed to be this species have been observed by the author in Ripley County, and there is an unpublished report of its occurrence in Monroe County.

HABITAT: Typically *Liparis loeselii* is an orchid of calcareous wetlands with high levels of peat or peaty sand. Fens, sedge meadows, marshes, forested seep springs, marly lake borders, mats of floating peat, and moist calcareous sands in dunal swales are all important habitats. In these environments the orchid most commonly occurs in areas devoid of dense plant growth (e.g., areas of high marl or sand content), and/or areas cropped by occasional mowing or light grazing. However, even where dense vegetation is predominant *L. loeselii* may occur, as searches in thick growths of *Carex stricta* hummocks have yielded several individuals. Species observed growing with *Liparis loeselii* in the various types of calcareous wetlands include *Carex hystericina, C. leptalea, C. sterilis, C. stricta, Cladium mariscoides, Epilobium coloratum, Glyceria striata, Panicum implicatum, Pilea pumila, Potentilla fruticosa, Rhynchospora capillacea, Scirpus americanus,* and *Selaginella eclipes.*

Liparis loeselii is capable of tolerating considerable shade, but sites with full sun are favored. Shade plants are normally larger and somewhat

Liparis loeselii (Loesel's twayblade). June 1989, La Grange Co. Lee Casebere. x2.

etiolated compared with the compact and erect ones growing in the open. Some grow "epiphytically." In one forested seep spring I observed dozens of plants growing on fallen moss-covered logs.

Not all plants of *Liparis loeselii* grow in calcareous or wet substrates. Sue Ulrich of Warren County led me to a west-central Indiana population that grew in a dry, brushy old field with soil acidic in reaction. The site harbored typical old-field species such as *Daucus carota*, *Fragaria virginiana*, *Pedicularis canadensis*, *Poa pratensis*, *Potentilla simplex*, and *Rumex acetosella*. Additional plants included *L. liliifolia* and the small, rare *Botrychium simplex*. Old fields and young regrowth forests are the habitats for *L. loeselii* in Sullivan and Montgomery counties as well. In the latter, the orchid was growing with *Agrimonia parviflora*, *Anenome virginiana*, *Galium triflorum*, *Parthenocissus quinquefolia*, *Poa compressa*, *Polygonum virginianum*, *Rhus radicans*, and

L. loeselii (Loesel's twayblade). June 1989, La Grange Co. Lee Casebere. x3.

Viburnum prunifolium. *Liparis loeselii* also occurs in acidic wetlands, growing with such acid-loving plants as *Drosera rotundifolia*, *Osmunda regalis*, *Sphagnum* spp., *Vaccinium corymbosum*, and *Woodwardia virginica*.

DISCUSSION: Although most of our native orchids that are undergoing range extension are advancing northward (e.g., *Corallorhiza odontorhiza*, *Spiranthes ovalis* var. *erostellata*, *S. vernalis*, and *Tipularia discolor*), *Liparis loeselii* is apparently moving south. For example, Deam (1940) depicts *L. loeselii* for only the northern one-quarter of the state, whereas today the orchid occurs almost to the Ohio River. It is doubtful that the discrepancy in range results from a historical lack of field work in southern Indiana, as the region was one of the more thoroughly botanized in the state. A more likely reason is that *L. loeselii* is actively colonizing new habitats and territory. Why it is able to occupy these habitats now and not historically is open to speculation. One possibility is that a genotype of *L. loeselii* with greater habitat amplitude than formerly existed here entered the state and is just now reaching southern Indiana. See *Corallorhiza odontorhiza* for a discussion of what appears to be a similar phenomenon with that species.

Vegetatively *Liparis loeselii* is very similar to *L. liliifolia*, but the leaves of *L. loeselii* are generally narrower, shorter, and yellower than those of *L. liliifolia*. Measurements from Indiana specimens reveal *L. loeselii* leaves averaging 3 cm wide (taken at the widest point) and 9 cm long, compared to 5 cm wide and 10 cm long for *L. liliifolia*. The greater disparity in width than length illustrates the comparative narrowness of *L. loeselii* leaves. However, these traits are variable, leaving determinations based on them alone somewhat tentative.

Liparis loeselii is autogamous, and Catling (1980) has shown that rain assists in the process. Raindrops hit the anther-cap, forcing the attached pollen masses onto the stigmatic surface of the flower. Consequently, there is a greater percentage of fruit development when rainy periods coincide with anthesis.

MALAXIS
Swartz

According to Luer (1975) the genus name is from the Greek word *malaxis*, meaning "a softening," in reference to the soft, pliable leaves of the group. Fernald (1950) states that the derivation is from "*malacos*," for weak or delicate, referring to the frail character of the circumboreal *Malaxis paludosa*. *Malaxis* is a genus of over 200 species, most of which occur in Asia. There are eight species in the U.S., but only one known for Indiana (M. *unifolia*), with a possible second (M. *monophyllos*—see discussion under that species in the Excluded Species section).

Our North American taxa typically have a single, basal leaf which subtends a raceme of greenish flowers. The plants are very tiny, making their discovery difficult. *Malaxis unifolia* has the smallest flowers of any of our Hoosier orchids.

Because of the excellent possibility for the occurrence of *Malaxis monophyllos* in Indiana, the following key is given.

MALAXIS
A.   Lip apex appearing as if two-lobed, with a third, indistinct middle lobe; flowers on pedicels 3–10 mm long..........................
.... *Malaxis unifolia*
AA.   Lip apex with one acuminate lobe, considerably longer than the two rounded lateral lobes; flowers on pedicels less than 3 mm long... *Malaxis monophyllos*

Malaxis unifolia Michaux

COMMON NAME: green adder's-mouth.
SPECIFIC EPITHET DERIVATION: *unifolia* = "one leaf," in reference to the single leaf of the species.

DESCRIPTION: Plant glabrous throughout, 11–15 cm tall. **Roots** fibrous, **attached to a corm. Leaf 1,** shiny, ovate to ovate-lanceolate, 3–4 cm long x 2.5–3 cm wide. Inflorescence initially a compact raceme, elongating as anthesis progresses, from 25–50 flowers, each subtended by a minute bract. **Lip 1–2 mm long x 0.5–1.5 mm wide, green, cordate-ovate, tridentate at apex, with the lateral teeth much longer than the middle one. Petals** green, **filiform,** 1 mm long x 0.2 mm wide. Sepals green, elliptic-lanceolate, 1.5–2 mm long x 0.5 mm wide.

BLOOMING PERIOD: mid-June to late July.

RANGE: Seven widely scattered counties are known to have harbored this diminutive orchid, but of these only Elkhart, Lake, and Monroe counties have extant populations. Virtually all regions of the state could harbor *Malaxis unifolia*, but the best habitats are in the Northwestern Morainal, Northern Lakes, and Highland Rim natural regions.

HABITAT: All collections of green adder's-mouth have come from acidic substrates, including sand (Lake and La Porte counties), sphagnum moss (Elkhart, Kosciusko and Noble counties), and thin soil over sandstone and shale (Monroe County). The substrate for the Vigo County population is unknown, but it most likely is acidic also. Blatchley (1897) described the Monroe County population as occurring with *Medeola virginiana, Isotria verticillata,* and clumps of *Polytrichum commune* (hair-cap moss). A separate Monroe County population, discovered in 1989 by Cloyce Hedge, Darrell Breedlove, Bill Bull, and the author, occurs in nearly identical habitat. There, on a steep mossy slope under a canopy of red oak, American beech, red maple, and sugar maple, approximately 30 *M. unifolia* plants were found in association with *Amelanchier arborea, Amphicarpaea bracteata, Antennaria plantaginifolia, Athyrium filix-femina, Carex picta, Desmodium nudiflorum, Hamamelis virginiana, Isotria verticillata, Mitchella repens, Panicum dichotomum, Polystichum acrostichoides, Solidago caesia,* and *Vaccinium pallidum.* These associated species are typical of the vast chestnut oak forests of

Malaxis unifolia (green adder's-mouth). June 1988, Lake Co. Lee Casebere. x3.

the Highland Rim Natural Region, leading one to believe that the potential habitat for the green adder's-mouth is enormous there.

In 1987 Ken Klick discovered over two dozen plants of *M. unifolia* growing in moist sand within a copse of quaking aspen and black oak. This Lake County site, which is commonly flooded by shallow water in the winter, is part of a large mosaic of sand prairie and oak barrens. Associates include *Aralia nudicaulis, Coreopsis tripteris, Eryngium yuccifolium, Gaylussacia baccata, Pteridium aquilinum,* and *Rubus hispidus.*

At the Elkhart County site green adder's-mouth was observed growing in full sun in a sphagnum bog (Aldrich et al., 1986) with *Carex lasiocarpa, Drosera rotundifolia, Eriophorum viridicarinatum, Menyanthes trifoliata, Osmunda regalis, Potentilla palustris, Rhus vernix, Scirpus acutus, Spiraea tomentosa,* and *Thelypteris palustris.*

M. unifolia (green adder's-mouth). June 1988, Lake Co. Lee Casebere. x3.

The La Porte County *Malaxis* site consists of a wet forest bordering a sphagnum bog, where the orchid grew with *Acer rubrum, Carex crinita, Fraxinus americana, Larix laricina, Maianthemum canadense, Nyssa sylvatica, Rhus vernix,* and *Woodwardia virginica* (associates information taken from label of *Wilhelm and Dritz 6882,* MOR).

DISCUSSION: The green adder's-mouth is without question our smallest and most inconspicuous native orchid. Upon viewing it, one cannot help but be amazed that it is ever discovered, as its diminutive size and green pigmentation make it virtually impossible to detect. This, rather than actual rarity, may account for the paucity of records for this orchid. However, several people, the author included, have looked diligently for it in many places to no avail.

I think the greatest potential for discovery of new populations of *Malaxis* occurs in the Highland Rim Natural Region, Brown County Hills Section. Excellent habitat is ubiquitous (and essentially unbotanized) there. Although currently only two populations are known for the region, a thorough inventory would surely reveal more. The dry and dry-mesic forest communities situated on steep, mossy slopes dominated by *Carex picta* are likely to prove most productive.

Of the species of native orchids occurring in Indiana, *Malaxis unifolia,* along with *Corallorhiza odontorhiza,* has the most southerly global distribution, being known at least as far south as Guatemala and Honduras.

PLATANTHERA
L. C. Richard

Of the genera represented in Indiana, *Platanthera* has the fourth highest number of species worldwide (about 200—only *Malaxis*, *Spiranthes*, and *Liparis* have more). It is the number-one genus for total species diversity in Indiana (11).

Platanthera, from the Greek *platys*, for "broad," and *anthera*, for "anther," is in reference to the wide anther typical of the group. First used in 1818, the name *Platanthera* was virtually absent in the major works produced by this century's North American botanists until its use by Luer (1972) in his *The Native Orchids of Florida*. In the previous decades most botanists included members of the group in the genus *Habenaria*. Although not all contemporary botanists have accepted the changeover, most have. Those recognizing *Platanthera* have not dissolved *Habenaria*, however. According to Luer (1975), *Habenaria* is best used to describe a group of species that are primarily tropical in distribution. The closest occurrence of one to Indiana, that being *Habenaria repens*, is coastal North Carolina. *Habenaria* is recognized by its tuberously thickened roots, two-parted petals and lip divided into three linear divisions, and, most diagnostic, a pair of stigmatic processes (growths) protruding around and below the spur opening. In contrast, *Platanthera* has fleshy roots without tubers, undivided petals, a lip without three linear parts, and a nectary opening free of stigmatic processes.

Although it is difficult to refrain from using the name *Habenaria*, I think Luer's treatment is a good one, and therefore utilize *Platanthera* in this work for our species of "Habenaria."

PLATANTHERA

A.   Lip margins conspicuously fringed or jagged.............................. B.

    B.   Main body of lip unlobed; flowers orange..........................
       .... *Platanthera ciliaris*

    BB.   Main body of lip three-lobed; flowers not orange...........C.

       C.   Flowers purple..D.

           D.   Lip lobes fringed, with divisions at least one-third of the lobe length; pollinaria positioned close to one another, less than 2 mm apart; plants of saturated muck soils........................
              ....*Platanthera psycodes*

           DD.   Lip lobes merely jagged, with shallow divisions less than one-third the lobe length; pollinaria widely separated, commonly 3–5 mm apart; plants of ephemerally wet silt-loam soils ....*Platanthera peramoena*

       CC.   Flowers green or creamy-white.............................. E.

           E.   Petals linear, with an entire or finely toothed

margin; flowers normally green ....
.... *Platanthera lacera*

    EE. Petals wedge-shaped (broadest at tip), with distinct teeth or short fringing at the top margin; flowers normally creamy-white............
.... *Platanthera leucophaea*

AA. Lip margins entire or with a few shallow lobes ....F.

    F. Leaves basal, two in number (may be one in sterile plants), and rounded..G.

        G. Upper sepal and petals converging to form a hood over the column; lip curved forward and upward; flowers greenish; flowering stalk bractless below the inflorescence .... *Platanthera hookeri*

        GG. Upper petals widely spreading from the upper sepal, not forming a column hood; lip curved downward and back; flowers mostly white; flowering stalk with one or more bracts below the inflorescence.............
.... *Platanthera orbiculata*

    FF. Leaves one to several occurring along stem, or if appearing basal (as in sterile plants), then lanceolate to oblanceolate in shape ....H.

        H. Lip blunt at tip, either entire or three-lobed...........I.

            I. Lip apex entire; basal portion of lip bearing a nose-like projection (tubercle); major stem leaves 2 or more...J.

                J. Lip broad, about as wide as long, yellowish-green; only the lowest floral bracts longer than the flowers; plants of southern floodplain forests; blooms in July .... *Platanthera flava* var. *flava*

                JJ. Lip elongated, longer than broad, green; floral bracts typically longer than all but the uppermost flowers; plants mostly of wet sites with sandy, organic substrates; blooms mostly in June..........
.... *Platanthera flava* var. *herbiola*

            II. Lip apex with three teeth, or entire; basal portion of lip without a tubercle; stem with only one major stem leaf................................
.... *Platanthera clavellata*

    HH. Lip tapering to a slender point .... K.

            K. Flowers green, the lip gradually widening toward its base ....
.... *Platanthera hyperborea*

            KK. Flowers white, the lip abruptly widened at the base......................
.... *Platanthera dilatata*

Platanthera ciliaris (Linnaeus) Lindley

[Syn: *Habenaria ciliaris* (Linnaeus) R. Brown]

COMMON NAMES: orange fringed-orchid, yellow fringed-orchid.

SPECIFIC EPITHET DERIVATION: *ciliaris* = "eyelash," in reference to the fringed character of the lip.

DESCRIPTION: Plant glabrous throughout, 45–65 cm tall. Roots fleshy and tuberously thickened. Leaves 2–5, oblong-lanceolate to lanceolate, 7–12 cm long x 1.5–3.5 cm wide. Inflorescence a loose raceme of 20–30 flowers, each subtended by a lanceolate bract 10–15 mm long x 3–4 mm wide. **Lip** 10–12 mm long x 7–9 mm wide (including fringe), **orange**, oblong-elliptic, **with a margin of numerous filiform fringe hairs**, and **a basal spur** 20–25 mm long. **Petals orange**, linear, **with a fringed apex**, 4–5 mm long x 1–1.5 mm wide. **Sepals orange**, ovate, 5–7 mm long x 5–6 mm wide.

BLOOMING PERIOD: mid-July to mid-September.

RANGE: Confined to the northern three tiers of counties, with one remarkable exception, viz., Harrison County.

HABITAT: In northern Indiana *Platanthera ciliaris* occurs primarily in two habitat types: sphagnum bogs and moist sand flats. In all cases these environments are decidedly acidic and possess ample and continuous soil moisture. Another ingredient is light; the orchid does poorly in areas of low light, and is virtually absent from densely shaded sites. Consequently, maintenance of populations requires periodic disturbance, such as fire, to remove or suppress competing vegetation.

Sphagnum bogs are prime habitat for *Platanthera ciliaris*. At a large bog in La Porte County the orange fringed-orchid grows abundantly on sphagnum moss hummocks in openings between tamarack, red maple, and tall *Ilex verticillata* and *Vaccinium corymbosum* shrubs. In this classic bog habitat the orchid grows with *Chamaedaphne calyculata, Cypripedium acaule, Osmunda cinnamomea, O. regalis, Rhynchospora alba, Sarracenia purpurea,* and *Vaccinium oxycoccos*.

Moist sand flats also are important habitats for *P. ciliaris* in Indiana. Typically only a few plants are seen together in these habitats, although at at least one site, in La Grange County, the orchid is locally common. The moist pine savannas of the southeastern U.S. coastal plain are re-

markably similar floristically to our sand flats, including the presence of *P. ciliaris*. Yet, in contrast to its occurrence in Indiana, the orchid is relatively common there. Its failure to colonize freely areas of seemingly suitable habitat here reflects the conservative reproduction and habitat selection commonly seen in species on the edges of their ranges.

Some of the species associated with *Platanthera ciliaris* in open sand-flat habitat are *Aletris farinosa, Aronia melanocarpa, Gaultheria procumbens, Liatris spicata, Lycopodium inundatum, Pteridium aquilinum, Rubus hispidus, Sorghastrum nutans, Spiraea tomentosa,* and *Vaccinium angustifolium*. In a lightly forested, wet sand flat in La Grange County the orchid grows under a canopy of red maple and black gum, with *Aronia melanocarpa, Carex intumescens, Gaylussacia baccata, Ilex verticillata, Lysimachia quadrifolia, Maianthemum canadense, Nemopanthus mucronatus, Rubus hispidus, Sphagnum* spp., *Trientalis borealis, Vaccinium atrococcum,* and *Viburnum cassinoides* in the understory. Not far from this site a single *P. ciliaris* was growing on a relatively dry sand flat forested with black oak (*fide* Lee Casebere). This habitat is evidently unusual for the species in Indiana.

In his personal collection journal Clapp indicated that he collected *Platanthera ciliaris* on August 4, 1835, in the barrens near New Albany. A voucher specimen exists to verify his note (*Clapp s.n.,* WAB). The specimen was most likely collected in the extensive barrens region on the Mitchell Karst Plain, where grassy-bordered sinkhole ponds were plentiful. Those conditions would have been ideal for *P. ciliaris*, as sinkhole depressions in general are moist, sunny, and acidic (described today as Baxter/Crider silt loams). Most of the barrens and undisturbed sinkhole wetlands are now virtually gone from southern Indiana's landscape, and the hope of finding *P. ciliaris* there today is remote.

Another habitat possibility for *Platanthera ciliaris* in southern Indiana is found on the Knobstone Escarpment just west of New Albany. There xeric forests of Virginia pine and chestnut oak blanket the steep knobs composed of acidic shale and siltstone. Within those forests natural openings (glades) occur where sun-loving species flourish. Although obviously not moist, the openings nevertheless might provide suitable habitat for *P. ciliaris*, as the orchid occurs in similar environments farther south in its range. In the mountains of North Carolina and elsewhere in the southern Appalachians it commonly grows in dry forest clearings,

ABOVE: *Platanthera ciliaris* (orange fringed-orchid). July 1987, La Grange Co. Lee Casebere. x1.

OPPOSITE: *P. ciliaris*. July 1990, La Grange Co. Lee Casebere. x½.

old fields, and along graded roadsides. In addition, there are records of *P. ciliaris* from dry upland habitats in nearby south-central Ohio (Braun, 1967).

DISCUSSION: The orange fringed-orchid is undeniably a spectacular organism. During the dog days of summer when few other plants are in bloom *Platanthera ciliaris* stands ablaze in glory, putting on an unforgettable display for those willing to battle the heat and mosquitoes. Perhaps the latter elements were getting to Pepoon (1927) when he wrote that "the flowers show curious semblances to witches' heads." Regardless of perspective, we are fortunate to have *Platanthera ciliaris* in Indiana, especially considering that the orchid is on the edge of its range here. Interestingly, the northern Indiana populations, with those in adjacent southern Michigan, northeastern Illinois, and northwestern Ohio, form an isolated range separated by over 200 miles from the nearest documented occurrences in far south-central Ohio and southeastern Missouri, and those in Harrison County, Indiana.

Platanthera clavellata (Michaux) Luer

[Syn: *Habenaria clavellata* (Michaux) Sprengel]

COMMON NAMES: club-spur orchid, small green wood orchid.

SPECIFIC EPITHET DERIVATION: *clavellata* = "small club," in reference to the club-shaped spur of the species.

DESCRIPTION: **Plant glabrous** throughout, 20–30 cm tall. Roots fleshy, slender. **Leaves normally 2–3, with the lowest considerably larger than the others. Lowest leaf oblanceolate, 9–11** cm long x 1.5–2 cm wide. **Inflorescence a short, few-flowered raceme of 7–10 flowers tilted at an angle away from the main axis,** each subtended by a lanceolate bract 4–6 mm long x 1–1.5 mm wide. **Lip** 4–5 mm long x 2 mm wide, pale green, oblong-cuneate, **shallowly tridentate at apex, with a club-shaped spur** from the lip base 9–11 mm long. Petals pale green, ovate, 4–5 mm long x 2 mm wide. Sepals pale green, ovate, 4–6 mm long x 2 mm wide.

BLOOMING PERIOD: early July to late August.

RANGE: Occurs predominantly in the northern third of the state,

particularly in the Northern Lakes and Northwestern Morainal natural regions. There are scattered populations in southern Indiana, mostly in the south-central counties. Clapp listed it for the New Albany area (Floyd County), having noted it on August 20, 1833. Although the record is surely correct, I have not seen a voucher specimen to support the claim. There is an obvious absence of occurrences in the central counties (generally equalling the Central Till Plain Natural Region), this due primarily to drainage of wetlands and unsuitability of the remaining habitats.

HABITAT: As if in hiding, this orchid typically makes its home in the almost impenetrable jungle of intertwining branches of shrubs and small trees that occur within and/or bordering our bogs, fens, and seep springs. Only rarely does it grow out in the open where it can be readily seen. *Platanthera clavellata* is normally found on the hummocks formed at the base of other vegetation, or on fallen, rotting logs. Other than for mosses and liverworts, this underworld is relatively competition-free, allowing the orchid to become abundant in places. It is particularly fond of growing on mossy hummocks underneath alder (*Alnus incana* and *A. serrulata*), poison sumac (*Rhus vernix*), and the fronds of *Osmunda* ferns (*Osmunda cinnamomea* and *O. regalis*). In these environments it grows with *Acer rubrum, Aronia melanocarpa, A. prunifolia, Bartonia virginica, Botrychium simplex* (locally), *Carex atlantica* var. *atlantica, C. bromoides, Cornus racemosa, Cypripedium acaule, Dryopteris carthusiana, D. cristata, Ilex verticillata, Lindera benzoin, Onoclea sensibilis, Oxypolis rigidior, Platanthera lacera, Rubus hispidus, Sphagnum* spp., *Symplocarpus foetidus,* and *Viola pallens.*

Platanthera clavellata also grows in moist, organic sands bordering vernal pools. In such an environment in La Porte County it occurs along a buttonbush (*Cephalanthus occidentalis*) swamp with the surrounding forest dominated by red maple, red oak, and tulip tree. Associates include *Maianthemum canadense, Mitchella repens, Nyssa sylvatica,* and *Sassafras albidum.* In similar environments in sunnier situations, *P. clavellata* may occur with *Aletris farinosa, Bartonia virginica, Calopogon tuberosus,* and *Xyris torta* (Swink, 1966).

Platanthera clavellata also occurs in open fens, but rarely. There it grows with *Cladium mariscoides, Drosera rotundifolia, Eleocharis rostellata, Lysimachia quadriflora, Parnassia glauca, Pedicularis lanceolata, Potentilla fruticosa, Solidago ohioensis,* and *Zigadenus elegans* (fide Lee Casebere).

PRECEDING PAGE: *Platanthera clavellata* (club-spur orchid). July 1990, La Grange Co. Lee Casebere. x1.

ABOVE: *P. clavellata.* July 1990, La Grange Co. Lee Casebere. x1¾.

Further south in Indiana *P. clavellata* becomes more habitat specific, occurring only in acid seep springs. The orchid has such a fidelity to acid seep springs that all reports of its occurrence (in the south) from other habitats are suspect.

DISCUSSION: As may not be evident from the range map, *Platanthera clavellata* is actually one of the more common wetland orchids. With a little patience, searching through suitable habitat will almost always turn up specimens. However, being one of the smallest and least colorful orchids, as well as an inhabitant of some of the most inhospitable environments, *P. clavellata* is not commonly seen. One of the best ways to find the small green wood orchid is to "muscle" into the thickets of alder or poison sumac, stoop to the level of the hummocks, and scan for the orchid. By getting at the orchid's level, one can find many plants that otherwise would have been missed.

Platanthera clavellata is our only *Platanthera* with flowers that are positioned at a 45–degree angle from vertical. All others have flowers more or less in a vertical plane. *P. clavellata* is also the smallest Indiana *Platanthera*. Its size, in combination with its flower angle and possession of a single, oblanceolate leaf, distinguishes this orchid from all others.

Platanthera dilatata (Pursh) Lindley *ex* Beck

[Syn: *Habenaria dilatata* (Pursh) Hooker]

COMMON NAMES: tall white bog-orchid, bog candles.

SPECIFIC EPITHET DERIVATION: *dilatata* = "broadened," in reference to the dilated base of the flower's lip.

DESCRIPTION: Plant glabrous throughout, 30–45 cm tall. Roots fleshy, thickened toward the base. Principal leaves 4–6, linear-lanceolate, 5–10 cm long x 7–10 mm wide. Inflorescence an elongated raceme of 25–35 flowers, each subtended by a lanceolate bract 8–11 mm long x 2 mm wide. **Lip** 5–7 mm long x 2–3 mm wide (at the base), **white, lanceolate with an abrupt dilation at the base, and a spur** from the lip base 5–6 mm long. **Petals white**, ovate-lanceolate, falcate, 4–5 mm long x 1–1.5 mm wide. **Dorsal sepal white**, ovate, 4–5 mm long x 3 mm wide. Petals and dorsal sepal converge to form a hood over the column. **Lateral sepals white**, lanceolate, spreading, 5–7 mm long x 1–2 mm wide.

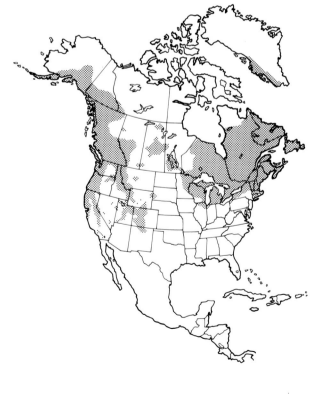

BLOOMING PERIOD: late May to late June.

RANGE: This boreal orchid reaches the southern edge of its midwestern range in Indiana, with occurrence in the state only from a few-square-mile area in St. Joseph County. See Discussion for details of reports from elsewhere in the state.

HABITAT: In Indiana, as elsewhere in most of its range, *Platanthera dilatata* requires constant saturation of its root zone with cold water. It also is a calciphile, at least in the eastern U.S., where it is most often found growing in fens and marly lake borders. Its calciphilic nature is particularly evident at the one site where it still occurs in Indiana. There the orchid grows in marly, spring-fed rivulets that snake through a small calcareous fen.

Another growth requirement of *Platanthera dilatata* is high light level. Habitats dominated by trees or shrubs that otherwise may be suitable will not likely have this orchid. However, "full-sun" species can persist in extremely tiny openings in forested communities, so don't discount overgrown fens as a possible habitat for *P. dilatata*.

OPPOSITE: *Platanthera dilatata* (tall white bog-orchid). June 1989, St. Joseph Co. Lee Casebere. x³/₄.

ABOVE: *P. dilatata*. May 1987, St. Joseph Co. Perry Scott. x1½.

At the fen in St. Joseph County, *Platanthera dilatata* grows with *Cacalia plantaginea, Carex cryptolepis, C. sterilis, Cirsium muticum, Deschampsia cespitosa, Equisetum arvense, Glyceria striata, Parnassia glauca, Potentilla fruticosa, Sarracenia purpurea,* and *Silphium terebinthinaceum.*

DISCUSSION: *Platanthera dilatata* is certainly one of the most attractive and rarest of Indiana orchids. To my knowledge, its graceful wand of fragrant white flowers has adorned only one area in Indiana, that in St. Joseph County. Unfortunately, most of the area where *P. dilatata* occurred has been destroyed, leaving at last count only nine individuals of the orchid remaining in an overall population that probably once numbered in the hundreds, if not thousands.

Peter E. Hebert of Notre Dame was the first to collect *Platanthera dilatata* in Indiana, doing so in 1932 in an area in St. Joseph County known as "Six Mile Swamp." Over a 15–year period following Hebert's discovery the area yielded several additional specimens of the orchid, most to such great Hoosier botanists as Charles Deam, Ray Friesner, and John Potzger. As early as 1935, however, it became evident that the plants were in danger. One of Deam's specimen labels from a 1935 collection (*Deam 56098*, IND) states that the site was being "heavily

Platanthera dilatata   153

grazed and doubtless will soon be exterminated. F. J. Hermann was with me and he took a specimen and we left about a half dozen for the cows." Another Deam label, from 1946 (*Deam 64566*, IND) states: "This bog and springy area is now being drained."

Following Deam's ominous statement, it appeared that no tall white bog-orchids would ever be seen again in St. Joseph County, or for that matter, the state, as no individuals were seen in Indiana for several decades thereafter. Then on June 5, 1984, nearly 40 years after the last *Platanthera dilatata* was seen in Indiana, a population of 7 plants was discovered by an excited group of biologists consisting of Jim Aldrich, John Bogucki, Lee Casebere, Marge and Vic Riemenschneider, and myself. The orchids occur in a small fen that was discovered by Bogucki and is apparently a remnant of the former Six Mile Swamp where *P. dilatata* was first seen. True to Deam's prophetic statement, virtually all of the wetland was drained, and is now in cultivation. However, one tiny remnant persists, and amazingly it still supports *Platanthera dilatata.*

There are reports of *Platanthera dilatata* populations from elsewhere in the state (Nieuwland, 1913; Deam, 1940; Swink and Wilhelm, 1979—citing Deam, 1940; Case, 1987), but I feel these are the result of mistaking *P. hyperborea* for *P. dilatata.* The Porter County and Lake County specimens (*Nieuwland 940*, ND and *Nieuwland s.n.*, ND, respectively) cited by Deam (1940) are *P. hyperborea*, as are the *Deam 64569* (IND) and *Friesner 20466* (BUT) specimens from La Porte County. All of these have lips without any significant basal dilation, and instead have a more gradual widening toward the base characteristic of *P. hyperborea* (see Fig. 9).

Of the three sheets of specimens collected by L. M. Umbach comprising *Umbach 1761*—all originally labeled *Habenaria* (*Platanthera*) *hyperborea*—one was annotated by A. M. Fuller (in 1932) and F. W. Case (in 1961) as *Platanthera dilatata*. The specimens, collected in 1907 from "swales" in Millers (now Gary), are housed, one sheet each, at the University of Wisconsin (WIS), the University of Michigan (MICH), and the Milwaukee Public Museum (MIL). Only the MIL specimens were annotated *P. dilatata*. The MICH specimens were annotated by Case as *Habenaria hyperborea*, and both he and Fuller anno-

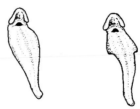

FIGURE 9. Comparison of lips of *Platanthera hyperborea* (left) and *P. dilatata*

154 ***Platanthera dilatata***

tated the WIS specimens as *H. hyperborea* also (Fuller evidently did not see the MICH specimens, as there is no annotation by him). After carefully inspecting the three sheets of *Umbach 1761* together, it is my conclusion that all of the collections are the same species, viz., *Platanthera hyperborea*. Although the lips differ slightly in shape from specimen to specimen, they nevertheless are easily within the range of variability found in *P. hyperborea*. None of them possesses the diagnostic dilated lip base of *P. dilatata*. Thus, I feel the original determination by Umbach was correct.

Indiana plants of *Platanthera dilatata* belong to variety *dilatata*. It is distinguished from the other North American varieties—var. *albiflora* (Chamisso) Ledebour, and var. *leucostachys* (Lindley) Luer—by its slender spur, equal to or shorter than its lip.

Platanthera flava (Linnaeus) Lindley var. *flava*

[Syn: *Habenaria flava* (Linnaeus) R. Brown *ex* Sprengel var. *flava*; *Habenaria scutellata* (Nuttall) F. Morris]

COMMON NAME: southern tubercled orchid.

SPECIFIC EPITHET DERIVATION: *flava* = "yellow," in reference to the color of the flowers.

DESCRIPTION: Plant glabrous throughout, 30–40 cm tall. **Roots fleshy, apparently growing for several dm, from which new plants arise. Principal leaves 2, a third greatly reduced,** elliptic-lanceolate, 12–14 cm long x 2.5–3 cm wide. Inflorescence an elongated raceme of 20–30 flowers, each subtended by a lanceolate bract 6–10 mm long x 2 mm wide. **Most bracts, except possibly for those at the lowermost end of the raceme, as long as or shorter than the flowers. Lip** 3–4 mm long x 1.5–2 mm wide, **yellowish-green, suborbicular-quadrate, with a tooth or lobe on each side of the base, and a tubercle in the middle of the lip. Spur from base of lip** 5–6 mm long. Petals yellowish-green, ovate, 2 mm long x 1–1.5 mm wide. Sepals green, ovate, 2 mm long x 1–1.5 mm wide.

BLOOMING PERIOD: early July to late September.

Map shows combined ranges for both varieties.

RANGE: Known only from Jackson and Posey counties. Deam (1912) cited an 1877 Schneck specimen taken from Foote's Pond, Gibson County (Deam erroneously listed Foote's Pond for Posey County), but I have not encountered any Schneck specimen. Oddly, the Schneck collection is not referenced in the *Flora of Indiana* (Deam, 1940).

HABITAT: *Platanthera flava* var. *flava*, like some populations of its northern counterpart variety *herbiola*, occurs in swamps and ephemeral woodland pools. At a site in Jackson County *P. flava* var. *flava* grows in shallow, abandoned river channels deep within a large tract of bottomland forest. The old channels are commonly ponded during the winter and spring seasons, with water provided directly from precipitation and flooding from a nearby river. During the summer and autumn growing seasons the pools are generally reduced to exposed mud and dense vegetation. This habitat is apparently similar to that where Deam found the orchid in Posey County. He noted finding a "large colony . . . growing in a bare place under a large clump of buttonbush where it must have been submerged much of the year" (Deam, 1940). The Posey County site (precise locality unknown, but general habitat and associates determinable) and the one in Jackson County possess a strong southern affinity, harboring such species as sweetgum, swamp chestnut oak, red maple, bald cypress, water locust, pecan (the latter three from Posey County only), *Campsis radicans*, *Cephalanthus occidentalis*, *Chasmanthium latifolium*, *Glyceria striata*, *Iris virginica*, *Lindera benzoin*, *Ranunculus septentrionalis*, and *Saururus cernuus*.

DISCUSSION: Since Linnaeus described and named *Platanthera flava* (as *Orchis flava*) botanists have noted consistent differences between the northern and southern populations of the species. The distinctiveness between them is so great that some early botanists considered them as separate species. Charles Deam belonged to this group, as he referred to variety *flava* as *Habenaria scutellata* (and variety *herbiola* as *Habenaria flava*). Today most botanists (although see last paragraph) recognize the entities of *P. flava* at the varietal level, as var. *flava* and var. *herbiola*. Regardless of treatment they are clearly separable, as can be seen by a comparison of traits given in Table 2.

Luer (1975) states that the two varieties of *Platanthera flava* intergrade where their ranges overlap, and that recognition of the intergrades

OPPOSITE: *Platanthera flava* var. *flava* (southern tubercled orchid). July 1990, Jackson Co. Mike Homoya. x³/₄.

ABOVE: *P. flava* var. *flava*. July 1990, Jackson Co. Lee Casebere. x3.

Table 2. Characteristics used to distinguish *P. flava* var. *flava* and *P. flava* var. *herbiola*

variety *flava*	variety *herbiola*
principal leaves	
normally 2	normally 3
floral bract	
only the lower bracts longer than the flowers	most bracts longer than the flowers they subtend
flower color	
greenish-yellow	green
lip	
as broad as long, square to rounded in shape (quadrate to suborbicular)	longer than broad (oblong)
habitat	
floodplain swamps and forests; soil silt-loam	upland depressions, floodplain forests, prairies; soil sandy and/ or highly organic (rarely silt-loam) alluvium, outwash, lacustrine deposits
distribution	
strictly southern quarter of state	throughout the state, but mostly northern
prime flowering	
early July to early August	early June to early July

as one or the other variety is merely a matter of opinion. In Indiana the plants are not so problematic. Southern Indiana is one of the few areas where the two varieties occur in the same range, and yet no intergradation is evident. This suggests that the two taxa may possibly be reproductively isolated, and thus merit species level status. Obviously, more research is needed to solve this taxonomic problem.

Platanthera flava (Linnaeus) Lindley var. *herbiola* (R. Brown) Luer

[Syn: *Habenaria flava* (Linnaeus) R. Brown var. *herbiola* (R. Brown) Ames and Correll]

COMMON NAMES: northern tubercled orchid, tubercled rein-orchid.

SPECIFIC EPITHET DERIVATION: *flava* = "yellow," in reference to the color of the flowers; *herbiola* = "little plant," possibly in reference to the type (of the variety) being described. Fernald (1950) gives "grass-green" as the meaning of *herbiola*.

DESCRIPTION: Plant glabrous throughout, 30–40 cm tall. **Roots fleshy, apparently growing for several dm, from which new plants arise. Leaves 3–4,** elliptic-lanceolate, 8–12 cm long x 2–3 cm wide. Inflorescence an elongated raceme of 15–30 flowers, each subtended by a lanceolate bract 10–15 mm long x 2 mm wide. **Most bracts longer than the flowers. Lip** 3–5 mm long x 1–3 mm wide, **greenish, oblong, with a tooth or lobe on each side of the base, and a tubercle in the middle of the lip near the base. Spur from base of lip** 5–6 mm long. Petals green, ovate, 2–3 mm long x 1–1.5 mm wide. Sepals green, ovate, 2–3 mm long x 1–1.5 mm wide.

BLOOMING PERIOD: late May to early August.

RANGE: Occurs predominantly in the northern half of the state, but three occurrences are from the far southern counties of Daviess, Harrison, and Jackson.

HABITAT: There are two principal habitats in Indiana for *Platanthera flava* var. *herbiola:* woodland ponds and swamps, and sand prairie. Most populations are found in the former habitat, especially in wet depressions that are inundated periodically (usually in winter and spring) but are normally free of surface water by flowering time. Borders of buttonbush (*Cephalanthus occidentalis*) swamps are particularly good habitats, as are black ash swamps. At one such site in De Kalb County I found this orchid growing as densely as 30 plants per square meter, all under a canopy of black ash, bur oak, and American elm. *Aesculus glabra, Athyrium filix-femina, Corylus americana, Cryptotaenia canadensis, Geranium maculatum, Iris virginica, Rhus radicans, Rosa palustris,* and *Viburnum lentago* occur in the immediate surroundings.

Map shows combined ranges for both varieties.

FOLLOWING PAGE: *Platanthera flava* var. *herbiola* (northern tubercled orchid). June 1989, Daviess Co. Mike Homoya. x¹/₂.

At a somewhat similar site in Daviess County the swamp border was shaded by black willow, red maple, and American elm. Although the orchid also was found in dense shade, the greatest numbers of individuals were found in an area of the swamp formerly cleared of timber and now in regrowth. The greater light levels were apparently responsible for the orchid's proliferation, as well as for the many co-occurring species, viz., *Boehmeria cylindrica*, *Carex lupulina*, *Cinna arundinacea*, *Eupatorium perfoliatum*, *Glyceria striata*, *Impatiens capensis*, *Juncus effusus*, *Oxypolis rigidior*, *Pedicularis lanceolata*, *Rosa palustris*, and *Saururus cernuus*.

In great contrast to the forested environments there is sand prairie, where, unlike in the shaded swamp, *Platanthera flava* var. *herbiola* grows exposed to full sunlight. Wet-mesic swales are the favored habitat of the orchid in the sand prairie, although in such environments this orchid is not a common plant. *Andropogon gerardii*, *Calamagrostis canadensis*, *Calopogon tuberosus*, *Onoclea sensibilis*, *Osmunda regalis*, *Platanthera lacera*, *Pycnanthemum virginianum*, *Sorghastrum nutans*, *Spartina pectinata*, *Spiraea alba*, and *Tradescantia ohiensis* are known associates of *P. flava* var. *herbiola* in Indiana sand prairies.

P. flava var. *herbiola* (northern tubercled orchid). June 1976, Lake Co., Illinois. Marlin Bowles. x1.

The majority of *Platanthera flava* var. *herbiola* stations occur on sand or peat/muck substrates. Even most disjunct southern localities are situated in local deposits of sand. Sheviak (1974) noted this for Illinois plants as well. The one known exception occurs in Jackson County, where a few plants of var. *herbiola* were found growing on the border of a floodplain oxbow. The soil is a silt-loam alluvium. The site has a canopy of red maple and blue beech, with *Boehmeria cylindrica*, *Cephalanthus occidentalis*, *Cinna arundinacea*, *Onoclea sensibilis*, *Ranunculus septentrionalis*, *Rudbeckia laciniata*, *Scutellaria lateriflora*, and *Triadenum tubulosum* in the understory.

DISCUSSION: Another of the "green" orchids, *Platanthera flava* is also one of the more uncommon species in Indiana. It is encountered only by the most astute observer, and even then it may be passed over as some weed, or as some other species of "green" orchid. It is commonly confused with *Coeloglossum viride*, probably because both have green flowers, and long bracts subtending each flower. It is also sometimes confused with *Platanthera hyperborea*, as well as *P. clavellata*.

The easiest way to distinguish *P. flava* from the others is to look for

the presence of a tubercle or "nose" projecting outward from the upper portion of the lip. No other Indiana orchid has such a feature. The tubercle is more than an interesting floral ornament. It serves to deflect the head and probing proboscis of a feeding insect (such as a moth or mosquito) into one of two pathways leading to a nectar-filled spur (Stoutamire, 1971; Luer, 1975). By forcing the insect to go around the tubercle, the insect's proboscis is likely to attach to a viscidium that, upon withdrawal of the proboscis from the spur, brings along the pollinium.

The petals and sepals of *Platanthera flava* are quite fleshy, and commonly persist on the developing ovaries throughout much of the growing season. The lip deteriorates, but it too may persist in the dried condition. This in effect creates an extended blooming period, freeing one from the need to rely only on vegetative characters in order to determine plants found late in the growing season.

Although *Platanthera flava* var. *herbiola* is predominantly a northern species, the first Indiana specimen came from Harrison County, collected in 1840 by Dr. C. W. Short of Kentucky (*Short s.n.*, MO). He found the orchid in The Barrens, a region that harbored many interesting and unusual plants, several of which no longer occur there. *Platanthera flava* var. *herbiola* is apparently one of them. Clapp noted in his annotated copy of Riddell (1835) having collected this species in the "Barrens," but no date was recorded. The collection may have preceded that made by Short, but I have seen no specimen.

Platanthera hookeri (Torrey) Lindley

[Syn: *Habenaria hookeri* Torrey in A. Gray]

COMMON NAME: Hooker's orchid.

SPECIFIC EPITHET DERIVATION: *hookeri*, in honor of William Hooker, an English botanist.

DESCRIPTION: Plant glabrous throughout, 25–30 cm tall. Roots several, fleshy. **Leaves 2, opposite, basal, orbicular to broadly elliptic**, 10 cm long x 6–7 cm wide. Inflorescence a loose raceme of 15–20 flowers, each subtended by a lanceolate bract 1–1.5 cm long x 3 mm wide. **Stem below flowers without bracts. Lip** 1–1.2 cm long x 3–4 mm wide, **triangular-lanceolate, strongly curved upward**, yellowish-green, **with a spur** from the lip base 2 cm long. **Petals lanceolate, falcate**, yellowish-green, 5–7 mm long x 2 mm wide. Dorsal sepal ovate, green, 5–8 mm long x 4 mm wide. **Petals and dorsal sepal converge to form a hood over the column**. Lateral sepals elliptic-lanceolate, strongly reflexed, green, 10 mm long x 3 mm wide.

BLOOMING PERIOD: late May to late June.

RANGE: Confined to the counties bordering Lake Michigan (Lake Michigan Border Section—Northwestern Morainal Natural Region). Although unknown from elsewhere in the state, the extreme northeastern counties might reveal a few individuals, as specimens have been procured in adjacent Michigan counties (Case, 1987). Van Gorder (1894) reported *Platanthera hookeri* for Noble County, but his specimens are *P. orbiculata*.

HABITAT: Because of its extreme rarity, little is known about the habitat of *Platanthera hookeri* in Indiana. All of the collections from Indiana are quite old, and these provide little information regarding habitat other than brief one or two-word notations such as "pine woods," "low thickets," and "wet woods." The best information we have comes from Valdemar Schwarz, a long-time orchidologist from Blue Island, Illinois. He has observed *P. hookeri* growing in Porter County under a canopy of white pine, with understory associates consisting of *Acer rubrum*, *Actaea alba*, *Cornus rugosa*, *Cypripedium calceolus* var. *pubescens*, *Juniperus communis* var. *depressa*, *Parthenocissus quinquefolia*, *Pyrola elliptica*, *P. rotundifolia*, and *Quercus rubra* (V. Schwarz, personal communication).

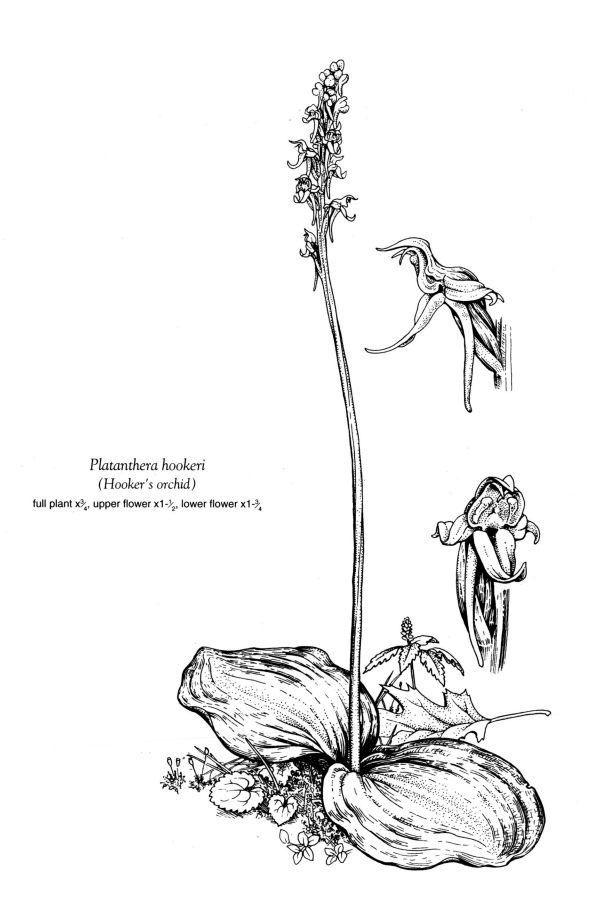

Platanthera hookeri
(Hooker's orchid)

full plant x$\frac{3}{4}$, upper flower x1-$\frac{1}{2}$, lower flower x1-$\frac{3}{4}$

According to Case (1987), mixed hardwood forests dominated chiefly by American beech and sugar maple are the prime habitats for *P. hookeri* in southern Michigan. Small, rather disturbed examples of such habitats occur in northern Indiana, and could thus harbor the orchid.

DISCUSSION: No longer known to occur in Indiana, Hooker's orchid was evidently last seen here by Valdemar Schwarz. For several consecutive years Schwarz observed a population of approximately 10–15 plants in Indiana Dunes State Park, Porter County, only to watch it eventually succumb for unknown reasons. He last observed the species there in September of 1969. Ironically, the single plant was laden with ripening capsules, as if to make "one last stand" before it and the population vanished forever. See Schwarz's photograph of *P. hookeri*, taken at the park, in the Introduction, section on Orchid Conservation.

There are primarily three reasons why Hooker's orchid is no longer in Indiana today. First and foremost is habitat destruction. Many of the areas where it was known have since been developed, particularly by industry. Related to this is the second reason; habitat alteration. Chemical deposition, changes in hydrology, alteration of fire regimes, and a host of other possibilities may have played an important role in the orchid's disappearance. Lastly, the orchid was on the very edge of its range here, not particularly common, and restricted to a small geographic area, suggesting a species extremely vulnerable to extirpation.

Plants of *Platanthera hookeri*, both in sterile and flowering condition, have been confused with *P. orbiculata*. The vegetative similarities are obvious, as both orchids have paired, suborbicular to orbicular leaves. However, the leaves of *P. hookeri* are less glossy than those of *P. orbiculata*, and normally are not as large and orbicular. The flowers are easier to distinguish. The lateral petals of *P. hookeri* join with the dorsal sepal to form a hood, whereas in *P. orbiculata* the lateral petals spread freely upward. The lip is curved upward in *P. hookeri*, giving the flower in profile an appearance of "ice tongs" (Case, 1987). An easy way to remember this is to think of the alliteration coined by Morris and Eames (1929), "Hooker's Hooks." The lip of *P. orbiculata* curves down and back toward the flower stalk. See the key for additional differences.

Platanthera hyperborea (Linnaeus) Lindley

[Syn: *Habenaria hyperborea* (Linnaeus) R. Brown in Aiton]

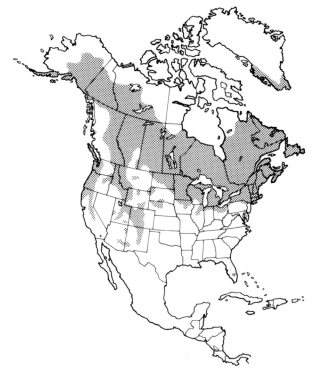

Platanthera hyperborea (northern green orchid). July 1988, La Grange Co. Lee Casebere. x1.

COMMON NAMES: northern green orchid, green-flowered bog-orchid.

SPECIFIC EPITHET DERIVATION: *hyperborea* = "over the north," in reference to the far northern range of the species.

DESCRIPTION: Plant glabrous throughout, 37–45 cm tall. Roots fleshy, thickened toward the base. Leaves 3–4, oblong-lanceolate, 8–12 cm long x 1.5–3 cm wide. Inflorescence an elongated raceme of 30–40 flowers, each subtended by a lanceolate bract 1–2 cm long, 3–4 mm wide. **Lip** 3–4 mm long x 1.5–2 mm wide, **green, lanceolate, but not abruptly dilated, with a spur** from the lip base, 3–4 mm long. **Petals green,** lanceolate, falcate, 3–4 mm long x 1 mm wide. **Dorsal sepal green,** ovate, 2–3 mm long x 2 mm wide. Petals and dorsal sepal converge to form a hood over the column. **Lateral sepals green,** lanceolate, spreading, 3–4 mm long x 1–2 mm wide.

BLOOMING PERIOD: early June to late July.

RANGE: Another boreal orchid, *Platanthera hyperborea* is known in Indiana only from the northernmost tier of counties. Although not known farther south, it may occur there in the other counties making up the Northern Lakes Natural Region.

HABITAT: Like its similar-appearing relative, *Platanthera dilatata*, *P. hyperborea* occurs in wetlands composed of calcareous, peaty substrates saturated with cold ground water—fen, forested fen, panne, seep spring, and marsh. Also like *P. dilatata* is the orchid's preference for full sun, but it is much more tolerant of shade, occurring in dense shrub thickets and forested fens. Wherever it occurs it typically occupies the wettest areas, especially near open pools of water or along spring channels or animal runs.

In a few fens in northeastern Indiana, *Platanthera hyperborea* is locally common, occurring in open marl flats as well as areas shaded by tamarack, poison sumac, and shrub dogwood species (*Cornus racemosa, C. sericea*). Other plants growing with the orchid include *Carex leptalea, C. sterilis, C. tetanica, Cicuta bulbifera, Cypripedium calceolus* var. *parviflorum, C. candidum, Equisetum fluviatile, Lindera benzoin, Oxypolis rigidior, Parnassia glauca, Potentilla fruticosa, Rhamnus alnifolia, Sarrace-*

nia purpurea, Symplocarpus foetidus, Thelypteris palustris, Typha angustifolia, and *Zizia aurea.*

Across the state in the Lake Michigan Dunes region Swink (1966) noted *Platanthera hyperborea* growing in calcareous springy areas with *Caltha palustris, Galium triflorum, Glyceria striata, Ribes americanum, Rudbeckia laciniata,* and *Symplocarpus foetidus.* Bowles et al. (1986) noted the orchid growing along margins of pannes near Lake Michigan with *Cladium mariscoides, Hypericum kalmianum, Juncus arcticus, Populus deltoides, Rhynchospora capillacea, Salix myricoides,* and *S. syrticola.* Bowles (1987) also reported *P. hyperborea* growing in mesic sand prairie in Lake County, along with *Aster oolentangiensis, Calamagrostis canadensis, Coreopsis tripteris, Fragaria virginiana, Maianthemum canadense, Pycnanthemum virginianum, Rudbeckia hirta, Senecio pauperculus, Solidago ohioensis,* and *Sorghastrum nutans.*

P. hyperborea (northern green orchid). June 1983, Steuben Co. Lee Casebere. x2.

DISCUSSION: Of the orchids native to Indiana, *Platanthera hyperborea* (along with *Corallorhiza trifida, Cypripedium calceolus,* and *Spiranthes romanzoffiana*) ranges farthest north on Earth. The specific epithet, *hyperborea,* literally translated "above or over the north," certainly has meaning here, as the orchid is one of the few to occur within the Arctic Circle. It even occurs in Iceland, hence one of the common names, Iceland Orchis (Peattie, 1930). Based on geography, Indiana specimens of *P. hyperborea* can be attributed to var. *huronensis* (Nuttall) Luer. The validity of this variety is debatable, as it is based principally on size (var. *huronensis* being more robust than var. *hyperborea*). Indiana specimens exhibit a wide range of sizes, seemingly reflecting the environmental conditions in which they grew. Further study is needed.

As is evident in the photographs, *Platanthera hyperborea* and *P. dilatata* are morphologically similar. Obviously closely related, the two interbreed, resulting in populations that can be referred to only as the *P. dilatata–P. hyperborea* complex (Case, 1987), or as the putative hybrid *Platanthera X media* (Luer, 1975). The situation is particularly complicated in the western states, where other species are involved (Schrenk, 1978). Fortunately in Indiana the two species behave themselves, and can be easily distinguished from one another (at least when encountered in the field—herbarium specimens are not so easy!). See Figure 9 for a comparison of the lip shapes of *P. hyperborea* and *P. dilatata.*

Platanthera lacera (Michaux) G. Don in Sweet

{Syn: *Habenaria lacera* (Michaux) R. Brown}

COMMON NAMES: green fringed-orchid, ragged fringed-orchid.

SPECIFIC EPITHET DERIVATION: *lacera* = "torn," in reference to the fringed lip of the species.

DESCRIPTION: Plant glabrous throughout, 40–50 cm tall. Roots thickened, fleshy. Leaves 2–4, linear-lanceolate to oblong-lanceolate, 10–14 cm long x 1.5–2 cm wide. Inflorescence a loose raceme of 20–30 flowers, each subtended by a lanceolate bract 12–15 mm long x 2–4 mm wide. **Lip 8–12 mm long x 8–10 mm wide, green to light green**, ovate in general outline, **three-parted, with each lobe cut deeply into narrow fringes. Spur from base of lip 8–12 mm long. Petals linear-oblong, green, normally entire margined**, 3–4 mm long x 0.5–1 mm wide. Dorsal sepal green, ovate, 3 mm long x 2 mm wide. Lateral sepals green, ovate, oblique, 3–5 mm long x 2–3 mm wide.

BLOOMING PERIOD: early June to late July.

RANGE: Occurs statewide, although much more common in the northern counties.

HABITAT: Few orchids occur in as many different habitats as *Platanthera lacera*. Although some environmental conditions appear more favorable than others for its growth, the orchid is seemingly indifferent to moisture level, light level, soil texture, and pH (although mostly in acidic substrates). The range of habitats known to harbor *P. lacera* include mesic and dry-mesic sand prairie, wet sedge meadow, calcareous fen, sphagnum bog, acid seep spring, dry field, mesic flatwoods, and mesic upland forest.

The preferred habitats, as determined by frequency of plants encountered, are those that are moist, sunny, and mildly acid. Those conditions are much more likely to be found in northern Indiana, especially in the Northern Lakes, Northwestern Morainal, and Grand Prairie (Kankakee Sand Section) natural regions. In southern Indiana the orchid is less common, known there primarily from acid seep springs (with filtered light), mesic flatwoods, and dry old fields dominated by *Andropogon scoparius*. The occurrence of *P. lacera* in old fields illustrates the

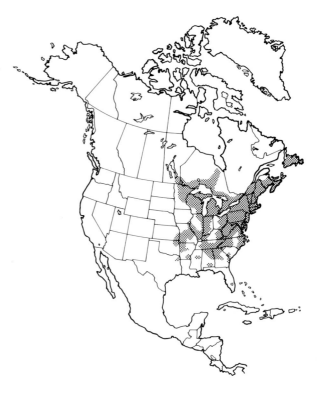

FOLLOWING PAGE: *Platanthera lacera* (green fringed-orchid). June 1990, Steuben Co. Lee Casebere. x³/₄.

orchid's versatility in habitat tolerance. No other *Platanthera* in Indiana would grow in such droughty soils.

Because of the variety of habitats in which the orchid occurs, a tremendous number of associated species could be listed. Therefore, only those from principal habitats are given here. *Platanthera lacera* is most common in prairie habitats, especially those that are moist and sandy. There the orchid grows with, among others, *Coreopsis tripteris*, *Euphorbia corollata*, *Fragaria virginiana*, *Helianthus mollis*, *Osmunda regalis*, *Pedicularis canadensis*, *Phlox glaberrima*, *Platanthera flava* var. *herbiola*, *Rudbeckia hirta*, and *Salix humilis*.

In acid seep springs, *Platanthera lacera* occurs with many of the same species that are found in the sphagnum bogs of northern Indiana, viz., *Bartonia virginica*, *Carex atlantica* var. *capillacea*, *C. bromoides*, *Dryopteris cristata*, *Ilex verticillata*, *Osmunda cinnamomea*, *O. regalis*, *Platanthera clavellata*, and *Rhus vernix*.

P. lacera (green fringed-orchid). June 1990, Steuben Co. Lee Casebere. x1½.

In southeastern Indiana *Platanthera lacera* grows in wet depressions within mesic flatwoods communities. There it occurs in the partial shade of white oak, red maple, American beech, sweetgum, and shagbark hickory. Present in the understory are *Carex debilis*, *C. gracillima*, *C. intumescens*, *Lobelia cardinalis*, *Parthenocissus quinquefolia*, *Rhus radicans*, and *Smilax rotundifolia*.

Associates in bog habitats include *Carex lasiocarpa*, *Drosera rotundifolia*, *Larix laricina*, *Potentilla fruticosa*, *Sarracenia purpurea*, and *Vaccinium macrocarpon*.

DISCUSSION: The green fringed-orchid is the most common *Platanthera* in Indiana, and yet it often goes unnoticed. Reasons are its overall green coloration (including the flowers), and its propensity for occurring at a locality one year and being absent the next. The claim that this is our most common *Platanthera* statewide would have been inaccurate in the early part of this century or before, as the orchid was unknown from the southern two-thirds of the state until 1922. Perhaps the orchid was overlooked in the south up to that time, or perhaps it indeed was absent. I suspect that the plants were not present, as many good botanists collected in southern Indiana during the late 1800s and early 1900s, and they certainly would have documented the orchid's presence.

Most likely *Platanthera lacera* is a newcomer to southern Indiana

Platanthera lacera 171

counties. Range expansion for native orchids is not unprecedented (see discussion under *Tipularia*, *Spiranthes ovalis*, and *Corallorhiza odontorhiza*). I observed range expansion of *P. lacera* in southern Illinois during the mid- to late 1970s. Unknown from the southern tip of Illinois until 1966 (Schwegman and Mohlenbrock, 1968), it subsequently began appearing for the first time in many localities, several of which had a long tradition of visits by botanists. By the late 1970s, botanists were seeing it regularly. Although such colonization has not been as pronounced in southern Indiana (yet), the phenomenon is the same.

Platanthera X *andrewsii*, a hybrid between *Platanthera lacera* and *P. psycodes*, occurs in the northern Great Lakes region and the northeastern U.S., but is unknown from Indiana. Its occurrence here is possible, however, as there is some overlap in the blooming periods of the two species for hybridization.

Platanthera leucophaea (Nuttall) Lindley

[Syn: *Habenaria leucophaea* (Nuttall) A. Gray]

COMMON NAME: eastern prairie fringed-orchid.

SPECIFIC EPITHET DERIVATION: *leucophaea* = "off-white," in reference to the creamy-white color of the flowers.

DESCRIPTION: Plant glabrous throughout, 45–55 cm tall. Roots fleshy, thickened, especially near their base. Leaves 3–4, oblong-lanceolate, 10–17 cm long x 1.5–2.5 cm wide. Inflorescence a loose raceme of 18–25 flowers, each subtended by a lanceolate bract 15–25 mm long x 3–4 mm wide. **Lip 17–20 mm long x 13–16 mm wide, creamy-white, broadly ovate in general outline, three-parted with each lobe cut deeply into narrow fringes. Spur from base of lip 20–30 mm long. Petals creamy-white, spatulate, with a finely toothed margin,** 8–10 mm long x 4–5 mm wide. Dorsal sepal white to greenish-white, ovate, 7–10 mm long x 4–5 mm wide. Lateral sepals white to greenish-white, obliquely ovate, 7–9 mm long x 4–5 mm wide.

BLOOMING PERIOD: late June to late July.

RANGE: Known principally from the northern one-fourth of the state, with an outlying population from Hamilton County.

172   *Platanthera leucophaea*

Platanthera leucophaea
(eastern prairie fringed-orchid)
full plant x1, silhouette x⅓

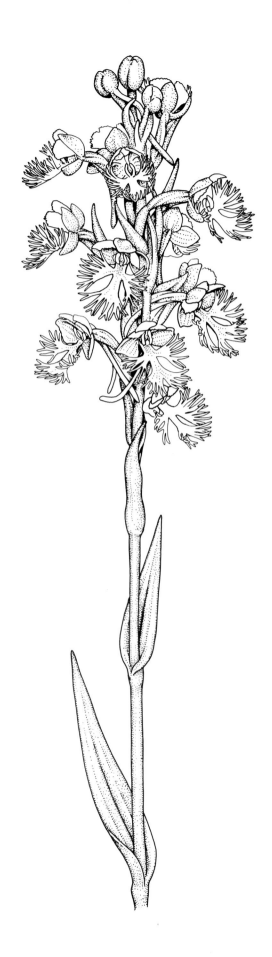

HABITAT: Although *Platanthera leucophaea* is principally a plant of grasslands over the western part of its range (Bowles, 1983), most Indiana collections are from wetland habitats. Such habitats, as described on herbarium labels, include "sedge marsh"; "wet marsh"; "tamarack marsh"; "sedge border" (of a lake); "bog"; and "low prairie." Most of the sites harboring these habitats occurred near natural lakes in the Northern Lakes Natural Region, and, as can be determined from remaining remnants, possess more features in common with northern wetlands than midwestern tallgrass prairie.

The northern wetland affinity of the habitat is perhaps best illustrated by label information from *Deam 20669*, IND. Deam collected the orchid from a lakeside sphagnum and sedge border in La Grange County, where it grew with *Calopogon tuberosus*, *Drosera rotundifolia*, *Eriophorum*, *Pogonia*, *Sarracenia purpurea*, *Scheuchzeria palustris*, and *Vaccinium macrocarpon*. These species are classic bog plants, indicating a natural community very different from a prairie. The orchid's use of bog habitats is apparently not atypical for the Great Lakes region however, as both Bowles (1983) and Case (1987) report the orchid for Michigan from bog mats composed of sedges and/or sphagnum moss. It should be noted that these bogs are not the highly acid, extremely mineral-poor (ombrotrophic) type, of which Indiana has only one sizable example, but rather are the type with an apparent influx of groundwater. In these groundwater-fed bogs the acidic sphagnum zones occur as relatively shallow layers of floating peat. Other parts of these bogs may have a decidedly fen-like character, thus indicating an input of groundwater.

Although fen communities are not typical habitats for *Platanthera leucophaea* in the Great Lakes region (Bowles, 1983; Case, 1987), some of our historic collections have come from fens. Bowles (personal communication) suggests that in general most fens are too alkaline for *P. leucophaea*, thus explaining its apparent absence in existing Indiana fens. Possibly the former collections from fen communities were from localized pockets of less alkaline substrates that now have either been destroyed or altered in some fashion and made unsuitable.

Of the approximately 20 specimens of *P. leucophaea* examined for this work, only one came from what was described as prairie. The paucity of collections from prairie habitat should not be interpreted as an avoidance of prairie by *P. leucophaea* in Indiana, but rather as a reflection of the almost complete destruction of the habitat before it could be properly inventoried. Certainly this orchid must have occurred commonly throughout the extensive prairies of northwestern Indiana, but after the prairie's destruction the only *P. leucophaea* plants available for the early botanists to discover were in wetlands.

DISCUSSION: No other orchid in Indiana has suffered the consequences of habitat destruction as much as *Platanthera leucophaea*. Other orchid species are extirpated from the state, to be sure, but none were ever as common here as *P. leucophaea*. Its occurrence in prairie remnants in widely separated cemeteries in the Midwest suggests to me that the

174   *Platanthera leucophaea*

orchid must have been common throughout the midwestern prairie landscape, a landscape that extended into and occupied much of northwestern Indiana. One can only imagine the great numbers of *P. leucophaea* prior to the coming of the settlers.

Even considering the extensive habitat destruction that has taken place in Indiana, and the fact that *Platanthera leucophaea* has not been seen here in over fifty years, it is still difficult to accept the possibility that it no longer occurs in Indiana. Several attempts were made in 1989 to locate this orchid, including efforts by search teams who scoured historic sites as well as potential habitats. Although no *P. leucophaea* was found, the hope remains that it will again occur here. Several populations in recent years have been found in other states in disturbed habitats, including one area in Ohio formerly planted in corn that was allowed to revert to wetland vegetation (Allison Cusick, personal communication). However, such occurrences are extremely uncommon and enigmatic, and are mentioned only to alert readers of the possibility.

Sheviak and Bowles (1986) have identified a new western species of orchid that until recently was classified as *Platanthera leucophaea*. All known specimens of the new species, *P. praeclara*, come from west of the Mississippi River. It is extremely unlikely that it occurs here. *Platanthera praeclara* strongly resembles *P. leucophaea*, but is larger flowered and possesses a distinctly different column structure. The latter effectively isolates it from genetic exchange with *P. leucophaea;* consequently the two are separable as species. A similar pollinator-isolated species pair is *P. psycodes* and *P. grandiflora*.

Almost every year I receive reports of discoveries of *Platanthera leucophaea* in Indiana, but after seeing the plants (or photographs of them) it becomes clear that they are actually *P. lacera*. Such mistakes are not uncommon. Some pale specimens of *P. lacera* could pass for "white," leading the uninitiated to identify the plants as *P. leucophaea*. Careful inspection of the flowers allows for easy determination of the two. The upper petals of *P. lacera* are mostly linear to linear-oblong and entire-margined, whereas *P. leucophaea* has broad, wedge-shaped petals that are moderately fringed along the apex.

Platanthera orbiculata (Pursh) Lindley

[Syn: *Habenaria orbiculata* (Pursh) Torrey]

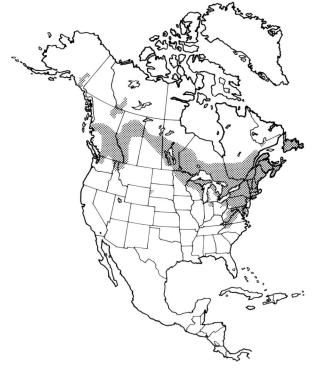

COMMON NAME: large round-leaved orchid.

SPECIFIC EPITHET DERIVATION: *orbiculata* = "circular," in reference to the large, circular leaves of the species.

DESCRIPTION: Plant glabrous throughout, 25–30 cm tall. Roots fleshy and thickened. **Leaves 2, opposite, basal, orbicular to elliptic**, 12–14 cm long x 10–12 cm wide. Inflorescence a loose raceme of 10–15 flowers, each subtended by a lanceolate bract 8–10 mm long x 2–3 mm wide. **Stem below inflorescence with 2–4 bracts. Lip 10–12** mm long x 2–3 mm wide, **white to greenish-white, entire and linear-oblong. Spur from base of lip** to 20 mm long. **Petals ovate-lanceolate, falcate**, white to greenish-white, 8 mm long x 3 mm wide. **Dorsal sepal white to greenish white, suborbicular**, 5 mm long x 5 mm wide. Lateral sepals white to greenish-white, ovate to ovate-lanceolate, somewhat falcate, 8–10 mm long x 6–7 mm wide.

BLOOMING PERIOD: early to mid-June (possibly later).

RANGE: This species is known only from three collections, one each from Marshall, Noble, and Wells counties. The stations in Marshall and Noble counties are within the Northern Lakes Natural Region, and that in Wells County in the Bluffton Till Plain Section of the Central Till Plain.

HABITAT: Little is known about the Indiana habitat of *Platanthera orbiculata*. All that can be determined is provided in the label data from the three collections, and from reports by Deam (1940) and Van Gorder (1894). The Noble County collection, made by W. B. Van Gorder in 1884, was taken from "rich woods." The site was in sections 35 and 36 of Allen Township of Noble County, in what was probably an admixture of sandy, forested ridges and low, swampy depressions.

The second collection from the Northern Lakes Natural Region was found by Charles Deam in 1927 along the Yellow River near the town of Plymouth, in Marshall County. There he reported finding ten plants growing in black, sandy soil near the base of a low north-facing slope densely shaded by sugar maple. Also in 1927, Deam found two plants growing under a beech tree in a mesic flatwoods near the town of

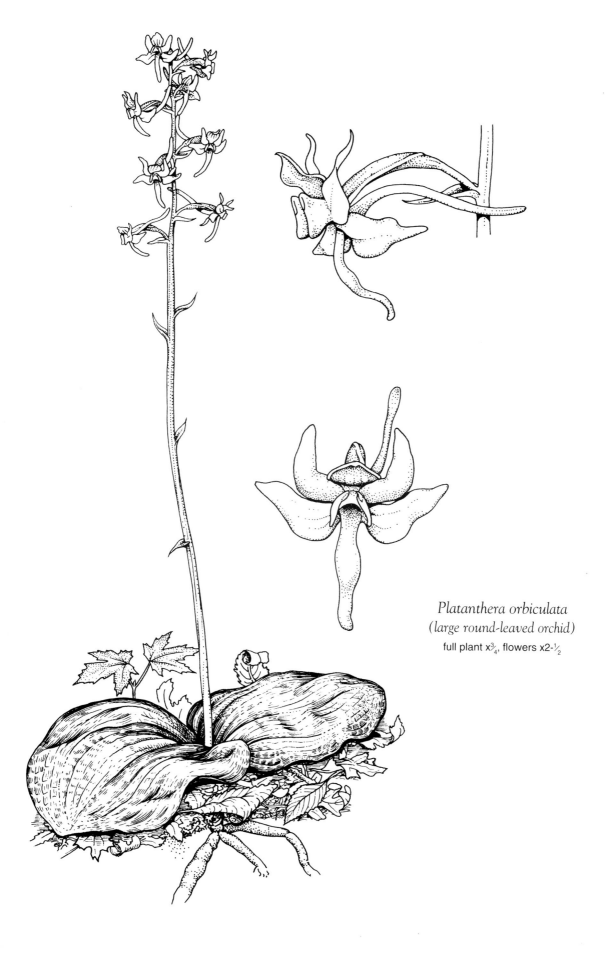

Platanthera orbiculata
(*large round-leaved orchid*)
full plant x$\frac{3}{4}$, flowers x2-$\frac{1}{2}$

Craigville, Wells County. It was the last collection (and possibly the last observation) of *Platanthera orbiculata* taken in Indiana. I have seen the site, finding it to be a rather ordinary mesic flatwoods of the type commonly scattered about the Central Till Plain in the form of 20-to-40 acre woodlots. These communities typically have American beech, sugar maple, bur oak, swamp white oak, Shumard oak, American basswood, and shagbark hickory as dominants. Understories are rich with herbaceous species, as well as enormous mosquitoes!

DISCUSSION: It seems amazing that this boreal orchid was ever collected in Indiana, especially after several fruitless searches through the forests and swamps of northeastern Indiana. But knowing that it did indeed occur in our landscape at one time is all the more motivation to continue the hunt. I consider the Wells County occurrence exceptional (flatwoods of the Central Till Plain are generally not good orchid habitats), and so I would not concentrate search efforts in that county or elsewhere in the Central Till Plain. Certainly the best areas for investigation are found in the Northern Lakes and Northwestern Morainal natural regions. All good-quality mesic forests in those regions, especially those interspersed with swamp forest, should be carefully searched.

Platanthera orbiculata was at an earlier time reputed to have medicinal properties. Riddell (1835) stated that the leaves of the orchid were "used and highly esteemed for dressing blisters," and Correll (1978) cites Pursh, who stated that it was known in the mountains by the name of heal-all.

Platanthera peramoena A. Gray

[Syn: *Habenaria peramoena* A. Gray]

COMMON NAME: purple fringeless-orchid.

SPECIFIC EPITHET DERIVATION: *peramoena* = "very loving," in reference to the beautiful, "lovely" flowers of the species.

DESCRIPTION: Plant glabrous throughout, 45–55 cm tall. Roots fleshy and thickened. Leaves 3–4, lanceolate to elliptic, 9–12 cm long x 2–3.5 cm wide. Inflorescence a loose raceme of 15–25 flowers, each subtended by a lanceolate bract 15–20 mm long x 3–4 mm wide. **Lip 15–19 mm long x 18–20 mm wide, rose-purple, broadly ovate in general outline, three-parted, each lobe wedge-shaped, shallowly toothed at the apex, with the middle lobe notched in the center. Spur from base of lip 20–25 mm long. Petals rose-purple,** spatulate, 6–7 mm long x 3–4 mm wide. **Dorsal sepal rose-purple,** ovate, 6–7 mm long x 2–4 mm wide. **Lateral sepals rose-purple,** obliquely ovate to suborbicular, 7–8 mm long x 5–7 mm wide.

BLOOMING PERIOD: mid-July to late August.

RANGE: Known only in the southern half of the state, but is widespread in all natural regions there. A recent documented observation from Hendricks County (*Hedge and Aldrich*, photo voucher) marks the northern limit of its range in Indiana.

HABITAT: *Platanthera peramoena* is found primarily in poorly drained floodplain habitats, but may occur well into uplands along ditches and borders of ponds and lakes. It occurs in forested sites, but the greatest vigor and numbers of individuals are achieved in exposed sites. Such open environments are normally the result of disturbance: ditches, infrequently mowed rights-of-way, sites with recent timber harvest, and abandoned agricultural fields and pastures. Associates of *P. peramoena* in disturbed sites include *Agrimonia parviflora*, *Asclepias syriaca*, numerous *Carex* species; e.g., *C. frankii*, *C. grayi*, *C. lupulina*, *C. shortiana*, and *C. tribuloides*, *Eupatorium fistulosum*, *Juncus effusus*, *Leersia oryzoides*, *Panicum clandestinum*, *Phlox glaberrima*, *P. paniculata*, *Pycnanthemum tenuifolium*, *Scirpus cyperinus*, *Senecio aureus*, *Solidago canadensis*, and *Typha latifolia*.

FOLLOWING PAGE: *Platanthera peramoena* (purple fringeless-orchid). July 1989, Monroe Co. Lee Casebere. x¹/₂.

In densely forested sites *Platanthera peramoena* is usually uncommon; small, rather spindly-looking plants with pale flowers are typical for such environments. Associates noted growing with the orchid there include *Amorpha fruticosa, Amphicarpaea bracteata, Carex muskingumensis, C. typhina, Cinna arundinacea, Elymus virginicus, Festuca subverticillata, Impatiens capensis, Parthenocissus quinquefolia, Pilea pumila, Prunella vulgaris, Ranunculus hispidus, Rhus radicans,* and *Senecio aureus,* along with the canopy trees red maple, American elm, sycamore, pin oak, swamp white oak, swamp chestnut oak, sweetgum, black gum, and blue beech.

In most situations *Platanthera peramoena* occurs on substrates composed of stream-deposited silt-loam soils that have an acidic reaction. However, the orchid is not limited to alluvial soils. It also occurs on leached till (primarily in the Bluegrass Natural Region), on "terra rosa" soils bordering sinkhole ponds and swamps (in the Highland Rim Natural Region), and lacustrine soils formed in basins of ancient glacial lakes in southwestern Indiana. In upland sites *P. peramoena* occurs in ditches, on soils not normally associated with wetlands.

P peramoena (purple fringeless-orchid). July 1989, Martin Co. Lee Casebere. x2¼.

DISCUSSION: *Platanthera peramoena* is one of the most brilliantly colored native orchids, and were it not for the general lack of success in its cultivation it would certainly be a popular ornamental flower. Fortunately, it is one of the more common native orchids, and can be seen by most anyone willing to venture along a lowland trail or drive the back roads of southern Indiana in July.

The beautiful rose-purple flowers of *Platanthera peramoena* are similar in color to the flowers of two of its common associates, *Phlox paniculata* and *P. glaberrima,* and because both *Phlox* species and the orchid bloom at about the same time, have similar sized inflorescences, and commonly occur in the same habitat, it is easy to confuse the three at a distance. Consequently, many "false alarms" have occurred for those anticipating that the pink-flowered plants along the trail or road ahead are *P. peramoena,* only to discover upon approach that they are *Phlox.*

Over the years many people have mistaken plants of *Platanthera peramoena* for *P. psycodes.* This is especially true of those having never seen actual examples of both taxa. The confusion appears to stem from a faulty interpretation of the lip fringe. Although *Platanthera peramoena* may have some fringing of the lip, it is never to the degree of that found

in *P. psycodes*. Generally, the lip margins of *P. peramoena* are merely jagged and cut normally less than one-third the lobe length, whereas in *P. psycodes* the cut is a full one-third or more. Also, the flowers of *P. peramoena* are generally much larger than those of *P. psycodes* (commonly twice the size). As well, the habitats and range of the two are very different. *Platanthera peramoena* grows in southern Indiana in heavy silt-loam soils that are ephemerally wet, whereas *P. psycodes* occurs primarily in northern Indiana in sandy muck soils saturated with cool ground water.

Because of the apparent difficulty in correctly assessing lip fringe length, consideration of other characters may prove more helpful to arrive at a correct determination. Clearly the most significant morphological difference between the two species can be seen in a comparison of their columns. As pointed out by Stoutamire (1974), the pollinaria of *P. peramoena* are widely separated on the column, with viscidia positioned for lateral attachment of pollinaria to the eyes of insect visitors. In *P. psycodes*, the pollinaria are closely spaced, the viscidia positioned for attachment to an insect's proboscis. These differences result in reproductive isolation between the species, providing strong evidence that the two are not as similar as they might appear.

In 1965, Charles Sheviak captured a tiger swallowtail (*Pterourus glaucus* Linnaeus) from within a Brown County population of *Platanthera peramoena* (Sheviak, personal communication). The butterfly bore one hemipollinarium of *P. peramoena* on its compound eye. This account is one of the few in the literature regarding pollination of *P. peramoena*.

P. peramoena (purple fringeless-orchid). July 1989, Monroe Co. Lee Casebere. x2.

Platanthera psycodes (Linnaeus) Lindley

[Syn: *Habenaria psycodes* (Linnaeus) Sprengel]

COMMON NAME: small purple fringed-orchid.

SPECIFIC EPITHET DERIVATION: *psycodes* = "butterfly," in reference to the shape and aspect of the flowers

DESCRIPTION: Plant glabrous throughout, 40–60 cm tall. Roots fleshy, thickened near their base. Leaves 3–4, lanceolate to elliptic, 10–12 cm long x 2–2.5 cm wide. Inflorescence a loose raceme of 25–40 flowers, each subtended by a linear-lanceolate bract 10–15 mm long x 1 mm wide. **Lip 7–9 mm long x 9–11 mm wide, lavender to rose-purple, broadly ovate in general outline, three-parted, with each lobe cut deeply into narrow fringes. Spur from base of lip** 13–14 mm long. **Petals purple,** obovate, with a finely toothed margin, 4–5 mm long x 2.5–3.5 mm wide. **Dorsal sepal purple,** elliptic, 4–5 mm long x 2.5–3 mm wide. **Lateral sepals purple,** obliquely ellipticovate, 5–6 mm long x 3 mm wide.

BLOOMING PERIOD: late June to mid-August.

RANGE: Occurs primarily in the northern quarter of the state, but also occurs (very locally) as far south as Owen County. The Northern Lakes and Northwestern Morainal natural regions are the principal areas of occurrence. The reports by Baird and Taylor (1878) for Clark County, by Clapp (in his collection journal of the early 1800s) for Floyd County, and by J. Coulter (1875) for Jefferson County, are likely errors of identification. There are no specimens to support their reports. Most likely the authors confused partially fringed individuals of *P. peramoena* for *P. psycodes*.

HABITAT: In Indiana *Platanthera psycodes* has a strong affinity for forested seepage communities, particularly those that are composed of saturated, circumneutral sandy-muck substrates. These wetland habitats typically are dominated by red maple, tamarack, black ash, American elm, and alder, and in areas where a broken canopy exists, thickets of *Cornus* spp., *Lindera benzoin*, *Rhus vernix*, *Salix* spp., and *Viburnum lentago* are characteristic. Species commonly associated with *P. psycodes* in forested seepages include *Caltha palustris*, *Carex bromoides*, *Circaea lutetiana*, *Glyceria striata*, *Impatiens capensis*, *Onoclea sensibilis*, *Oxypolis rigidior*, *Solidago patula*, and *Symplocarpus foetidus*.

Platanthera psycodes (small purple fringed-orchid). July 1990, La Grange Co. Lee Casebere. x½.

Springy stream corridors also are good habitat for *Platanthera psycodes*. One of the best ways to find the orchid is to walk the stream channel, keeping an eye open for any blush of purple on the bank. In using this technique, however, one must take care not to step into a deep hole!

In areas where the substrate is especially saturated with groundwater seepage the orchid may be found in sunnier, more exposed sites, although even there its leaves are usually provided some shade by surrounding vegetation. At one such site the orchid grows on mossy hummocks in a cat-tail marsh with *Aster puniceus, Epilobium coloratum, Impatiens capensis, Polygonum scandens, Rhus vernix, Rosa palustris, Salix sericea,* and *Saxifraga pensylvanica.*

P. psycodes (small purple fringed-orchid). July 1987, La Grange Co. Lee Casebere. x2½.

DISCUSSION: Not many of the Indiana orchids are as attractive as *Platanthera psycodes.* Its lacy purple flowers are certainly a welcome sight in the subdued light of a mosquito-infested swamp. Unfortunately the sight is becoming an uncommon one, not because the orchid is necessarily rare in its preferred habitat, but rather because of the extensive destruction of its wetland habitat. Consequently, most Hoosier wildflower enthusiasts are unfamiliar with the species.

Although alike in gross morphology, *Platanthera psycodes* is not as similar to *P. peramoena* as it appears. The two species prefer different habitats, occupy different ranges, and most importantly, have different pollination mechanisms. Thus, the two almost never come in proximity to one another, and when they do, they evidently never interbreed. For additional discussion of these differences, and how to distinguish the species, see the text for *P. peramoena.*

Although *Platanthera psycodes* does not interbreed with *P. peramoena,* it does do so with the seemingly dissimilar *P. lacera.* Because of their similar column structure, cross-pollination and fertilization can and do occur, ultimately resulting in a putative hybrid known as *P.* X *andrewsii.* Cross-pollination is usually not a common event, however, as the pollinators of *P. psycodes* are normally diurnal, whereas those of *P. lacera* are crepuscular and/or nocturnal (Stoutamire, 1974). Individuals of *P.* X *andrewsii* possess traits of both parents, but the inherited features may be expressed differently. Some individuals may have the floral morphology of one parent and the color of the other, and vice versa. There is no evidence of *P.* X *andrewsii* occurring in Indiana, although the possibility certainly exists.

Stoutamire (1974) reports that the hummingbird clear-wing hawk-moth (*Hemaris thysbe*) and a skipper known as long dash (*Polites mystic*)

are pollinators of *Platanthera psycodes*. Both moth and skipper occur in Indiana. Perhaps not coincidental is the more or less concomitant range in Indiana of the butterfly (see Shull, 1987) with that of the orchid. The significance of this co-occurrence is not known, as there are other possible pollinators of *P. psycodes* (such as the hawkmoth), and the long dash nectars on several other plant species.

POGONIA
Jussieu

The name *Pogonia*, from the Greek *pogon*, for "beard," refers to the bearded labellum typical of the genus. Formerly consisting of species now included in other genera, including *Triphora* and *Isotria*, *Pogonia* now is composed of only two or three species (Luer, 1975). *Pogonia* is separated from *Triphora* and *Isotria* by, among other traits, a denticulate column housing a terminal, decumbent anther with simple pollen grains (Ames, 1922). There is only one species endemic to North America, viz., our *P. ophioglossoides*. A similar species, *P. japonica*, occurs in China and Japan.

Pogonia ophioglossoides (Linnaeus) Jussieu

COMMON NAMES: rose pogonia, adder's-mouth, snake mouth.

SPECIFIC EPITHET DERIVATION: *ophioglossoides* = "resembling *Ophioglossum*," in reference to the resemblance of the foliage of the orchid to that of adder's tongue fern (*Ophioglossum*).

DESCRIPTION: Plant glabrous throughout, 20–25 cm tall. **Roots slender, fibrous, with rootshoots from which new plants arise. Leaf solitary,** on the lower half of the stem, ovate to elliptic, 5–6 cm long x 15–18 mm wide. **Inflorescence consisting of 1** (rarely 2) **flower**(s) terminating the stem. The floral bract foliaceous, oblong-elliptic to lanceolate, 3–3.5 cm long x 6–8 mm wide. **Lip 15–18 mm long x 5–7 mm wide, pink, spatulate, heavily fringed on the margin, with 3 rows of yellow bristles occurring lengthwise through the middle of the lip. Petals pink,** elliptic, 16–17 mm long x 5–6 mm wide. **Sepals pink,** elliptic-lanceolate, 17–19 mm long x 4–5 mm wide.

BLOOMING PERIOD: early June to late July.

RANGE: Known only from the northern one-third of the state, primarily in the Northern Lakes and Northwestern Morainal natural regions.

HABITAT: In Indiana *Pogonia ophioglossoides* occurs in four types of communities: bogs, wet sand flats, calcareous fens, and pannes. Open, sunny sphagnum bogs are perhaps the primary habitat for *Pogonia*, where typical associates include *Betula pumila, Calopogon tuberosus, Carex lasiocarpa, Drosera rotundifolia, Equisetum fluviatile, Menyanthes trifoliata, Osmunda cinnamomea, O. regalis, Potentilla palustris, Rhus vernix, Sarracenia purpurea, Thelypteris palustris, Vaccinium macrocarpon,* and at some sites, scattered *Larix laricina.*

Acidic sandy flats in the Kankakee Sand Section of the Grand Prairie Natural Region and in parts of the Northwestern Morainal Natural Region are also important *Pogonia* habitats. Here *Pogonia* typically occurs with an interesting array of sand-loving species, including *Aletris farinosa, Calopogon tuberosus, Drosera rotundifolia, Lycopodium inundatum, Osmunda cinnamomea, Rhexia virginica, Scleria triglomerata, Spiraea tomentosa, Utricularia subulata* (locally), and *Viola lanceolata.*

Pogonia ophioglossoides prefers the wet, marly portions of fens, growing with *Calopogon tuberosus, Drosera rotundifolia, Parnassia glauca, Potentilla fruticosa, Rhynchospora capillacea, Scirpus americanus, Scleria verticillata,* and *Triglochin maritimum. Pogonia* also is known from pannes immediately adjacent to Lake Michigan. There the orchid grows with many of the same species that occur in fens.

DISCUSSION: *Pogonia ophioglossoides* is one of several native orchids that can be seen while "bog-trotting" in the northern counties. The best opportunity for seeing *Pogonia* occurs in the Northern Lakes Natural Region, where more available habitat is present than anywhere else in the state. Even there the orchid is uncommon, and may not be seen after extensive searching. Its apparent absence in seemingly suitable habitat may be due to fluctuations of flowering plants, and a visit to a site with few or no plants evident in one year may reveal dozens in other years. Typically, at sites with *Pogonia*, one also finds *Calopogon*. The occurrence of *Calopogon* with *Pogonia* is apparently of particular benefit to *Calopogon*, as it exploits pollinators that visit the similar-looking *Pogonia* (Thien and Marcks, 1972). *Pogonia* offers pollinator reinforcement

OPPOSITE: *Pogonia ophioglossoides* (rose pogonia). June 1990, Steuben Co. Lee Casebere. x1.

ABOVE: *P. ophioglossoides.* June 1990, Steuben Co. Lee Casebere. x1¼.

Pogonia ophioglossoides   189

by providing nectar, whereas *Calopogon* does not; but naive bees do not know the difference.

SPIRANTHES

L. C. Richard

The name *Spiranthes* is formed by the combination of two Greek words: *speira,* meaning coil or spiral, and *anthos,* which equals flower. It thus reads as "coiled flower," in allusion to the spiraled arrangement of the flowers.

The derivation of its common name is less clear. Most authors believe the name "ladies'-tresses" refers to the similarities of shape between a woman's braid of hair and the orchid's arrangement of flowers. The other school of thought presents a not-so-modest etymology, stating that ladies'-tresses is a corruption of "ladies'-traces," an old English name for the criss-crossing traces (straps, lacings) used to tighten corsets! As similarly stated by Dana (1908), "ladies'-traces, from a fancied resemblance between its [the orchid's] twisted clusters and the lacings which played so important a part in the feminine toilet."

There are approximately 300 species (or as few as 30, according to some) of *Spiranthes* worldwide, making it the most diverse of the orchid genera indigenous to Indiana. The genus *Spiranthes* is represented in Indiana by nine species. Several of these are rather common, possibly occurring in every county, while others are quite rare, found only at a few sites or in very specialized habitats. The common *Spiranthes* colonize early successional habitats, such as the acid, sterile soils of fields dominated by little bluestem (*Andropogon scoparius*) and broom sedge (*Andropogon virginicus*).

Most people associate *Spiranthes* with the autumn season, noting it as one of the few species in bloom during the fall "colors." However, many species of the genus flower much earlier. It so happens that the most common ladies'-tresses, *Spiranthes cernua,* is a late bloomer, and being one of the larger species of the genus, it is much more visible than, say, the summer blooming *S. tuberosa,* a wisp of a plant virtually unnoticed by the untrained eye (see life-size illustrations of *Spiranthes* flowering spikes in Fig. 10). Most people are simply not seeing the earlier blooming species.

Determination of our *Spiranthes* species is perhaps the most challenging task for a beginning orchidologist. They are not as difficult to determine as many have stated, but, as with the mastery of any skill, practice and experience are necessary before a high degree of proficiency can be expected. Seeing plants in the field is critical, as herbarium specimens can be extremely difficult to determine. Utilizing information from Luer (1975), Sheviak (1982), Case and Catling (1983), Case (1987), and

S. tuberosa

S. lacera

S. ovalis

S. lucida

S. vernalis

FIGURE 10. Actual size comparisons of inflorescences
of the Indiana *Spiranthes*

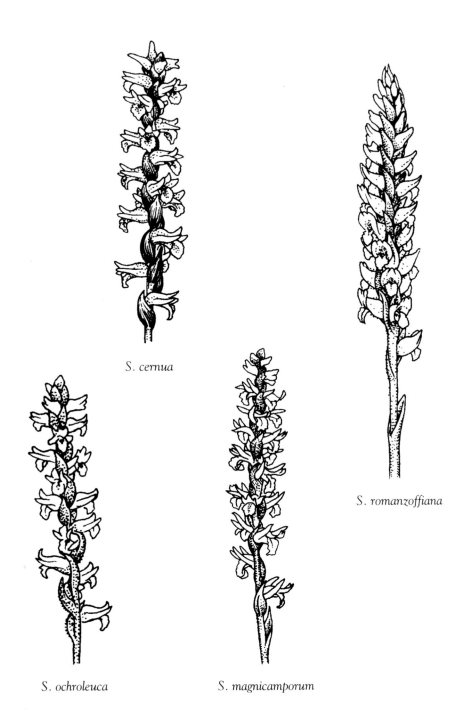

S. cernua

S. romanzoffiana

S. ochroleuca

S. magnicamporum

FIGURE 10. continued

this work, along with making frequent trips to the field to observe live specimens, one should be able to identify most *Spiranthes* successfully.

All of the *Spiranthes* in Indiana have a spike of flowers arranged in a single spiral. The spiral may be a graceful, single row of flowers, arranged like the steps of a spiral staircase; or it may be tightly wound, so much so that no spiral is discernible. Spiral patterns are commonly described by the number of ranks present—the row(s) of flowers evident within an inflorescence. For example, a single row of flowers gracefully spiraling around a stem is single-ranked, whereas those with several rows or ranks of flowers are referred to as multi-ranked. Rank number can be determined on most plants by looking down on the spike from above, noting any obvious rows of flowers. The rows may occur in straight, vertical lines, or have slight spiraling. In some species the specific number of ranks is not evident.

Traditionally most botanists have emphasized rank number as a taxonomic tool in separating species, as ranking pattern is normally consistent for a species. Generally, single ranks occur in *S. tuberosa*, *S. lacera* (especially those referable to var. *lacera*), and *S. vernalis*. *Spiranthes ovalis* var. *erostellata* and *S. romanzoffiana* typically have discernible rows of flowers, usually three, while the remaining multi-ranked species are so tightly wound that no spiral or ranks are evident.

Although using rank number is generally an effective way to identify *Spiranthes*, ranks are not always consistent. For example, *Spiranthes magnicamporum* is a multi-ranked species that normally does not have discernible rows of flowers, but I have seen individuals that are decidedly three-ranked. Moreover, some individuals of *S. lacera* have a single, graceful spiral, whereas others appear multi-ranked. Possibly the best method for handling the ranking pattern problem is to consider a species' phyllotaxy (Sheviak, 1982). The phyllotaxy of a *Spiranthes* inflorescence is expressed simply as the number of flowers (or think of it as steps) in a spiral that are necessary to have one flower directly above the flower starting the cycle. The phyllotaxy is expressed as a fraction, such as 1/6. For example, in a plant with 1/6 phyllotaxy, it takes six flowers in one cycle (spiral) around the stem before a flower is directly above the point (flower) of beginning. Similarly, in a plant with 1/3 phyllotaxy there are three flowers in the cycle before the vertical alignment of flowers occurs. Phyllotaxy is generally consistent among species, and thus is a better taxonomic tool than rank. It is particularly helpful in separating confusing specimens with atypical ranking.

Spiranthes has the peculiar trait of "right-handedness" and "left-handedness." These terms refer to the direction of spiraling of the flowers around the stem. On some plants, the spiral twists to the right (clockwise), in others, to the left (counterclockwise). This can most easily be seen in the orientation of the floral bracts on single-ranked species. If the curved tips of the bracts point to the right, the spiral is left-handed. Conversely, bracts pointing to the left have right-handed spirals. There is no consistency to the spiral direction, as separate plants of a given species may exhibit different patterns. In fact, a single plant may be right-handed one year, and left-handed the next! Obviously there is no apparent taxonomic significance to spiral direction. The problem of how and why different twisting directions come about has yet to be solved.

McDonald (1937) lists *Spiranthes* as one of the three orchid genera in Indiana that are hemicryptophytes.

SPIRANTHES

A.   Stems slender with small flowers, the lip of the lowest flowers 5 mm or less in length.. B.

B.   Plants flowering in May and June; lip with a bright yellow center.. *Spiranthes lucida*

BB.   Plants flowering in July and later; lip white or green...... C.

C.   Lip green-centered........................... *Spiranthes lacera*

CC.   Lip mostly white throughout................................ D.

D.   Flowers typically arranged in a graceful single spiral (phyllotaxy of one-fifth or less); lip generally expanded at the apex; leaves absent during flowering, or if present, basal only; plants of sunny grasslands and sparse woodland............................ *Spiranthes tuberosa*

DD.   Flowers typically in a tight spiral of the three vertical ranks (phyllotaxy of one-third or one-fourth); lip commonly narrowed toward the tip (appearance due in part to curling of lip edges); lower stem leaves spreading and conspicuous during flowering; plants of forest and edge environments.................................... ....*Spiranthes ovalis* var. *erostellata*

AA.   Stems stout with larger flowers, the lip of the lowest flowers averaging 7–10 mm in length .... E.

E.   Spiral of flowers normally single-ranked (phyllotaxy one-fifth or less); sepals strongly inrolled toward base; pubescence of inflorescence pointed; plants of dry grasslands; blooming in mid-June through July................. ....*Spiranthes vernalis*

EE.   Spike normally multi-ranked (phyllotaxy one-third or one-fourth); pubescence of inflorescence capitate (globular-shaped tip); sepals normally flattened at base; plants blooming mostly in September and October (or if earlier, plants of northern Indiana wetlands)..................F.

F.   Lip fiddle-shaped (constricted in the middle) and recurved; other flower parts strongly ascending; petals and sepals joined together to form a helmet-shaped hood; rare plant of northern Indiana wetlands ....*Spiranthes romanzoffiana*

FF. Lip not constricted in the middle; flowers nodding to ascending; petals and sepals variously arranged, but not forming a helmet; plants occurring throughout the state, or if rare and restricted, not of wetland habitats .... G.

G. Lateral sepals widely spreading, with tips commonly arching well above the petals; flowers strongly fragrant; leaves usually absent at flowering; plants normally of dry calcareous grasslands or dunes; diploid, sexually reproducing species with monoembryonic seeds.....................................
.... *Spiranthes magnicamporum*

GG. Lateral sepals normally appressed to the petals and parallel to them, or, if ascending, the sepal tips not raised above the distal area of the petals; plants of various habitats, but rarely dry calcareous grasslands .... H.

H. Flowers and especially the lateral sepals ascending, with the lip strongly curving from its base, giving the flower a "hump-backed" appearance; flowers clearly cream to yellowish-colored; basal lip tubercles prominent, noticeably larger than the next species (best seen in side-by-side comparison); plants of dry, acidic substrates; diploid, sexually reproducing species with monoembryonic seeds............................
.... *Spiranthes ochroleuca*

HH. Flowers normally nodding or horizontal, the sepals generally parallel to the flower body or slightly ascending, the lip not strongly curved from its base; flowers white to creamy-yellow; basal lip tubercles evident, but generally smaller than above species; plants of various habitats, ranging from dry, acid substrates to calcareous wetlands; polyploid, apomictic, highly variable species with polyembryonic seeds .... *Spiranthes cernua*

Spiranthes cernua (Linnaeus) L. C. Richard

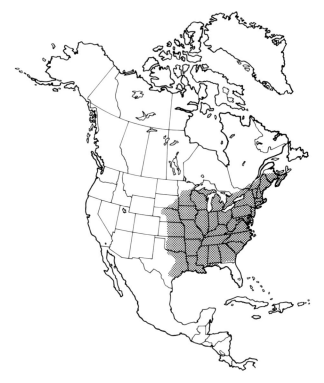

ABOVE, LEFT: *Spiranthes cernua* (nodding ladies'-tresses), "typical" plant. October 1989, Hamilton Co. Lee Casebere. x¼.

ABOVE, RIGHT: *S. cernua*, sand prairie ecotype. September 1989, La Grange Co. Mike Homoya. x½.

BELOW, LEFT: *S. cernua*, northern Indiana fen ecotype. September 1989, La Grange Co. Mike Homoya. x½.

BELOW, RIGHT: *S. cernua*, old-field ecotype. September 1988, Perry Co. Mike Homoya. x1.

COMMON NAME: nodding ladies'-tresses.

SPECIFIC EPITHET DERIVATION: *cernua* = "nodding," in reference to the downward angle of the flowers.

DESCRIPTION: Plant variable, especially between races. **Inflorescence and upper stem pubescent with capitate hairs, principal leaves glabrous,** 25–35 cm tall. Roots fleshy, slender to thick. Leaves 3–5, mostly basal, linear-lanceolate to oblanceolate, 10–13 cm long x 9–11 mm wide. Leaves of some plants absent at flowering. Inflorescence consisting of a tight spike of 25–40 flowers, each subtended by a lanceolate bract 8–11 mm long x 2–3 mm wide. **Spike multiranked, with a phyllotaxy of 1/3 or 1/4. Lip** 8–11 mm long x 3–5 mm wide, **white to cream, entire with a dilated base, commonly tinged with yellow centrally,** ovate, and 2 basal tubercles. Petals white to cream, linear-lanceolate, 7–10 mm long x 2 mm wide. Petals and dorsal sepal convergent. Lateral sepals appressed to spreading, horizontal to nodding to ascending.

BLOOMING PERIOD: late July to early November.

RANGE: This species occurs throughout Indiana, probably in every county. It is most common in the Highland Rim and Shawnee Hills natural regions, followed by the Northern Lakes and Northwestern Morainal regions. It is least common in the Central Till Plain, where conversion of the landscape to agriculture has eliminated most suitable habitat.

HABITAT: *Spiranthes cernua* occurs in a variety of habitat types, including old-field, dry woodland, prairie, marsh, fen, roadside, and abandoned gravel quarries. The kind of habitat utilized depends in great part on the genetic race of the species. In southern Indiana, where the old-field race of *S. cernua* occurs, the vast majority of plants occur on dryish upland sites with acidic substrates; e.g., soils derived from or consisting of sandstone, shale, chert, loess, various silt-loams, and clay. Conversely, wet, highly organic basic soils are the orchid's principal habitat in northern Indiana (where various other races are known). As might be expected, central Indiana appears to have an equal number of populations occurring in both wetland and upland habitats.

Old-field habitats provide the most important habitat for *S. cernua* in

southern Indiana. Such fields are commonly dominated by a host of native species, including *Andropogon gyrans*, *A. scoparius*, *A. virginicus*, *Asplenium platyneuron*, *Botrychium dissectum*, *Cornus florida*, *Eupatorium coelestinum*, *Hypericum prolificum*, *Liatris aspera*, *L. squarrulosa*, *Lobelia puberula*, *Potentilla simplex*, *Rudbeckia hirta*, and *Sabatia angularis*.

Another important habitat in southern Indiana is dry upland forest. Sheviak hypothesized (1974) that this may have been the primary habitat for *S. cernua* in Illinois prior to the extensive thinning and clearing of forests that followed settlement by Europeans in the early 1800s. *Spiranthes cernua* was most likely a relatively uncommon plant then, confined to woodland habitats and the few natural openings. In such a woodland habitat in Martin County I noted *S. cernua* growing in shallow sandy soil atop a massive sandstone cliff. There several small plants were present on a windswept slope in an elfin forest of stunted chestnut oak, blackjack oak, *Andropogon scoparius*, *Cunila origanoides*, *Danthonia spicata*, *Opuntia humifusa*, *Tephrosia virginiana*, and *Vaccinium arboreum*.

In northern Indiana, *Spiranthes cernua* typically shuns the dry habitats of its southern counterparts; most plants are confined to mesic and wetland habitats composed of gravel, sand, and organic substrates. Fen, sedge meadow, sand scrape, mesic prairie, and roadside ditch are important habitats for *S. cernua* in the north. In such environments an assortment of moisture-loving plants occurs with *S. cernua*, including, in the alkaline sites, *Carex granularis*, *C. leptalea*, *C. sterilis*, *Gentianopsis crinita*, *Muhlenbergia glomerata*, *Parnassia glauca*, *Potentilla fruticosa*, *Scirpus acutus*, *Solidago ohioensis*, and *Triglochin maritimum*. Where acidic conditions prevail (typically in sand deposits), associates include *Aletris farinosa*, *Andropogon scoparius*, *Drosera intermedia*, *Lycopodium inundatum*, *Rubus hispidus*, *Scleria pauciflora*, *S. triglomerata*, *Spiraea tomentosa*, and *Viola lanceolata*. Interdunal sand flats, sand scrapes, and sandy ditches are likely habitats to find the above.

DISCUSSION: *Spiranthes cernua* is part of a species complex that botanists are just beginning to understand. Until the past two decades or so one could safely refer to all Indiana nodding ladies'-tresses as *S. cernua*, but starting with the description of *S. magnicamporum* (Sheviak, 1973), and the resurrection of *S. ochroleuca* as a distinct species (Luer, 1975; Sheviak and Catling, 1980), we now have three species in the complex from Indiana.

Contrary to appearances, the designation of two additional species from the *Spiranthes cernua* complex is not a splitter's attempt to overemphasize the nuances of *S. cernua* morphology. The fact is, *S. cernua* is the "problem child," with *S. magnicamporum* and *S. ochroleuca* being the stable, diploid, sexually reproducing species that maintain some degree of morphological consistency. For example, there are at least five distinct races and forms of *S. cernua* in Indiana. *Spiranthes magnicamporum* and *S. ochroleuca* are not nearly so variable as this.

One of the most distinctive and beautiful races of *Spiranthes cernua* occurs in fens in the far northern counties. It has large, pure white flowers with a gaping throat and lateral sepals extending well beyond the rest of the flower. According to Sheviak (personal communication) the race is similar to if not the same as the "New England form" (see Figure 19 in Sheviak, 1982). If it is the same, then the Indiana populations represent a remarkable range extension to the west. Another distinctive race occurs primarily in southern Indiana. Known as the "old-field ecotype" of Sheviak (1974), this race most closely resembles S. ochroleuca both in habitat and morphology. In Indiana prairie habitats there occur at least three entities of S. cernua: the "low prairie race" (Sheviak, 1974), the "sand prairie ecotype" (Sheviak, 1974), and a form of the southern prairie complex (see Figure 21 of Sheviak, 1982). Some individuals of the low prairie race and the southern prairie complex are difficult to distinguish from S. magnicamporum. Consequently, extreme caution should be exercised in identifying plants looking like S. magnicamporum. In almost all cases the plants will be one of the prairie races of S. cernua.

Although the races look like distinct species, they have sufficient genetic and morphological features in common that they are grouped under one species, viz., Spiranthes cernua. They all are apparently of hybrid origin, being derived from crossings of several different taxa, including S. magnicamporum, S. ochroleuca, and possibly a "pure," ancestral Spiranthes cernua. All are polyploids with polyembryonic seeds, and all have relatively large, white to yellowish-colored flowers with lips that are dilated basally and mostly membranaceous (Sheviak, 1982). They also have the ability to produce seed apomictically, viz., without the fertilization of ovules (agamospermy). This latter trait helps explain the variability in the complex, as progeny of each successful cross of S. cernua with another taxon are capable of cloning themselves, and thus ultimately creating large, reproducing populations of new hybrids. For an in-depth study of the complexity of S. cernua biology, readers are encouraged to consult Sheviak (1982, 1991).

A specimen collected in Starke County in 1937 (Deam 58473, AMES) has inscribed on the sheet "Drawn by Dillon." The reference is apparently to an illustration made by Gordon Dillon, the renowned orchid illustrator from the Botanical Museum of Harvard University. Whether the illustration was published I do not know. Many of his illustrations can be seen in Correll's classic work, Native Orchids of North America (1978).

Spiranthes lacera (Rafinesque) Rafinesque

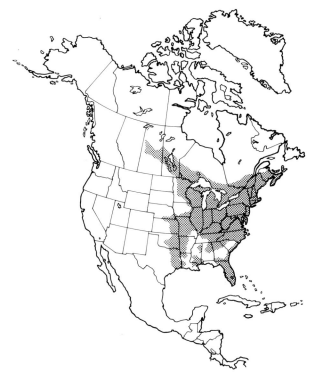

COMMON NAMES: slender ladies'-tresses, green-lip ladies'-tresses, cemetery orchid.

SPECIFIC EPITHET DERIVATION: *lacera* = "torn," in reference to the fringe on the lip.

DESCRIPTION: Plant mostly glabrous, although the inflorescence normally possesses some capitate hairs, 25–35 cm tall. Roots fleshy, slender to thickened, several clustered from the stem base. **Leaves 2–4, basal, ovate to elliptic, commonly absent at anthesis in var. (cf.) gracilis, to present in var. (cf.) lacera,** 2–3 cm long x 0.8–1.5 cm wide. Inflorescence consisting of a loose to moderately tight spike of 20–50 flowers, each subtended by a lanceolate bract 3–4 mm long x 1–1.5 mm wide. **Spike single-to multi-ranked, with a phyllotaxy of 1/5 or less. Lip** 3–5 mm long x 1.5–2 mm wide, **white with a green center, oblong with a finely lacerate apex,** and two basal tubercles. Petals white, linear, 3–5 mm long x 0.5–1 mm wide. Sepals white, oblong-lanceolate, 3–5 mm long x 0.5–1 mm wide. Petals and dorsal sepal convergent. **Lateral sepals somewhat spreading and downward angled.**

BLOOMING PERIOD: early July to early October.

RANGE: *Spiranthes lacera* occurs primarily in the southern half of the state, with relatively few occurrences in the north. In the south the orchid is most common in the Shawnee Hills and Highland Rim natural regions, while most collections in the north have come from the Northwestern Morainal Natural Region.

HABITAT: Like many ladies'-tresses, *Spiranthes lacera* is a plant of disturbed habitats. It prefers rather dry, sunny sites with little competition from other vegetation, although it can grow in thick turf that is periodically cropped. The species is most common in old fields, pastures, barrens, and thinly wooded rocky slopes. Its occurrence on wooded slopes indicates a tolerance for light shade, but it shuns heavily shaded sites. Species commonly associated with *S. lacera* in its typical sunny habitat include *Agalinis tenuifolia, Andropogon scoparius, Aristida* spp., *Chamaecrista fasciculata, Danthonia spicata, Lespedeza* spp., *Liatris* spp., *Lobelia puberula, Panicum anceps, Potentilla simplex, Prunella vulgaris, Sabatia angularis, Solidago canadensis* var. *scabra, S. nemoralis,* and *Tridens flavus.*

Spiranthes lacera (slender ladies'-tresses). August 1989, Harrison Co. Mike Homoya. x1.

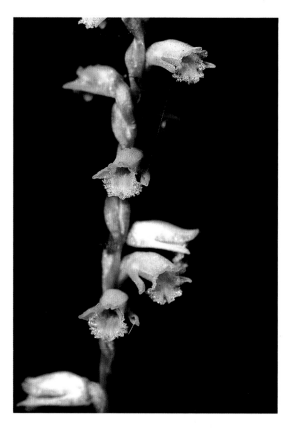

In the Chicago region (including northwestern Indiana) Swink and Wilhelm (1979) report *Spiranthes lacera* occurring in sand prairies, growing with *Agalinis purpurea*, *Andropogon gerardii*, *Euphorbia corollata*, *Helianthus occidentalis*, *Pycnanthemum virginianum*, *Solidago nemoralis*, and *Sorghastrum nutans*.

Because the leaves of *Spiranthes lacera* are basal and parallel to the ground, it generally avoids contact with mower blades, and thus is one of the few orchids that can grow in lawns (not the highly fertilized, manicured kind!). I have seen it in an unmown lawn of a recently abandoned house, as well as a neatly kept lawn of a college campus. Without doubt the greatest number of lawn occurrences are in cemeteries (thus the name "cemetery orchid"!). Perhaps its apparent greater frequency in lawns of cemeteries is due to the longer interval between mowings in some cemeteries, thereby allowing for a flowering spike to emerge and be seen.

S. lacera (slender ladies'-tresses). September 1990, Porter Co. Lee Casebere. x4.

DISCUSSION: *Spiranthes lacera* is an easily recognized ladies'-tresses; no other *Spiranthes* occurring in Indiana has a flower with a green lip. What is not always easy is the separation of this single taxon into the two varieties recognized by many authorities. The two varieties, var. *lacera* and var. *gracilis*, are distinct in the extreme, but the common occurrence of intermediates can cause frustration and the suspicion that only one highly variable entity exits. Nevertheless, some trends can be seen. The best examples of var. *lacera* occur in northern Indiana, and may in fact be the predominant taxon there. Conversely, var. *gracilis* is the more common in southern Indiana. Plants of var. *lacera* generally are smaller than var. *gracilis*, although this is variable and seemingly site-induced. The distance between the lowest flowers is much greater in var. *lacera*, resulting in a very loose spiral, whereas in var. *gracilis* the flowers are proximate to one another. The spiral in var. *gracilis* ranges from a graceful single-ranked spike (typical) to one very tight and multi-ranked. Leaves are commonly present in var. *lacera* during flowering, but are generally absent in var. *gracilis*. Variety *lacera* also tends to flower earlier than var. *gracilis*. Additionally, some authors report differences between the two varieties with respect to area of green pigmentation on the lip (Fernald, 1946; Braun, 1967; Case, 1987).

Of the species of *Spiranthes* with which *S. lacera* commonly occurs, only *S. tuberosa* and possibly *S. ovalis* should cause any confusion in

identification. In the absence of fresh flowers, the oblanceolate stem leaves of *S. ovalis*, and the glabrous rachis of *S. tuberosa*, separate them from the leafless (or ovate, basal leaves only) and normally pubescent *S. lacera*.

Spiranthes lucida (H. H. Eaton) Ames

COMMON NAMES: shining ladies'-tresses, wideleaf ladies'-tresses.

SPECIFIC EPITHET DERIVATION: *lucida* = "shining," in reference to the glossy leaves of the species.

DESCRIPTION: **Plant glabrous except for a few capitate hairs in the inflorescence,** 18–22 cm tall. Roots fleshy, several. **Leaves 3–4, basal, lanceolate to elliptic, 5–8 cm long x 10–15 mm wide**. Inflorescence consisting of a loose to tight spike of 15–20 flowers, each subtended by an ovate-lanceolate bract 8–12 mm long x 3 mm wide. **Spike** single- to multi-ranked. **Phyllotaxy normally 1/3 or 1/4.** Lip 4–5 mm long x 2–3 mm wide, **white with a vivid yellow center,** oblong, with a wavy apex, and 2 basal tubercles. **Petals white, oblanceolate, somewhat oblique,** blunt, 4–5 mm long x 1 mm wide. Sepals white, oblong-lanceolate, 4–5 mm long x 1 mm wide. Petals and dorsal sepal convergent. Lateral sepals appressed.

BLOOMING PERIOD: mid-May to late June.

RANGE: This species occurs primarily in the northern third of Indiana, but there are collections of it from as far south as Jefferson County. Dr. A. Clapp lists it in his journal for the New Albany area, but I have not seen a voucher specimen. Suitable habitat is generally wanting in that area, although the rocky flats and adjacent springy banks of the Falls of the Ohio may have been satisfactory. The Northern Lakes Natural Region boasts the greatest number of occurrences, followed by the Northwestern Morainal and Central Till Plain natural regions.

HABITAT: *Spiranthes lucida* is most common in wet calcareous substrates where other vegetation is suppressed or absent. These conditions are not common in Indiana, but can be found in some fens, lake borders eroded by wave action, and moist limestone outcrops. Areas of exposed marl, sand, and/or gravel are preferred in fens. This typically occurs

FOLLOWING PAGE: *Spiranthes lucida* (shining ladies'-tresses). June 1988, Madison Co. Lee Casebere. x1.

where water saturation is highest, such as along rivulets or where slopes are so steep and eroded that raw mineral substrate is exposed. Most plant species avoid these harsh conditions, or, if present, are dwarfed in stature, thus reducing competition for the *Spiranthes*. Typical species that occur with *S. lucida* include *Equisetum arvense*, *Juncus tenuis* var. *dudleyi*, *Lobelia kalmii*, *Lysimachia quadriflora*, *Parnassia glauca*, *Potentilla fruticosa*, *Rhynchospora capillacea*, *Selaginella eclipes*, *Senecio aureus*, and several sedges, namely *Carex granularis*, *C. hystericina*, *C. interior*, *C. sterilis*, and *C. viridula*.

A most interesting habitat for *S. lucida* occurs in southeastern Indiana, viz., mossy, dripping-wet ledges situated at the bases of limestone cliffs. Apparently the constant seepage and occasional scouring of the cliff base by floodwater create conditions not unlike those of exposed mineral soils in fen communities. Associates of *S. lucida* on these cliff communities include *Carex granularis*, *C. hystericina*, *Equisetum arvense*, *Eupatorium perfoliatum*, *Glyceria striata*, *Juncus tenuis* var *dudleyi*, *Lysimachia ciliata*, *L. nummularia*, *Salix caroliniana*, *Senecio aureus*, *Trifolium repens*, and *Zizia aurea*.

S. lucida (shining ladies'-tresses). June 1988, Madison Co. Lee Casebere. x2½.

Rocky stream banks are another fascinating but little known habitat of *Spiranthes lucida*. In 1951 Hoosier botanist Edna Banta (now deceased), in a letter to then–McCormick's Creek State Park naturalist William Overlease, reported *S. lucida* growing at the water's edge of McCormick's Creek within the park. From the location information she provided, the plants would have been growing on a rocky creekbank, and not on a wet cliff. According to Overlease (personal communication), he never found any of the plants after an intensive search in the park. Elsewhere in its range streambank habitat is not an uncommon haunt for this orchid (Luer, 1975; Correll, 1978; Brackley, 1985; Case, 1987), but I believe such a habitat in Indiana is rarely utilized, due primarily to excessive siltation.

Spiranthes lucida apparently thrives on disturbances within its preferred habitat. Ken Klick recently found it growing in an old, abandoned house site at the Indiana Dunes National Lakeshore (Marlin Bowles, personal communication), and I have seen Indiana's largest known population of the orchid growing most luxuriantly in and about old tire ruts of exposed raw marl in a Whitley County fen. There is also a 1979 collection from a quarry in Wayne County (*Hendricks s.n.*, Hayes Regional Arboretum Herbarium).

DISCUSSION: Although most Indiana *Spiranthes* species bloom in late summer or autumn, the consistent exception is *Spiranthes lucida.* It is a spring wildflower, blooming in the month of May and continuing into early July. No other *Spiranthes* is in bloom then (save for late June specimens of *S. vernalis*). Also diagnostic of *Spiranthes lucida* is its yellow lip and broad, shiny leaves. There are other *Spiranthes* that have a yellowish lip, but the yellow is typically a vague, dull yellow. The yellow on the lip of *S. lucida* is brilliant and unmistakable.

Spiranthes lucida is not a common plant in Indiana, at least as currently known. I have observed it only a few times, but those experiences lead me to believe that I and others may be overlooking it. Finding *Spiranthes lucida* rests upon two factors: locating suitable habitat, and persistent searching in wetland vegetation. Although the orchid does prefer open sites, it may also occur among taller vegetation, necessitating diligent efforts for finding it. In Missouri I found *S. lucida* growing in an almost pure stand of sweet flag (*Acorus calamus*), but only after parting the leaves of the sweet flag and carefully searching was I able to see the orchids.

Case (1987) suggests that *Spiranthes lucida* is overlooked because botanists avoid its habitat (streamside pastures, at least in the western Great Lakes region), especially during its blooming period. This could be the situation in Indiana as well. I am not aware of any Indiana records from pastures.

Spiranthes magnicamporum Sheviak

COMMON NAMES: Great Plains ladies'-tresses, prairie ladies'-tresses.

SPECIFIC EPITHET DERIVATION: *magnicamporum* = "of the Great Plains," in reference to the principal region of the species' occurrence.

DESCRIPTION: **Plant glabrous except for capitate hairs on the upper stem and inflorescence,** 25–35 cm tall. Roots several, very thick, fleshy. **Leaves** linear-lanceolate to oblanceolate, 10–15 cm long x 8–12 mm wide, **characteristically absent at anthesis.** Inflorescence a tight spike of 20–40 flowers, each subtended by a lanceolate bract 7–10 mm long x 2–3 mm wide. **Spike multi-ranked, with phyllotaxy of 1/3 or 1/4. Lip** 8–10 mm long x 3–5 mm wide, **white with a dull yellowish center, oblong-ovate, with a wavy margin distally, and 2 relatively small basal tubercles.** Petals white, linear-lanceolate, 8–10 mm long x 1–2 mm wide. Sepals white, lanceolate to linear-lanceolate, 8–10 mm long x 1–3 mm wide. Petals and dorsal sepal convergent. **Lateral sepals widely spreading, incurved apically and commonly arching above the flower.**

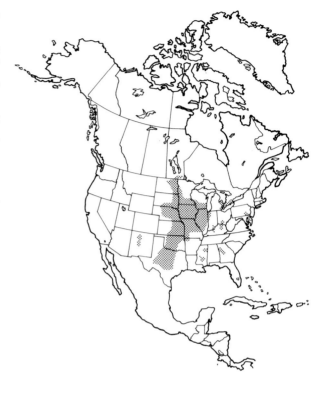

BLOOMING PERIOD: early September to early November.

RANGE: Known only from Clark and Lake counties. Although known as a prairie plant, *Spiranthes magnicamporum* is conspicuously absent from the Grand Prairie Natural Region. This absence is due not only to the massive conversion of the landscape to agriculture, but also to the rather acidic condition of much of the remaining substrate there. This is particularly evident in the Kankakee Sand Section. Records of *S. magnicamporum* from this region (e.g., Jasper, Newton, Pulaski counties) reported by Case (1987) are omitted here, as the specimens he used to substantiate their occurrence in those counties have since been determined by Sheviak to be prairie forms of *S. cernua*.

HABITAT: *Spiranthes magnicamporum* is confined primarily to prairie communities on dry, calcareous substrates, and because such environments are not common in Indiana, it is one of the rarest *Spiranthes*. The orchid is definitively known from only two widely separated communities in the state, viz., a southern Indiana limestone glade, and a dune and swale area bordering Lake Michigan.

The largest populations of *S. magnicamporum* occur on low, grassy

FOLLOWING PAGE:
Spiranthes magnicamporum (Great Plains ladies'-tresses). September 1990, Lake Co. Lee Casebere. x1.

dunes near Lake Michigan in Lake County. There hundreds of plants grow with *Andropogon scoparius, Coreopsis tripteris, Fragaria virginiana, Liatris spicata, Lithospermum canescens, Phlox pilosa, Ratibida pinnata, Rhus aromatica,* and *Sorghastrum nutans.* The orchids occur only on those dunes composed of calcareous sand. Beyond the influence of alkaline groundwater (from Lake Michigan) the dune substrate becomes acidic, and *S. magnicamporum* is absent.

The most xeric site in Indiana for *Spiranthes magnicamporum* is a limestone glade located in southern Clark County. There the plants grow in very harsh conditions, characterized by extremes of temperature, little or no soil, and low moisture. The orchids appear to flourish nevertheless. Associates of *S. magnicamporum* at the site include *Allium cernuum, Andropogon scoparius, Danthonia spicata, Dodecatheon meadia, Juniperus virginiana, Lithospermum canescens,* and the very rare *Leavenworthia uniflora.* Surprisingly, this *Spiranthes* is not known to occur in other limestone glades in southern Indiana (but it is found in glades in nearby counties in Kentucky).

S. magnicamporum (Great Plains ladies'-tresses), with ambush bug. September 1982, Lake Co. Lee Casebere. x2.

DISCUSSION: Like *Spiranthes ochroleuca, S. magnicamporum* is a sexually reproducing diploid with monoembryonic seeds. Described in 1973 by Charles Sheviak (Sheviak, 1973), this orchid is one of the newest species to be separated out of the *S. cernua* complex. Although formerly referred to as *S. cernua,* or some variety of it, there is no question about its identity as a distinctive species. In fact, it is much more distinctive than *S. cernua* and its many forms.

One of the first diagnostic features to be noted about *S. magnicamporum* is its fragrance. On more than one occasion botanists have approached populations of the orchid unbeknownst to them and detected their distinctive fragrance before seeing a plant! The fragrance is quite pleasant, described by many as having the scent of coumarin (a fragrant substance produced from seeds of tonka bean trees, of the genus *Dipteryx*).

Other characters that distinguish *S. magnicamporum* are its widely spreading lateral sepals, a thickened yellowish lip, its lack of leaves during flowering, a preference for dry calcareous habitats, and its late flowering period. These characters are best used in combination, as certain individuals of *S. cernua* exhibit traits of *S. magnicamporum.* For example, the lip of *S. magnicamporum* is quite yellow, especially on the undersur-

face, but so are the lips of *S. ochroleuca* and the old-field and prairie races of *S. cernua*. Additionally, the absence of leaves during flowering is characteristic of *S. magnicamporum* as well as the prairie races of *S. cernua*.

If used with caution, habitat and flowering period can be helpful in identifying *Spiranthes magnicamporum*. In ridge-and-swale habitats where both *S. magnicamporum* and *S. cernua* occur one can observe a nice zonation in habitat preference and flowering period between the two. *Spiranthes cernua* occurs in low, wet swales, and usually blooms earlier than the dune-inhabiting *S. magnicamporum*.

The widely spreading and ascending lateral sepals of *Spiranthes magnicamporum* are possibly the orchid's most distinguishing feature. The degree of sepal spreading is somewhat variable, even of flowers on the same plant, but normally there is such a noticeable separation of the sepals from the rest of the flower that one is able to see a gap when viewed from above.

A word of caution about identifying *Spiranthes magnicamporum*. Because some individuals of *S. cernua*, particularly those of the prairie races, bear such a remarkable resemblance to *S. magnicamporum*, an inspection of their seeds may be needed to make an accurate determination. *Spiranthes magnicamporum* has monoembryonic seeds that are short and broad in comparison to the long, narrow polyembryonic seeds of *S. cernua*. If the seeds of *S. cernua* are monoembryonic, which some are, then their embryos are commonly extruded outside the seed coat, whereas those in *S. magnicamporum* are completely internal. Note: Catling (1982) reports the presence of agamospermic races of *S. magnicamporum* in Ontario—these with polyembryonic seed—so seed may not always be conclusive. Readers are referred to Sheviak (1982) for more information on this complex problem.

Spiranthes ochroleuca (Rydberg) Rydberg

COMMON NAMES: yellow ladies'-tresses, yellow nodding ladies'-tresses.

SPECIFIC EPITHET DERIVATION: *ochroleuca* = "yellowish white," in reference to the color of the flowers.

DESCRIPTION: **Plant pubescent with capitate hairs on the upper stem and inflorescence, leaves and lower stem glabrous,** 25–35 cm tall. Roots fleshy, slender. **Leaves** 3–5, linear-elliptic to oblanceolate, mostly basal, **with sheathing bracts on the lower stem commonly foliaceous,** 13–17 cm long x 10–15 mm wide. Inflorescence a tight spike of 20–50 flowers, each subtended by a lanceolate bract 7–13 mm long x 2–3 mm wide. **Spike multi-ranked, with phyllotaxy of 1/3 or 1/4.** Lip 8–9 mm long x 3–5 mm wide, **cream to yellow, the latter especially in the center,** oblong-ovate, **with** a wavy margin distally, and **2 large basal tubercles.** Petals cream, linear-lanceolate, 8–9 mm long x 1–2 mm wide. Sepals cream, linear-lanceolate, 8–9 mm long x 1–3 mm wide. Petals and dorsal sepal convergent. **Lateral sepals appressed to lip, pointing upward** or horizontally.

BLOOMING PERIOD: mid-September to early November.

RANGE: Currently known with certainty only from Bartholomew, Brown, Jackson, and Monroe counties. Herbarium specimens determined to be this species have been reported for Porter County (Sheviak and Catling, 1980) and Steuben County (Case, 1987). The Porter County specimen has since been determined to be *Spiranthes cernua* (Sheviak, personal communication). Attempts to locate the specimen attributed to Steuben County have been unsuccessful; the specimen in question is supposedly located at the University of Michigan Herbarium, but a loan request for *S. ochroleuca* from that institution did not include any from Steuben County.

HABITAT: As noted elsewhere in its range, primary habitat for this species is well-drained, acidic substrates (Luer, 1975; Sheviak and Catling, 1980; Sheviak, 1982; Case, 1987). In Bartholomew and Brown counties, at the only localities of *Spiranthes ochroleuca* observed by the author, the orchid grows in full sun in eroded gullies of long abandoned old fields, powerline cuts through dry upland forest, and bladed shoulders of road rights-of-way. All of these habitats experience high summer

temperatures and drought. This is due in part to the substrate (typically composed of sandstone, shale, or exposed soil), and the southern and/or western aspect of the sites. Some plants inhabit slightly less harsh environments, such as lightly shaded forest edges. Typical associates of *S. ochroleuca* include *Andropogon scoparius*, *Aristida* spp., *Chamaecrista fasciculata*, *Danthonia spicata*, *Lespedeza hirta*, *L. virginica*, *Liatris squarrulosa*, *Pycnanthemum tenuifolium*, *Solidago hispida*, *S. juncea*, and *S. nemoralis*.

If *Spiranthes ochroleuca* does occur in northern Indiana, its habitat would most likely be similar to that in Michigan—sterile, sandy-acid openings in pioneer woodland composed of red maple, aspen, oak, *Aronia melanocarpa*, *Gaultheria procumbens*, and *Polytrichum* moss (see Case, 1987 for further details). I have searched diligently for the orchid in seemingly perfect habitats in La Grange and Steuben counties, but to no avail. If *S. ochroleuca* indeed occurs in northeastern Indiana, then it is apparently quite rare there. I have not searched for it in northwestern Indiana, but seemingly suitable habitat is abundant. Its occurrence there is doubtful, however.

DISCUSSION: *Spiranthes ochroleuca* is a diploid, sexually reproducing member of the *S. cernua* complex. Initially described in 1901 (Rydberg, in Britton, 1901), the identity of this orchid has been the subject of great controversy. Since 1901 it has been recognized as a species by some, relegated to varietal status by others, and ignored altogether by most! Charles Deam failed to recognize it beyond the varietal level, and even then stated that it did not occur in Indiana (Deam, 1940). The problem was due mainly to the extreme variability in *S. cernua*, with many assuming that *S. ochroleuca* was simply one of the variations of *S. cernua*. Only recently, with the work of Luer (1975) and Sheviak and Catling (1980), do we now have a good understanding as to why *S. ochroleuca* deserves species level rank.

I must admit that I was initially skeptical about the validity of this species, that is, until I carefully read Sheviak and Catling (1980) and studied the photos in Luer (1975), Case and Catling (1983), and Case (1987). After being convinced that *Spiranthes ochroleuca* was a good species, my biggest concern was to determine if the species actually occurred in Indiana; all earlier reports of *S. ochroleuca* had been discounted by Deam and others. In examining specimens for the orchid book project I encountered a specimen (*Starcs* 2146, IND) that in 1983 was annotated by Fred Case as possibly being *S. ochroleuca*. That specimen and two others (*Friesner* 11629 and *Friesner* 9520, BUT) were recently examined by Charles Sheviak and determined to be *S. ochroleuca*. I have since annotated a small number of additional collections of the species as well. On October 12, 1988 Cloyce Hedge and I observed living plants of *S. ochroleuca* in Bartholomew and Brown counties, thus verifying that the species still occurs in Indiana.

The most difficult task in identifying *Spiranthes ochroleuca* is differentiating it from the race of *S. cernua* ("old-field ecotype" of Sheviak,

Spiranthes ochroleuca (yellow ladies'-tresses). October 1988, Bartholomew Co. Lee Casebere. x3½.

1974) that occurs in southern Indiana. Evidently old-field *S. cernua* has inherited genetic material (through hybridization) from *S. ochroleuca* at some undetermined time in the past (Sheviak, personal communication), making the two taxa very similar in appearance. Nevertheless, when observed in the field the two can be distinguished, albeit some specimens with a great deal of difficulty (determination of herbarium specimens is extremely difficult, even for advanced students). The key characters that I find most useful are the yellowish color and the ascending nature of the flowers and lateral sepals. Even if the flowers are not ascending, the sepals normally are. These characters, when used with others listed in the key and Sheviak and Catling (1980), can lead to a correct determination most of the time.

Spiranthes ochroleuca should be searched for elsewhere in the state, particularly in the Brown County Hills and Knobstone Escarpment Sections of the Highland Rim Natural Region. Diligent searching in the Shawnee Hills has not revealed the orchid, but its occurrence there would not be too surprising. However, factors responsible for limiting the occurrence of *Isotria verticillata* in the Shawnee Hills may be in effect for *S. ochroleuca* as well.

Spiranthes ovalis Lindley var. *erostellata* Catling

Map shows combined ranges for all varieties.

COMMON NAMES: oval ladies'-tresses, little elephants.

SPECIFIC EPITHET DERIVATION: *ovalis* = "oval," in reference to the outline of the inflorescence. Fernald (1950) states that "oval" is in reference to the lip shape.

DESCRIPTION: Plant pubescent with capitate hairs on the upper stem and inflorescence, leaves and lower stem glabrous, 20–35 cm tall. Roots fleshy, slender. Leaves 2–3, oblong-elliptic to oblanceolate, 6–8 cm long x 5–8 mm wide. Inflorescence a tight spike of 20–40 flowers, each subtended by an ovate-lanceolate bract 4–6 mm long x 2–3 mm wide. **Spike multi-ranked, commonly in 3 vertical ranks, with a phyllotaxy of 1/3 or 1/4. Lip** 3–4 mm long x 1.5–2 mm wide, **white, ovate, recurved and commonly inrolled,** with a wavy margin distally, and 2 basal tubercles. Petals white, lanceolate, 3–4 mm long x 1 mm wide. Sepals white, lanceolate, 3–4 mm long x 1–1.3 wide. Petals and dorsal

sepal convergent. Lateral sepals appressed to lip, horizontal to downward angled.

BLOOMING PERIOD: late August to mid-October.

RANGE: Primarily restricted to the southern half of the state, but occurs farther north along the Wabash River corridor (Entrenched Valley Section—Central Till Plain Natural Region), and in Steuben County. The Steuben County population, discovered in 1986 by Doug Rood of Fort Wayne, represents a significant expansion of the orchid's range in Indiana. However, occurrences in far northern Indiana are not to be unexpected, as this orchid has been known from Kalamazoo County, Michigan, since 1966 (Case, 1987).

HABITAT: Of all the Indiana *Spiranthes*, *S. ovalis* var. *erostellata* is the most adapted to shade. In fact, it appears to require at least partial shade, for rarely does it grow in full sun. Conversely, it does not do well in densely shaded forests. It is most often found in edge habitats and young regrowth forests with a mosaic of filtered light and shade. Examples of productive sites include trailsides, shaded roadsides, forest openings (natural or otherwise), and young, uneven-aged forests developing on abandoned old fields. Associates of *S. ovalis* var. *erostellata* in these situations include sassafras, flowering dogwood, tulip tree, red cedar, persimmon, redbud, *Botrychium dissectum* var. *obliquum*, *Celastrus scandens*, *Juncus tenuis* var. *tenuis*, *Liparis liliifolia*, *Poa compressa*, *Potentilla simplex*, *Prunella vulgaris*, *Rhus radicans*, *Sanicula canadensis*, and *Spiranthes cernua*.

Although Luer (1975) and Correll (1978) report *S. ovalis* as generally occurring in damp situations, in Indiana it is most at home in dry to dry-mesic upland sites. I have never observed it in deep wetlands. However, I have seen the orchid growing in floodplain forests, indicating at least some tolerance for "wet feet." Populations show a preference for calcareous substrates, but are not limited to them. The greatest success I have had in finding this orchid has been in the limestone hills in the Bluegrass Natural Region, but I also have seen a few plants in acidic substrates in the Shawnee Hills and Highland Rim.

DISCUSSION: *Spiranthes ovalis* var. *erostellata* is not easily identified by the amateur. In fact, in one publication the great orchidologist Oakes Ames listed it under the category of "Doubtful Species" (Ames, 1905). Although it does somewhat resemble *S. cernua* in miniature, it is distinctive and readily identified from its more common congener. Overall this

PRECEDING PAGE: *Spiranthes ovalis* (oval ladies'-tresses). September 1988, Steuben Co. Lee Casebere. x1½.

ABOVE: *S. ovalis.* September 1988, Steuben Co. Lee Casebere. x3.

variety of *S. ovalis* is quite small, with flowers averaging less than 5 mm in length. The flowers are normally arranged in a three-ranked inflorescence that has an outline (at least early in anthesis) shaped like the head of a lance. Each flower possesses a recurved lip that is commonly inrolled distally, giving the flower the look (with some imagination) of a tiny elephant's trunk drooping between the tusk-like lateral sepals. The stem has long oblanceolate leaves that, unless damaged, are present at flowering time. In addition, *S. ovalis* var. *erostellata* is a plant of brushy and woodland habitats; rarely is it exposed to full sunlight.

Although *Spiranthes ovalis* var. *erostellata* is rather widespread statewide, and occurs in a ubiquitous habitat type, it is rarely encountered. The reasons are twofold: one, at any given site there are usually only a few individuals, and two, the plants are so small that they go undetected by most people.

Trying to find *S. ovalis* var. *erostellata* can be a laborious and frustrating exercise. Possibly the best way, although time-consuming and a strain on the eyes, is to scan the edge of hiking trails in potential habitats. Even with this strategy, success will not come easily.

All of Indiana's *Spiranthes ovalis* presumably belong to the variety *erostellata* Catling. Named for the absence of a rostellum (Catling, 1983b), this variety consequently lacks a viscidium, and thus is not capable of attaching pollinia to visiting insects. Cross fertilization with other flowers is prevented, but seed production is not hampered because the flowers self-pollinate (autogamy). Catling (1983b) suggests that there are benefits for the orchid being autogamous, such as avoidance of extinction in pollinator-poor environments, and saving of energy otherwise devoted to pollen transfer. These, plus the fixation of adaptive gene combinations, may explain the recent spread of *S. ovalis* into successional habitats in the northern part of its range.

Increased frequency and utilization of successional habitats is clearly a recent phenomenon for *S. ovalis* in Indiana. In the first half of this century the orchid was an extremely rare plant in Indiana, and although the difficulty in spotting it can account in part for the lack of early records, more likely it probably was not as common then as now. In Deam's *Flora of Indiana* (1940), only Crawford and Spencer counties were documented as having the species. Compare that distribution with today's and one can see a significant increase in the range and number of counties. The reason for the spread of *S. ovalis* var. *erostellata* is unclear, but it may be that we are observing the movement of a disturbance-adapted ecotype into Indiana. For discussion of similar phenomena, see *Corallorhiza odontorhiza*.

I have seen plants in Switzerland County with no open flowers evident on the spike, yet its ovaries were obviously swollen with developing seeds. This condition previously has not been reported for this species, although peloric individuals of other species of *Spiranthes*, notably *S. cernua*, are known to exhibit cleistogamy (Sheviak, 1982).

In the classic book *Our Wild Orchids* (Morris and Eames, 1929), an account is given of the authors' expedition to observe and photograph *Spiranthes ovalis* in Spencer County, Indiana. The trip was a success, as evidenced by the photos (plates 88 and 89) in the book. The subject of the photographs now exists as *Deam 39962* (IND). The legendary Edgar T. Wherry accompanied them on their search.

Spiranthes romanzoffiana Chamisso

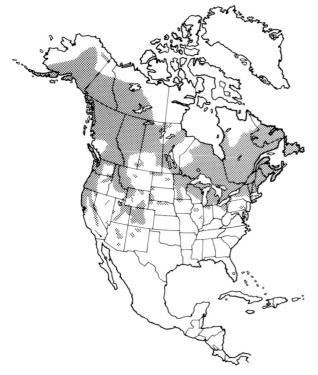

Spiranthes romanzoffiana (hooded ladies'-tresses). August 1989, Noble Co. Lee Casebere. x1.

COMMON NAMES: hooded ladies'-tresses, Romanzoff's ladies'-tresses.

SPECIFIC EPITHET DERIVATION: *romanzoffiana*, for Nicholas Romanzoff, a Russian minister of state.

DESCRIPTION: Plant pubescent with capitate hairs on the upper stem and inflorescence, leaves and lower stem glabrous, 25–35 cm tall. Roots fleshy, slender. Leaves 3–5, mostly basal, linear-lanceolate, 10–15 cm long x 8–12 mm wide. Inflorescence a tight spike of 15–30 flowers, each subtended by an ovate-lanceolate bract 12–15 mm long x 4–5 mm wide. **Spike multi-ranked, commonly in 3 vertical ranks, with a phyllotaxy of 1/3 or 1/4. Lip** 7–10 mm long x 4 mm wide, **white, with greenish veins centrally, pandurate, constricted above the middle, with a lacerate, greatly recurved apex and 2 small basal tubercles.** Petals white, linear-lanceolate, 7–10 mm long x 1–2 mm wide. Sepals white, lanceolate, laterals somewhat falcate, 7–10 mm long x 2.5–3 mm wide. **Sepals and petals convergent, ascending, forming a hood over the lip.**

BLOOMING PERIOD: mid-July to late August.

RANGE: This northern orchid is known in Indiana only from La Grange, Noble, and Porter counties, the likely southern limits of the orchid's range in Indiana. However, occurrences farther south are possible. There is a collection of *Spiranthes romanzoffiana* from Coles County, Illinois (Sheviak, 1974) that is only 40 miles distant from Terre Haute. That collection, from what was apparently a fen along the Shelbyville Moraine (the southern terminus of Wisconsinan glaciation), provides reason to believe that fens along the Shelbyville Moraine (and elsewhere) in Indiana may also harbor the orchid. Because of its relatively

high number of fens, the Northern Lakes Natural Region is a prime area for investigation.

HABITAT: Throughout its range *Spiranthes romanzoffiana* is typically a plant of neutral to alkaline wetlands (Luer, 1975; Correll, 1978; Case, 1987), and the Indiana localities are no exception. At the Noble County location several dozen plants of *S. romanzoffiana* occupy an open, marl flat saturated by groundwater seepage. The flat, a part of a graminoid fen, borders a small, natural lake where an interesting array of plants typical of the community are found, including *Drosera rotundifolia*, *Eleocharis rostellata*, *Lobelia kalmii*, *Lysimachia quadriflora*, *Parnassia glauca*, *Rhynchospora alba*, *Salix candida*, *Sarracenia purpurea*, *Scirpus acutus*, *S. americanus*, *Solidago ohioensis*, *Tofieldia glutinosa*, and *Utricularia intermedia*.

At the La Grange County site the orchids occur along a spring run in a fen, in association with many of the same species found at the Noble County site. The precise environment of the Porter County collection is not known, but most likely it was a fen community not greatly different from the ones described above.

DISCUSSION: Known from only three sites in the state, with one of these (Porter County) now destroyed, *Spiranthes romanzoffiana* is undoubtedly the rarest *Spiranthes* in Indiana. It was not known for Indiana until 1983, when Fred Case, author of *Orchids of the Western Great Lakes Region* (Case, 1987), discovered a specimen of it in the Deam Herbarium at Indiana University. The specimen, collected in Porter County on July 28, 1929, by Notre Dame botanist J. A. Nieuwland, was labeled only as *Spiranthes*. Although Case's discovery is significant, it offered little comfort to those hoping to observe a living plant in Indiana, for the collection site where Nieuwland procured the specimen, Baileytown, was destroyed years ago. Baileytown was a stopping point along the traction line between South Bend and Chicago, and was a popular collecting spot for botanists. Now a steel mill, the site is very close to what is currently called Cowles Bog. Even though Cowles Bog (which is actually a fen) is not the high-quality natural area it once was, there is a remote possibility that *S. romanzoffiana* could be there.

A great deal of excitement was generated in 1986 when Lee Casebere of the Indiana Department of Natural Resources found an estimated 30 individuals of *S. romanzoffiana* growing in a marl flat in Noble County. It

S. romanzoffiana (hooded ladies'-tresses). August 1986, Noble Co. Lee Casebere. x2.

was certainly one of the major orchid discoveries in Indiana. Casebere has since documented the occurrence of an additional Indiana population of *S. romanzoffiana*, from a La Grange County fen.

The paucity of occurrences of *Spiranthes romanzoffiana* in Indiana is perplexing, as many sites with seemingly suitable habitat exist. Although the orchid is certainly rare, it is possible that additional populations have been missed because of the superficial resemblance of *S. romanzoffiana* to *S. cernua*, the latter a *Spiranthes* sometimes not examined carefully because of its commonness. Any *Spiranthes* in flower in late July and early August in wetland habitats should be closely inspected.

Spiranthes tuberosa Rafinesque

[Syn: *Spiranthes grayi* Ames]

COMMON NAMES: little ladies'-tresses, Beck's ladies'-tresses.

SPECIFIC EPITHET DERIVATION: *tuberosa* = "tuberous," in reference to the orchid's single swollen root.

DESCRIPTION: Plant glabrous throughout, 20–30 cm tall. **Root solitary, tuberous. Leaves 2–3, ovate, basal, absent at anthesis,** 2–3 cm long x 1 cm wide. Inflorescence a loose, graceful spike of 10–20 flowers, each subtended by an ovate-lanceolate bract 2–3 mm long x 0.5–1 mm wide. **Spike single-ranked, with phyllotaxy of 1/5 of less. Lip 2–3 mm long x 1.5–2 mm wide, white, ovate, broad and wavy at the apex,** with 2 basal tubercles. Petals white, linear-oblong, 2–3 mm long x 0.5–1 mm wide. Sepals white, linear-lanceolate, 2–3 mm long x 0.5–1 mm wide. Petals and dorsal sepal convergent. Lateral sepals somewhat spreading.

BLOOMING PERIOD: late July to mid-September.

RANGE: Occurs primarily in the Shawnee Hills and Highland Rim natural regions, with a few collections from the Bluegrass. It undoubtedly occurs in the uplands of the Southwestern Lowlands Natural Region and although unknown from northern Indiana, there is an excellent possibility for it there, as seemingly suitable habitat exists in the Northern Lakes and Northwestern Morainal natural regions, and

the Kankakee Sand Section of the Grand Prairie Natural Region. Its occurrence in northern Indiana is even more probable considering that populations exist in south-central Michigan (Case, 1987).

HABITAT: *Spiranthes tuberosa* is most commonly found in sterile, dry sites where little or no competition is provided from associated plants. Open eroded slopes in old fields, rocky roadbanks, exposed ledges of sandstone cliffs, and thinly wooded forests on xeric, south-facing slopes are the primary haunts of this orchid. At these sites it is restricted to acidic, well-drained soils, especially those with ample fragments of sandstone, shale, and chert.

Old fields, especially those resulting from abandonment during the Great Depression, are particularly good places to find *Spiranthes tuberosa*. These fields are typically free of exotic weeds, and rather acidic, poor sites, as evidenced by extensive patches of lichens (*Cladina* and *Cladonia*) and bare soil. Nevertheless, the fields may be dominated by an interesting assortment of native species, such as *Andropogon gyrans*, *A. scoparius*, *Aster undulatus*, *Carex hirsutella*, *Chamaecrista fasciculata*, *Desmodium ciliare*, *Liatris squarrosa*, *Linum virginianum*, *Potentilla simplex*, *Pycnanthemum tenuifolium*, *Solidago nemoralis*, *Strophostyles umbellata*, *Stylosanthes biflora*, *Viola pedata*, and red cedar.

Xeric forests also are good habitats for *Spiranthes tuberosa*, although the orchid is usually not found in great numbers there. These thinly wooded sites are normally on steep, south-facing slopes that are windswept of leaves, and characterized by gnarled growths of chestnut oak, blackjack oak, scarlet oak, and locally, Virginia pine. Typical herbs present include *Cunila origanoides*, *Danthonia spicata*, *Hieracium* spp., *Krigia biflora*, *Panicum depauperatum*, *Solidago bicolor*, *Viola pedata*, and *V. triloba*.

DISCUSSION: Without question *Spiranthes tuberosa* is Indiana's daintiest ladies'-tresses orchid. In fact, it challenges *Malaxis unifolia* for having the smallest flowers of all Indiana orchids. Naturally this trait makes it one of the least conspicuous orchids, but it is not particularly difficult to find in its preferred habitat. It is much more predictable and easier to find than *S. ovalis*, for instance.

Despite its size, *Spiranthes tuberosa* is one of our most attractive orchids. Its graceful spire of tiny, clear white flowers is irresistible. Upon examining the flowers under magnification, its beauty is even more evident. As in many orchids, but especially here, the flower's cellular tissue appears to be composed of rounded, polished crystals, a condition I refer to as "jewelaceous."

Pressed specimens of *Spiranthes tuberosa* and *S. lacera*, especially old ones, are sometimes difficult to separate. In most cases, *S. tuberosa* is slightly smaller and glabrous throughout, has uniform coloration in the flowers, and if present, possesses a single tuberous root. *Spiranthes lacera* is a larger plant that commonly has some hairs within the inflorescence. It also possesses multiple roots and a contrasting darker area on the lip (that was formerly green in fresh condition).

Spiranthes vernalis Engelmann & Gray

COMMON NAMES: spring ladies'-tresses, vernal ladies'-tresses.

SPECIFIC EPITHET DERIVATION: *vernalis* = "of the spring," in reference to the species' blooming date (although most of its anthesis in Indiana is in summer).

DESCRIPTION: **Plant pubescent with pointed hairs on upper stem and inflorescence, leaves and lower stem mostly glabrous, 50–80 cm tall.** Roots thick and fleshy. Leaves 2–3, mostly basal, linear to linear-lanceolate, 10–17 cm long x 6–10 mm wide. Inflorescence a loose, graceful spike of 30–40 flowers, each subtended by an ovate-lanceolate bract 10–12 mm long x 4–5 mm wide. **Spike normally single-ranked, with phyllotaxy of 1/5 or less.** Lip 7–9 mm long x 4 mm wide, **white with a yellow center,** ovate, with a wavy-margined apex and 2 basal tubercles. Petals white, oblong-oblanceolate, 6–8 mm long x 1–2 mm wide. Sepals white, lanceolate, 6–8 mm long x 1–3 mm wide. Petals and dorsal sepal convergent. **Lateral sepals somewhat spreading and inrolled along their length.**

BLOOMING PERIOD: mid-June to late July.

RANGE: Currently known in Indiana only from Crawford, Dubois, Harrison, Lawrence, Perry, and Washington counties, but other southern Indiana counties are expected to have this species.

HABITAT: *Spiranthes vernalis*, like several southern Indiana *Spiranthes*, thrives in acidic, dry old fields exposed to full sunlight. In general, areas suitable for *S. cernua* (old-field type) and *S. tuberosa* are suitable for *S. vernalis*. At some sites native barrens species predominate: e.g., *Andropogon scoparius, Carex hirsutella, Danthonia spicata, Euphorbia corollata, Liatris spicata, L. squarrosa, Lobelia spicata, Potentilla simplex, Pycnanthemum tenuifolium, Silphium terebinthinaceum, Solidago nemoralis,* and *Sorghastrum nutans.* Species at some of the more disturbed *S. vernalis* sites include *Achillea millefolium, Andropogon scoparius, Chamaecrista fasciculata, Festuca elatior, Polygala sanguinea, Rhus copallinum, Strophostyles umbellata,* and *Tridens flavus.*

DISCUSSION: The first Indiana record of *Spiranthes vernalis* was from a collection made by Fred and Maryrose Wampler (12 July 1986 *F. & M. Wampler s.n.,* IND). They discovered a large ladies'-tresses orchid growing in an abandoned pasture just west of Mitchell while looking for wildflower subjects to use for their book. The Wamplers and I have made

FOLLOWING PAGE: *Spiranthes vernalis* (spring ladies'-tresses). July 1989, Crawford Co. Lee Casebere. x½.

subsequent attempts to locate additional plants at the site, but with no success. It is apparently extirpated. An illustration of this Lawrence County specimen can be seen on Plate 47 of *Wildflowers of Indiana* (Wampler, 1988).

Although I had given up hope that additional plants would be found at the Mitchell site, I felt certain that somewhere in southern Indiana *Spiranthes vernalis* would again be found. My confidence was supported with the knowledge of the orchid's occurrence in Kentucky counties bordering the Ohio River. Then, in 1989, a flurry of collections and observations of *S. vernalis* were made in Indiana, including one population each in Dubois County (24 June 1989 *Spurgeon s.n.*) and Perry County (6 July 1989 *Dillon s.n.*), and three populations in Crawford County, two by Jeff Dillon (7 July 1989 *Dillon s.n.*, and 13 July 1989 *Dillon s.n.*), and one by Katie and Brian Abrell on 15 July 1989 (not collected, but pho-

tographed). Additional collections were made in 1990 from Harrison and Washington counties.

I believe we are witnessing a very recent movement of the orchid into Indiana. In the state's long botanical history many have botanized extensively in southern Indiana, some looking specifically for orchids. I feel certain that this orchid of old fields would have been collected long ago had it been here. It is certainly not a case of mistaken identity, as *S. vernalis* has several characteristics that make it easily identifiable. First, although not blooming in spring as the name *"vernalis"* implies (except possibly for some plants blooming at the very end of the calendar spring), no other *Spiranthes* of southern Indiana fields blooms as early as *S. vernalis*. The second diagnostic feature of *S. vernalis* is its impressively large size. Although variable, it is commonly taller than other Indiana *Spiranthes*, attaining heights of two feet or more! The third and perhaps best character is the presence of dense, pointed non-glandular hairs in the inflorescence. No other Indiana *Spiranthes* has these.

S. vernalis (spring ladies'-tresses). July 1990, Crawford Co. Lee Casebere. x2½.

Nuttall

The botanical name (*Tipularia*) and common name (crane-fly orchid) of this genus reflect the similarity in appearance between the orchid's flowers and a flying insect known as the crane-fly, of the genus *Tipula*. The resemblance is remarkable, with the flowering stalks giving an impression of a swarm of flying gnats, mosquitoes, or small crane-flies. It would not be unreasonable to suspect that the flowers, imitating the body form of these flying insects, pose for the purpose of attracting a "mate" and thus get an unwitting carrier to transport pollen from one flower to the next. However, such is not the case (see discussion in the species account).

Worldwide only three species of *Tipularia* exist, two in Asia and our *T. discolor* of North America. All three species produce a single leaf which appears at a time separate from the appearance of the inflorescence (Luer, 1975).

Tipularia discolor (Pursh) Nuttall

COMMON NAME: crane-fly orchid.

SPECIFIC EPITHET DERIVATION: *discolor* = "different colors, or faded," in reference to the dull, mottled coloration of the flowers. It may also refer to differences in color of upper and lower leaf surfaces.

DESCRIPTION: Plant glabrous, 35–45 cm tall. Roots fleshy, attached to a connected series of 2–3 corms. **Leaf solitary, ovate,** 6–7 cm long x 4–6 mm wide, **dark green above (commonly spotted with purple), wine-purple below, evident from autumn to spring only.** Inflorescence a raceme of 30–40 **flowers on a purplish-brown scape,** each flower subtended by a minute, almost imperceptible bract. **Lip** 4–5 mm long x 1–2 mm wide, **translucent, pale purple, 3–lobed, the lateral lobes short, acute, the middle lobe long and narrow, lanceolate, and dilated apically, with a basal spur** 13–18 mm long x 0.5–1 mm wide. Petals oblong-elliptic, pale purple, 4–5 mm long x 1 mm wide. Sepals similar to petals, 4–5 mm long x 1.5–2 mm wide.

BLOOMING PERIOD: mid-July to late August.

RANGE: With the exception of a disjunct population in La Porte

PRECEDING PAGE:
Tipularia discolor
(crane-fly orchid).
August 1989,
Jennings Co. Lee
Casebere. x1.

RIGHT: *T. discolor*.
August 1989,
Crawford Co. Lee
Casebere. x2.

BOTTOM: *T. discolor*,
winter leaf. March
1989, Spencer Co.
Mike Homoya. x⅓.

County, the crane-fly orchid is restricted to the southern half of Indiana. By far, most of the populations occur in the Shawnee Hills and Highland Rim natural regions, followed by the Bluegrass (primarily in flatwoods) and Southwestern Lowlands.

HABITAT: Habitats of the crane-fly orchid range from mesic to dry, flat to rugged, and old growth to regrowth forests. However, it is more common in some habitats than others, particularly depending on the region of state; e.g., mesic and dry-mesic upland forests are the orchid's principal habitats in the Shawnee Hills and Highland Rim, whereas mesic flatwoods are preferred in the Bluegrass Natural Region. Acidic to neutral substrates are apparently critical, as the orchid is noticeably absent from areas composed mainly of basic soils. In upland forest sites typical overstory trees include American beech, sugar maple, tulip tree, white, red, and black oak, shagbark hickory, and mockernut hickory. Understory species commonly associated with *Tipularia* include flowering dogwood, pawpaw, *Aplectrum hyemale*, *Athyrium filix-femina*, *Botrychium dissectum*, *Epifagus virginiana*, *Polystichum acrostichoides*, *Rhus radicans*, *Solidago caesia*, *S. flexicaulis*, *Stellaria pubera*, and *Viburnum acerifolium*.

In the mesic flatwoods of the Bluegrass Natural Region overstory trees include sweetgum, American beech, tulip tree, red maple, and black gum. Understory associates include *Botrychium oneidense*, *Dryopteris carthusiana*, *Euonymus americanus*, *Goodyera pubescens*, *Mitchella repens*, and *Rhus radicans*.

At the La Porte County site, the orchid grows in a mesic, sandy flatwoods dominated by red oak and scattered paper birch (*fide* Tom Post).

DISCUSSION: In many respects, the life history of *Tipularia* is like that of the puttyroot, *Aplectrum hyemale*. It produces a single over-wintering leaf in September that disappears the following spring, and it sends forth a leafless flowering stalk during the regular growing season. The major difference between the life histories of these two organisms is the flowering date: *Aplectrum* is a spring bloomer, while *Tipularia* blooms in summer.

Tipularia is generally more common than *Aplectrum* where their ranges overlap. Part of the reason for this is the ability of *Tipularia* to colonize regrowth forests readily, even those on sites formerly cultivated. *Aplectrum* is less likely to grow in such conditions, although it does so sporadically. It also is usually easier to locate flowering individuals of *Tipularia*, even though their dark, narrow spikes are not conspicuous. This is because *Tipularia* commonly grows in drier habitats than *Aplectrum*, and thus there are normally fewer associated plants present to obscure the flowering stalk.

Tipularia discolor is clearly advancing its range. In the *Flora of Indiana* (Deam, 1940) there are eight counties shown for *Tipularia*, all in the far south-central and southeastern parts of the state. Compare Deam's map with the current one, and a north and western range expansion is evident. Further evidence of this expansion can be seen in Illinois, where *Tipularia* was unknown until its discovery in Pope County in 1958

Tipularia discolor   231

(Mohlenbrock, 1970). Since that initial discovery, the orchid has been documented in at least four additional Illinois counties, including the counties bordering Missouri. Not surprisingly, it was recently discovered for the first time in Missouri (Don Kurz, personal communication). The discoveries of *Tipularia* in Berrien County, Michigan, in 1972 (Case, 1987) and La Porte County, Indiana, in 1987 (*Post* 474, MOR), may reflect a recent range extension, although with the many disjunct occurrences of southern species in the Dunes region, it is possible that the orchid occurs there as a relict.

The range expansion of *Tipularia* is most likely a natural phenomenon not unlike natural movements of native plants in the past, except that we have had the opportunity to observe and document it. Many factors may be responsible for its expansion, but it may simply be a function of time, having taken this long for it to occupy suitable habitats in our area.

The flowers of *Tipularia* are unique among North American orchids in that they are not bilaterally symmetrical. Instead, the sepals and petals are positioned so that the flower is lopsided, with an unlike number of petals and sepals to either side of the column. Moreover, the flowers are angled to one side of the main stem, with some angled to the right, others to the left. Stoutamire (1978) observed that this floral positioning controls the placement of pollinaria on pollinators. The pollinators, nocturnal moths called millers, have pollinaria attached to their right eye when visiting "right-handed" flowers, and to their left eye when visiting left-handed flowers. The significance, if any, of floral positioning is unclear, as both right- and left-handed flowers appear to be pollinated with equal frequency. Whatever the reason, it must work, as *Tipularia* commonly produces capsules and is one of the most common woodland orchids in southern Indiana, if not the most common.

Another curious aspect of *Tipularia* pollination is the retention of the anther-cap to the pollinarium following the latter's removal from the column. Apparently unique among North American orchids, this anther-cap retention promotes outcrossing (Catling and Catling, 1991a). By retaining the anther-cap, the moth-transported pollinia cannot attach to the stigmatic surface of any flowers visited. This remains true until the anther-cap falls away, which it usually does after a period of 8 minutes or more. With the naked pollinia now free to pollinate, the vectoring moth is likely to have traveled to a *Tipularia* plant other than the one supplying the pollinarium, and thus outcrossing is achieved.

One of the mysteries of the crane-fly is its possession of dark purple spotting on the surface of the leaf. These unexplained spots occur in a random pattern and are variously sized. Rarely does a leaf have an unblemished surface. Case (1987) described them as "brownish rust spots," but Dr. Joseph Hennen of Purdue University found no rust (a type of fungus) present. Because many of the spots appear to be raised above the surrounding surface leaf tissue, with corresponding dimples underneath, I suspect that the spots are the result of mechanical damage, possibly by a sucking insect or mite. However, no organisms were found after an examination by entomologists of the Indiana Division of Entomology. Another possibility is that the spots simply may be concentrations of pigment, genetically determined, without any outside causative agent.

TRIPHORA
Nuttall

Approximately ten to twelve species compose this New World genus. In North America only our *Triphora trianthophora* extends northward beyond the subtropical climate of southern Florida.

The Greek *tri*, for "threefold," combined with *phoros*, for "bearing," produces *Triphora*, a name in reference either to the number of flowers produced per plant (commonly three), or the number of crests or ridges of the labellum.

Triphora, long known as a member of the genus *Pogonia*, differs from it by technical differences in column morphology and features of the pollinia (Ames, 1922). In addition, *Triphora* produces stolons, whereas *Pogonia* does not. These differences, plus others, have led botanists to consider the two as no longer closely related, as was originally believed (Luer, 1975; Dressler, 1981).

Triphora trianthophora (Swartz) Rydberg in Britton

COMMON NAME: nodding pogonia, three-birds orchid.

SPECIFIC EPITHET DERIVATION: *trianthophora* = "bearing three flowers," in reference to the common number of flowers per plant.

DESCRIPTION: **Plant glabrous,** 16–20 cm tall. **Roots slender, forming tubers from which new plants arise. Leaves 3– 5, ovate, clasping the purplish-green, zigzag stem, 8–12 mm long x 5–9 mm wide. Inflorescence a loose raceme of (2) 3 (4) flowers,** each subtended by an ovate bract 6–10 mm long x 3–6 mm wide. **Lip** 12–15 mm long x 6–8 mm wide, **3–lobed, obovate in general outline, the lateral lobes ovate, the middle lobe suborbicular, white to pinkish-purple, with 3 green interrupted ridges centrally.** Petals elliptic to oblanceolate, falcate, white to pinkish-purple, 12–15 mm long x 3–4 mm wide. Sepals similar to petals, but the dorsal sepal not falcate.

BLOOMING PERIOD: late July to mid-September.

RANGE: Occurs statewide, with the greatest number of populations located in the west-central part of the state, especially in the Entrenched Valley Section of the Central Till Plain. There are surprisingly few records and collections from the unglaciated portions of the Shawnee Hills and the Highland Rim.

HABITAT: Nodding pogonia occurs most commonly in rich, mesic forests composed of American beech, red oak, tulip tree, sugar maple, white ash, black walnut, and pawpaw. It thrives in areas with considerable leaf mold, some plants even growing in the decayed wood of fallen logs and bark shed from standing dead trees. High amounts of organic matter apparently are not critical to the orchid's survival, however, as I have seen plants growing on lightly eroded patches of soil where little or no humus was evident. Similarly, Deam (1940) reported finding a large colony growing on a bare, sandy flat in a wooded ravine.

Although *Triphora* occurs in greatest abundance in deeply dissected terrain, it typically shuns the steep slopes and occurs instead on the flats and/or gentle slopes above and below the deep ravines. My greatest success in locating plants has been to walk the break of an upland flat where it meets the upper edge of a steep-sloping ravine. However, plants can turn up just about anywhere there is suitable moisture and shade, including mesic floodplain forests and borders of swamps.

234   *Triphora trianthophora*

Some of the species recorded growing with *Triphora* in Indiana include *Actaea alba, Amphicarpaea bracteata, Brachyelytrum erectum, Carex hirtifolia, Desmodium nudiflorum, Dryopteris marginalis, Epifagus virginiana, Galium triflorum, Hydrophyllum appendiculatum, Osmorhiza longistylis, Panax quinquefolium, Parthenocissus quinquefolia, Pilea pumila, Podophyllum peltatum,* and *Polystichum acrostichoides.*

DISCUSSION: I think that of all the Indiana orchids, the flowers of *Triphora* provide the closest approximation of how the general public thinks an orchid should look. With a little magnification, *Triphora* flowers do bear a slight resemblance to those of *Laelia*, a tropical American orchid genus grown for its beauty and use in the horticulture market. Indeed, the coloration of the darker pigmented flowers of *Triphora* may best be described as "orchid"!

Typically having three flowers per stem (hence the common name three-birds orchid), *Triphora* has the curious habit of opening one flower at a time in synchrony with others in the population. This phenomenon, called thermoperiodicity, is best explained by Luer (1975): "All mature buds [of *Triphora*] open at the same time on the same day. Frequently, a few degrees decrease in the average night temperature is followed 48 hours later by the mass flowering of a colony, or all the colonies in that region subject to similar meteorological conditions. Sometimes the flowering occurs without a demonstrable drop in the night air temperature. Flowering is probably induced by a delicate combination of factors still unknown. It is not dependent upon precipitation." Luer goes on to state that, in combination with the above factors, day length may be responsible for triggering the precise moment that flowers open together during the day. Given that each flower lasts but a day, and that it sometimes takes up to a week for the next round of flower buds in the population to open, you must time your visit perfectly in order to observe blooming. Many a *Triphora* have I seen without an open flower!

Another factor that makes *Triphora* sometimes difficult to observe is its periodic dormancy. Plants plentiful in one year may be few or absent the next. *Triphora*, although photosynthetic during its short duration above ground, functions primarily as a saprophyte, and emerges from its subterranean chambers primarily for the purpose of reproduction. Thus, unless conditions are favorable for blooming, *Triphora* is perfectly content to remain underground and unseen. A visit to a population in subsequent years will likely reveal flowering plants again.

Plants of *Triphora trianthophora* with capsules on erect peduncles have been identified as variety *schaffneri* Camp. Camp (1940) cites a specimen (*Deam* 7202, IND) from Parke County, but the variety is not genuine, as erect capsules ultimately develop on all fruiting plants; they simply are the final developmental stage of capsule maturation (Medley, 1979).

Excluded Species

Calypso bulbosa (Linnaeus) Oakes

Dr. Clapp of New Albany, Indiana, placed marks next to this species as printed in his annotated copies of *A Synopsis of the Flora of the Western States* (Riddell, 1835) and *Manual of the Botany of the Northern United States* (Gray, 1848) (see Introduction, History of Indiana Orchidology). Clapp's marks indicate that he collected the said species within a twenty-mile radius of New Albany, north of the Ohio River. Other than the marks, no other notes appear next to the name *Calypso*. I have not encountered any specimens of *Calypso* collected by Clapp.

Calypso bulbosa is a boreal species that comes no closer to Indiana than the northern half of the lower peninsula of Michigan; its occurrence in southern Indiana is therefore extremely doubtful. I suspect that Dr. Clapp may have marked *Calypso* for what was really *Calopogon*. Although Clapp did not check *Calopogon* in his modified botany manuals, there are specimens with his labels (I think they are accurate—but see concern about label accuracy in discussion under *Malaxis monophyllos*, below) in the Wabash College collection. The occurrence of *Calopogon tuberosus* in appropriate habitats in southern Indiana is quite possible, particularly in the former barrens area of Harrison County where Clapp collected.

Goodyera repens (Linnaeus) R. Brown

This species was reported by Bradner (1892) for Steuben County. Given that he did not report *Goodyera pubescens*, a species that does occur in Steuben County, and that he applied incorrect names to other plants (e.g., *Spiranthes praecox* for *S. cernua*), it seems safe to assume that his report for *G. repens* is incorrect. Most likely Bradner mixed the specific epithets *repens* and *pubescens* inadvertently. If he indeed intended to identify the plants in question as *G. repens*, he was probably mistaking them for juvenile or depauperate specimens of *G. pubescens*. However, Case (1987) noted a collection of *G. repens* from Oakland County, Michigan, only four counties away from Steuben County, and thus it is not impossible for Bradner to have seen the orchid here. Without a voucher, however, it must be excluded.

Malaxis monophyllos (Linnaeus) Swartz var. **brachypoda**
(A. Gray) Morris and Eames

This species has been reported from at least three different localities in the state: one each for Carroll County (Thompson, 1892); Floyd County (Coulter, Coulter, and Barnes, 1881; Cunningham, 1896; Coulter, 1900; Deam, Yuncker and Friesner, 1951); and Porter County (Pepoon, 1927; Peattie, 1930). With the exception of a specimen of suspicious origin attributed to Floyd County, none of the reports are documented with a voucher. However, the orchid's occurrence in Indiana is not impossible, recognizing that we have suitable habitat in northern Indiana not far from known stations in nearby Allegan and Kalamazoo counties, Michigan, and Kane County, Illinois.

The report for Carroll County, made by Maurice Thompson (1892), is easily discounted. Aside from the fact that no voucher exists, Thompson's article in which the *Malaxis* is printed includes other plants that are obvious errors of determination or listing. Carroll County might have had appropriate habitat for the orchid, but its southerly location is probably too warm for the orchid's climatic tolerances.

The reports by Pepoon (1927) and Peattie (1930) may be accurate. Pepoon stated, and later paraphrased by Peattie, that a few plants occurred "in a cold tamarack swamp near Dune Park." Dune Park, not to be confused with Indiana Dunes State Park, was located in Porter County, and has since been destroyed. It apparently was a supreme natural area, harboring many rare and interesting plants (Wilhelm, 1990). The "cold tamarack swamp" would have been a perfect habitat for the *Malaxis*, as such is a primary habitat for it elsewhere.

Pepoon (1927) attributes his report of the *Malaxis* to "Clarke," a name for whom I have not determined an exact identity. Nor have I encountered any additional reports or collections to verify Pepoon's report. It is conceivable that the plants were confused with *Malaxis unifolia*, an orchid that is currently known from the Dunes area. Given that M. *unifolia* definitely occurs in the Dunes, and all reports of M. *monophyllos* from the Dunes are unverified, logic indicates that a misdetermination was made by Clarke, and the error was repeated in print by Pepoon and Peattie, as well as Fernald (1950). However, the seemingly suitable habitat once available at Dune Park, and the proximity of known stations of M. *monophyllos* in other states, suggest that Clarke's determination may have been correct.

A most interesting report of *Malaxis monophyllos* from southern Indiana was first made by Coulter, Coulter, and Barnes (1881). They cite a collection from the "Knobs" of Floyd County, made in 1836 by Clapp. The report was carried further in print by several authors (see above), until Deam (1940) excluded the report based on the lack of a voucher specimen, and because no note of such a collection was found in Clapp's annotated copies of Riddell (1835) and Gray (1848) (see Introduction, section on History of Indiana Orchidology). However, a specimen of M. *monophyllos* attributed to

Dr. Clapp was later found in the Wabash College Herbarium after the publication of Deam's Flora, and the record was thus accepted (Deam, Yuncker, and Friesner, 1951).

I have seen the Clapp specimen, and although it is mostly in fruit and has but a few yellowed flowers, it is nevertheless clearly *M. monophyllos*. On the specimen label is handwriting that reads: "Dr. Clapp, Knobs of Indiana, 1836." Also on the label is the machine-printed name "J. M. Coulter, Hanover College." Although the collection is properly identified and appears legitimate, I have such serious reservations about the specimen's indicated site of origin that I cannot accept the record for Indiana.

I trace the problem to the existing specimen label. In 1875, J. M. Coulter procured most if not all of the substantial collection of the late Dr. Clapp (Coulter, 1876). Shortly after obtaining the specimens Coulter completely remounted and relabeled all of them, a dangerous activity if not done with extreme care. Because of the distinct possibility of errors in remounting and relabeling specimens, the specimen may have been wrongfully labeled.

The main reason for my disbelief of the label locality information is the virtual impossibility of *Malaxis monophyllos* having grown at the latitude and environment of the "Knobs" of Floyd County, Indiana. The habitat within the Knobs is not specified on the label, but Stanley Coulter (1900) reported that the orchid grew "in moist woods in the southern counties." Where Coulter procured this information I do not know. "Moist woods" is not particularly informative and can be interpreted to indicate a variety of habitats, including ravine forests, floodplain forests, and possibly even wetlands. The Knobs region is characterized by rugged hills for the most part, and generally does not have wetland communities associated with it, but it does have what could be termed moist woods. Regardless of whatever "moist woods" refers to, *Malaxis monophyllos* is principally a plant of boreal wetlands characterized by alkaline, cold water seepage; i.e., fens, coniferous swamps, and springy stream borders, and it is highly unlikely that the orchid could occur in southern Indiana, especially in the Knobs. Thus, if Clapp did indeed collect *M. monophyllos* in the Knobs, it would have been a truly remarkable and most unusual find.

If Coulter did write inaccurate locality information for the *Malaxis monophyllos* specimen (which I think he did), one must still account for Clapp's possession of the specimen. Clapp was known to have traveled to the northeastern U.S. on several occasions, well within the range of *M. monophyllos*, and there on one of his botanical forays he may have collected the specimen. Another possibility is that Clapp might have acquired the specimen in a plant exchange, an activity which he is reported to have partaken with other botanists (Coulter, 1876). I therefore conclude that Clapp's specimen of *M. monophyllos* is not of Indiana origin, but most likely came from the northeastern U.S.

Platanthera blephariglottis (Willdenow) Lindley

Nieuwland (1913) reported this species for Lake Maxinkuckee in Marshall County on the authority of "Clarke." Presuming that Nieuwland was referring to H. W. Clark, one of the principal investigators of the Lake Maxinkuckee biological survey, it should be noted that Clark did not report *Platanthera blephariglottis* in his findings of the survey (Evermann and Clark, 1920). Given that Clark's report postdated Nieuwland's, it appears safe to assume that Clark never observed *P. blephariglottis* at Lake Maxinkuckee.

Platanthera blephariglottis is known to occur very close to Indiana's borders in Berrien County, Michigan (Sheviak, 1974; Swink and Wilhelm, 1979). There is also a collection from central Illinois, and a report for Cook County, Illinois (Higley and Raddin, 1891), believed to be correct (Sheviak, 1974). Such close occurrences suggest the real possibility of some day finding this orchid in Indiana.

Platanthera grandiflora (Bigelow) Lindley

There is a long history of confusion regarding *Platanthera grandiflora* and its most similar-looking congener, *P. psycodes*. Only relatively recently, with the publication by Stoutamire (1974) on the relationships of the two, did their taxonomy become clear. As well, it is now evident that *P. grandiflora* is far removed from our range, occurring no closer than eastern Ohio, and that any references to its occurrence here should be regarded as false.

Such is the case with the report made by Baird and Taylor (1878) for Clark County. They listed all three of the North American purple *Platanthera*s: *P. grandiflora*, *P. peramoena*, and *P. psycodes*. Almost certainly, only *P. peramoena* was truly observed; those identified as *P. grandiflora* and *P. psycodes* were most likely large individuals of *P. peramoena* with petals that had unusually deep serration on the margins. Clark County is beyond the range of known occurrences of *P. grandiflora* and *P. psycodes*, but more importantly, it does not appear to possess suitable habitat for them.

In light of the above information, I was surprised to encounter a specimen of *Platanthera grandiflora* attributed to Indiana. The specimen, clearly recognizable as *P. grandiflora* by its large flowers, open inflorescence, and large, widely separated pollinaria, was presumably taken by Dr. W. C. Ohlendorf at Miller's Station, Indiana in 1884 (*Ohlendorf s.n.*, MU). Unfortunately, I must exclude this record, as the evidence suggests that the specimen was not taken at the locality indicated. The specimen is labeled *Habenaria* (*Platanthera*) *ciliaris*. Although mistakes happen in identification and naming of plants, it is unlikely that one would make such a significant error as this. *Platanthera ciliaris* is obviously different from *P. grandiflora*, the two having very dissimilar flower shape and color. Only an error made in haste, or a lapse in thought, could account for the use of *P. ciliaris* for this plant. It appears that Ohlendorf, a Chicago area resident, sent a specimen or specimens to one E. Wilkinson, a graduate of Oberlin College and resident of Richland County, Ohio (Michael Vincent, personal communication). Wilkinson evidently labeled the specimen ("Herb. of E. Wilkinson" is machine-printed across the top of the specimen label) with Ohlendorf's name, the plant name, and locality and date, as the handwriting is in the same script as used on other E. Wilkinson labels.

The questions that now arise are: did Wilkinson make the error in incorrectly naming the plant; did he use the name provided by Ohlendorf; or did he (or an assistant) place a properly written label, one intended for an Ohlendorf specimen, on a specimen (the one in question) taken from elsewhere? I suspect the latter. *Platanthera ciliaris* did occur in Lake County, Indiana, and it is very possible that Ohlendorf collected the species there and shipped it to Wilkinson. Wilkinson, upon receiving the *P. ciliaris* specimen from Ohlendorf, properly prepared a label for it, but for some reason placed it not on the appropriate specimen, but on a plant that was collected from elsewhere, quite possibly northeastern Ohio, where *P. grandiflora* is known to occur.

It should be apparent that many unknowns exist regarding the above information, and consequently, I am not totally convinced that label mixing indeed happened (for example, is there a corresponding specimen of *P. ciliaris* somewhere that is incorrectly labeled?). The only way we can confirm with certainty the occurrence of *Platanthera grandiflora* in Indiana is to locate a properly labeled specimen taken from here, or better yet, to locate an extant population. Although I am doubtful of either event happening, neither is an impossibility. There are several species of plants that occur in the Dunes region that are disjuncts of greater distances than the distance between the known range of *P. grandiflora* and Lake County, Indiana. *Isotria medeoloides* is one such example. Thus, I will not be totally surprised if *P. grandiflora* is some day found here.

Spiranthes praecox (Walter) S. Watson in A. Gray

Reported by Baird and Taylor (1878) for Clark County, and Bradner (1892) for Steuben County. Cunningham (1896) and Coulter (1900) accepted the reports as valid, but Deam (1940) excluded them, based on the fact that neither Bradner nor Baird and Taylor listed *Spiranthes cernua*, a common species that they most likely observed. *Spiranthes praecox* is a southeastern Coastal Plain species far removed from our area. Its closest occurrences are in Arkansas, Mississippi, and North Carolina. It superficially resembles *S. cernua* , but differs from it in many ways: arrangement of flowers on the stem, lip pattern, and flowering season. Because of these differences, and its distant range, I concur with Deam's decision to exclude *S. praecox* from our flora.

Spiranthes tortilis (Swartz) L. C. Richard

This species was marked as occurring on "dry knobs" in the New Albany area by Dr. Clapp in his interleaved copy of *A Synopsis of the Flora of the Western States* (Riddell, 1835) (see Introduction, History of Indiana Orchidology). Riddell erroneously listed *Spiranthes tortilis* for the region of his flora (which included Indiana), when in fact it is known in the U.S. only from the southern tip of Florida. The confusion apparently was because of the orchid's similarity to *S. lacera*, the latter a species relatively common in the Midwest. Because of the great distance from Floyd County to the nearest *S. tortilis* population, the specimen Clapp noted certainly must have been *S. lacera*. *Spiranthes tortilis* therefore is excluded.

Appendix A:
Checklist and Pronunciation Guide

This is a list of the 46 taxa of orchids occurring wild in Indiana. In addition to the botanical and common names, a phonetic spelling is provided as a pronunciation guide. The pronunciations are those that are commonly used by American botanists—they do not necessarily follow strict Latin pronunciation rules.

☐ *Aplectrum hyemale*	(ā-plec′-trum hī-e-mā′-le; hī-e-mal′-ē)	puttyroot
☐ *Arethusa bulbosa*	(ar-e-thö′-sȧ bul-bō′-sȧ)	dragon's mouth
☐ *Calopogon tuberosus*	(kal-o-pō′-gon tö-ber-ō′-sus)	grass-pink
☐ *Coeloglossum viride*	(see-lō-gloss′-um vir′-i-dē)	long-bracted orchid
Corallorhiza	(kō-rall′-ō-rhī-zȧ; kôr′-a-lō-rhī′-zȧ)	
☐ *C. maculata*	(mak-ū-lā′-tȧ)	spotted coral-root
☐ *C. odontorhiza*	(ō-don-tō-rhī′-zȧ)	autumn coral-root
☐ *C. trifida*	(trif′-i-dȧ)	early coral-root
☐ *C. wisteriana*	(wis-tēr′-ē-ā-nȧ; wis-tēr′-ē-a-nȧ)	spring coral-root
Cypripedium	(sip-ri-pē′-dē-um)	
☐ *C. acaule*	(ā-câl′-ē)	pink lady's-slipper
☐ *C. X andrewsii*	(an-drö′-zē-ī)	Andrews' lady's-slipper
☐ *C. calceolus*	(kal-sē-ō′-lus; kal-sē′-ō-lus)	
var. *parviflorum*	(pär-vi-flôr′-um)	small yellow lady's-slipper
☐ *C. calceolus*		
var. *pubescens*	(pū-bes′-enz)	large yellow lady's-slipper
☐ *C. candidum*	(kan-dī′-dum; kan′-di-dum)	white lady's-slipper
☐ *C. reginae*	(rē-jī′-nē; rej′-i-nē)	showy lady's-slipper
☐ *Epipactis helleborine*	(ep-i-pak′-tis hel-e-bō-rī′-nē)	broad-leaved helleborine

☐	*Galearis spectabilis*	(gā-lē-ār′-is; gal′-ē-ār′-is spek-tab′-i-lis)	showy orchis
☐	*Goodyera pubescens*	(good-yer′-a pū-bes′-enz)	downy rattlesnake plantain
☐	*Hexalectris spicata*	(hex-a-lek′-tris spī-kā′-tà)	crested coral-root
☐	*Isotria verticillata*	(ī-sō′-tri-à vēr-ti-si-lā′-tà)	large whorled pogonia
	Liparis	(lip′-à-ris; lī-pār′-is)	
☐	*L. liliifolia*	(lil-ē-i-fō′-lē-à)	lily-leaved twayblade
☐	*L. loeselii*	(le-sel′-ē-ī)	Loesel's twayblade
☐	*Malaxis unifolia*	(mà-lax′-is ū-ni-fō′-lē-à)	green adder's-mouth
	Platanthera	(plà-tan′-thēr-à; plat-an-thēr′-à)	
☐	*P. ciliaris*	(sil-ē-ār′-is)	orange fringed-orchid
☐	*P. clavellata*	(kla-ve-lā′-tà)	club-spur orchid
☐	*P. dilatata*	(dil-a-tā′-tà; dil-a-tä′-tà)	tall white bog-orchid
☐	*P. flava* var. *flava*	(flā′-và)	southern tubercled orchid
☐	*P. flava* var. *herbiola*	(hēr-bē-ō′-là)	northern tubercled orchid
☐	*P. hookeri*	(hook′-ēr-ī)	Hooker's orchid
☐	*P. hyperborea*	(hī-pēr-bōr′-ē-à)	Northern green orchid
☐	*P. lacera*	(la′-cēr-à)	green fringed-orchid
☐	*P. leucophaea*	(lö-cō-fē′-à)	Eastern prairie fringed-orchid
☐	*P. orbiculata*	(ôr-bik′-ū-lā′-tà)	large round-leaved orchid
☐	*P. peramoena*	(pār-à-mē′-nà)	purple fringless-orchid
☐	*P. psycodes*	(sī-cō′-dēz)	small purple fringed-orchid
☐	*Pogonia ophioglossoides*	(pō-gō′-nē-à off-ē-ō-glâ-sō′-i-dēz; off-e-o-glâ-soy′-dēz)	rose pogonia
	Spiranthes	(spī-ran′-thēz)	
☐	*S. cernua*	(sērn′-ū-à)	nodding ladies'-tresses
☐	*S. lacera*	(la′-cēr-à)	slender ladies'-tresses
☐	*S. lucida*	(lö′-si-dà)	shining ladies'-tresses
☐	*S. magnicamporum*	(mag-ni-cam-pôr′-um)	Great Plains ladies'-tresses
☐	*S. ochroleuca*	(ok-rō-lö′-kà)	yellow ladies'-tresses
☐	*S. ovalis*	(ō-val′-is; ō-vāl′-is)	
	var. *erostellata*	(ē-ros-te-lāt′-à; ē-ros-te-lat′-à)	oval ladies'-tresses
☐	*S. romanzoffiana*	(rō-man-zof′-ē-ā-nà)	hooded ladies'-tresses
☐	*S. tuberosa*	(tö-be-rō′-sà)	little ladies'-tresses
☐	*S. vernalis*	(vēr-nā′-lis; vēr-nal′-is)	spring ladies'-tresses
☐	*Tipularia discolor*	(tip-ū-lār′-ē-à dis′-kul-ēr)	crane-fly orchid
☐	*Triphora trianthophora*	(trī-fôr′-à; trif′-ôr-à trī-an-thof′-ôr-à)	nodding pogonia

Key to Pronunciation

a as in pat   i as in pin
ā as in fate   ī as in pine
ä as in far   o as in not
âs in fall   ō as in go
ã as in care   ö as in move
à as in polka   ô as in for
e as in pet   u as in cut
ē as in be   ū as in mute
ẽ as in her

The syllables to be accented are marked with ʹ.

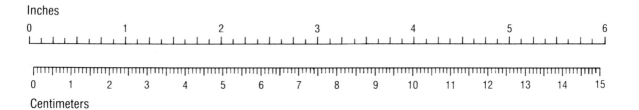

Inches

0   1   2   3   4   5   6

0 1 2 3 4 5 6 7 8 9 10 11 12 13 14 15

Centimeters

Appendix B:
Scientific and Common Names of Plants Cited in the Text

Only non-orchid taxa not identified in text by both scientific and common name are listed here. Nomenclature follows Gleason and Cronquist (1991). Where exceptions occur, the equivalent name in Gleason and Cronquist, followed by "GC," is given.

NAME	COMMON NAME	NAME	COMMON NAME
Abies balsamea	BALSAM FIR	*Allium tricoccum*	WILD LEEK
Acer rubrum	RED MAPLE	*Alnus incana*	SPECKLED ALDER
Achillea millefolium	YARROW	*Alnus serrulata*	SMOOTH ALDER
Actaea alba	WHITE BANEBERRY	*Amelanchier arborea*	JUNEBERRY
		Amorpha fruticosa	INDIGO BUSH
Adiantum pedatum	MAIDENHAIR FERN	*Amphicarpaea bracteata*	HOG PEANUT
Aesculus glabra	OHIO BUCKEYE	*Andropogon gyrans*	ELLIOTT'S BROOM SEDGE
Agalinis purpurea	PURPLE FALSE FOXGLOVE	*Andropogon scoparius* (= *Schizachyrium scoparium*, GC)	LITTLE BLUESTEM GRASS
Agalinis tenuifolia	SLENDER FALSE FOXGLOVE		
Agave virginica	FALSE ALOE	*Andropogon virginicus*	BROOM SEDGE
Agrimonia parviflora	SWAMP AGRIMONY	*Anemone virginiana*	TALL ANEMONE
		Antennaria plantaginifolia	PUSSY TOES
Aletris farinosa	COLIC ROOT		
Allium cernuum	NODDING WILD ONION	*Aralia nudicaulis*	WILD SARSAPARILLA

NAME	COMMON NAME	NAME	COMMON NAME
Arisaema triphyllum	JACK-IN-THE-PULPIT	*Carex albolutescens*	WHITE-YELLOW SEDGE
Aristida spp.	THREE-AWN GRASS	*Carex annectens* (= *C. vulpinoidea* var. *ambigua*, GC)	CONNECTED SEDGE
Aronia melanocarpa	BLACK CHOKEBERRY	*Carex atlantica* var. *atlantica*	ATLANTIC SEDGE
Aronia prunifolia	PURPLE CHOKEBERRY	*Carex atlantica* var. *capillacea*	HOWE'S SEDGE
Asarum canadense	WILD GINGER	*Carex bromoides*	BROME SEDGE
Asclepias syriaca	COMMON MILKWEED	*Carex careyana*	CAREY'S SEDGE
Asimina triloba	PAWPAW	*Carex cryptolepis*	MARL SEDGE
Asplenium platyneuron	EBONY SPLEENWORT	*Carex debilis*	TYPICAL SEDGE
Aster macrophyllus	BIG-LEAVED ASTER	*Carex frankii*	FRANK'S SEDGE
Aster oolentangiensis	SKY-BLUE ASTER	*Carex gracillima*	GRACEFUL SEDGE
Aster puniceus	SWAMP ASTER	*Carex granularis*	GRANULAR SEDGE
Aster shortii	SHORT'S ASTER	*Carex grayi*	BUR SEDGE
Aster undulatus	WAVY-LEAVED ASTER	*Carex hirsutella* (= *C. complanata* var. *hirsuta*, GC)	OLD-FIELD SEDGE
Athyrium filix-femina	LADY FERN	*Carex hirtifolia*	HAIRY SEDGE
Bartonia virginica	SCREWSTEM	*Carex hystericina*	BOTTLEBRUSH SEDGE
Betula pumila	DWARF BIRCH		
Boehmeria cylindrica	FALSE NETTLE	*Carex interior*	INLAND SEDGE
Botrychium dissectum	LACE-FROND GRAPE FERN	*Carex intumescens*	SWOLLEN SEDGE
Botrychium oneidense	BLUNT-LOBED GRAPE FERN	*Carex jamesii*	GRASS SEDGE
Botrychium simplex	LEAST MOONWORT	*Carex lasiocarpa*	HAIRY-FRUITED SEDGE
Botrychium virginianum	RATTLESNAKE FERN	*Carex laxiculmis*	LOOSE-STEMMED SEDGE
Brachyelytrum erectum	LONG-AWNED WOOD GRASS	*Carex leptalea*	BRISTLY-STALKED SEDGE
Cacalia plantaginea	PRAIRIE INDIAN PLANTAIN	*Carex louisianica*	LOUISIANA SEDGE
Calamagrostis canadensis	BLUE JOINT GRASS	*Carex lupulina*	HOP SEDGE
		Carex meadii	MEAD'S SEDGE
Caltha palustris	MARSH MARIGOLD	*Carex muskingumensis*	SWAMP SEDGE
Campsis radicans	TRUMPET CREEPER	*Carex pensylvanica*	PENNSYLVANIA SEDGE
Cardamine bulbosa	BULBOUS CRESS	*Carex picta*	PAINTED SEDGE

NAME	COMMON NAME	NAME	COMMON NAME
Carex plantaginea	PLANTAIN-LEAVED SEDGE	*Cornus rugosa*	ROUND-LEAVED DOGWOOD
Carex richardsonii	RICHARDSON'S SEDGE	*Cornus sericea*	RED-OSIER DOGWOOD
Carex shortiana	SHORT'S SEDGE	*Cornus* spp.	SHRUB DOGWOOD
Carex sterilis	STERILE SEDGE		
Carex stipata	CROWDED SEDGE	*Corylus americana*	AMERICAN HAZELNUT
Carex stricta	ERECT SEDGE	*Cryptotaenia*	HONEWORT
Carex swanii	SWAN'S SEDGE	*canadensis*	
Carex tribuloides	CALTROP SEDGE	*Cunila origanoides*	DITTANY
Carex typhina	CAT-TAIL SEDGE	*Cystopteris protrusa*	FRAGILE FERN
Carex viridula	GREEN SEDGE	*Danthonia spicata*	POVERTY OAT GRASS
Castilleja coccinea	INDIAN PAINT BRUSH		
		Daucus carota	WILD CARROT
Caulophyllum	BLUE COHOSH	*Decodon verticillatus*	SWAMP LOOSESTRIFE
thalictroides			
Celastrus scandens	CLIMBING BITTERSWEET	*Delphinium tricorne*	DWARF LARKSPUR
Cephalanthus	BUTTONBUSH	*Deschampsia cespitosa*	TUFTED HAIR GRASS
occidentalis			
Chamaecrista	PARTRIDGE PEA	*Desmodium ciliare*	HAIRY TICK TREFOIL
fasciculata			
Chamaedaphne	LEATHERLEAF	*Desmodium*	POINTED TICK TREFOIL
calyculata		*glutinosum*	
Chasmanthium	SPIKE GRASS	*Desmodium*	BARE-STEMMED TICK TREFOIL
latifolium		*nudiflorum*	
Cicuta bulbifera	BULBLET-BEARING WATER HEMLOCK	*Dicentra canadensis*	SQUIRREL CORN
		Dicentra cucullaria	DUTCHMAN'S BREECHES
		Dioscorea quaternata	WILD YAM
Cimicifuga racemosa	FALSE BUGBANE	*Dirca palustris*	LEATHERWOOD
Cinna arundinacea	COMMON WOOD REED	*Dodecatheon meadia*	SHOOTING STAR
		Drosera intermedia	NARROW-LEAVED SUNDEW
Circaea lutetiana	ENCHANTER'S NIGHTSHADE		
		Drosera rotundifolia	ROUND-LEAVED SUNDEW
Cladium mariscoides	TWIG RUSH		
Claytonia virginica	SPRING BEAUTY	*Dryopteris*	SPINULOSE SHIELD FERN
Conopholis americana	CANCER ROOT	*carthusiana*	
Coreopsis tripteris	TALL COREOPSIS	*Dryopteris cristata*	CRESTED SHIELD FERN
Cornus alternifolia	ALTERNATE-LEAVED DOGWOOD		
		Dryopteris marginalis	MARGINAL SHIELD FERN
Cornus racemosa	GRAY DOGWOOD		

NAME	COMMON NAME	NAME	COMMON NAME
Eleocharis rostellata	BEAKED SPIKE RUSH	*Filipendula rubra*	QUEEN OF THE PRAIRIE
Elymus virginicus	VIRGINIA WILD RYE	*Fragaria virginiana*	WILD STRAWBERRY
Epifagus virginiana	BEECH DROPS	*Fraxinus americana*	WHITE ASH
Epigaea repens	TRAILING ARBUTUS	*Galium concinnum*	SHINING BEDSTRAW
Epilobium coloratum	CINNAMON WILLOW HERB	*Galium triflorum*	SWEET-SCENTED BEDSTRAW
Equisetum arvense	FIELD HORSETAIL	*Gaultheria procumbens*	WINTERGREEN
Equisetum fluviatile	WATER HORSETAIL	*Gaylussacia baccata*	HUCKLEBERRY
Erigeron pulchellus	ROBIN'S PLANTAIN	*Gentianopsis crinita*	FRINGED GENTIAN
Eriophorum spp.	COTTON GRASS	*Geranium maculatum*	WILD GERANIUM
Eriophorum viridicarinatum	GREEN-KEELED COTTON GRASS	*Glyceria striata*	FOWL MEADOW GRASS
		Hamamelis virginiana	WITCH HAZEL
Eryngium yuccifolium	RATTLESNAKE-MASTER	*Helianthus hirsutus*	OBLONG SUNFLOWER
Erythronium americanum	YELLOW TROUT LILY	*Helianthus mollis*	DOWNY SUNFLOWER
Euonymus americanus	STRAWBERRY BUSH	*Helianthus occidentalis*	WESTERN SUNFLOWER
Euonymus obovatus	RUNNING STRAWBERRY BUSH	*Hepatica acutiloba*	SHARP-LOBED HEPATICA
		Hepatica americana	ROUND-LOBED HEPATICA
Eupatorium coelestinum	MISTFLOWER	*Hieracium* spp.	HAWKWEED
Eupatorium fistulosum	HOLLOW JOE PYE WEED	*Hybanthus concolor*	GREEN VIOLET
Eupatorium perfoliatum	COMMON BONESET	*Hydrangea arborescens*	WILD HYDRANGEA
Eupatorium rugosum	WHITE SNAKEROOT	*Hydrophyllum appendiculatum*	GREAT WATERLEAF
Euphorbia corollata	FLOWERING SPURGE	*Hydrophyllum canadense*	CANADA WATERLEAF
Euthamia graminifolia	FLAT-TOPPED GOLDENROD	*Hypericum kalmianum*	KALM'S ST. JOHN'S WORT
Festuca elatior	MEADOW FESCUE	*Hypericum prolificum*	SHRUBBY ST. JOHN'S WORT
Festuca subverticillata	NODDING FESCUE	*Hypoxis hirsuta*	YELLOW STAR GRASS
		Ilex verticillata	WINTERBERRY

NAME	COMMON NAME	NAME	COMMON NAME
Impatiens capensis	SPOTTED TOUCH-ME-NOT	*Lobelia kalmii*	BOG LOBELIA
		Lobelia puberula	DOWNY LOBELIA
		Lobelia spicata	PALE SPIKED LOBELIA
Iris cristata	DWARF CRESTED IRIS	*Lycopodium digitatum*	TRAILING GROUND PINE
Iris virginica	BLUE FLAG		
Juncus arcticus var. *littoralis*	LAKE SHORE RUSH	*Lycopodium inundatum*	BOG CLUB MOSS
Juncus effusus	COMMON RUSH	*Lysimachia ciliata*	FRINGED LOOSESTRIFE
Juncus tenuis var. *dudleyi*	DUDLEY'S RUSH	*Lysimachia nummularia*	MONEYWORT
Juncus tenuis var. *tenuis*	ROADSIDE RUSH	*Lysimachia quadriflora*	NARROW-LEAVED LOOSESTRIFE
Juniperus communis var. *depressa*	COMMON JUNIPER	*Lysimachia quadrifolia*	WHORLED LOOSESTRIFE
Juniperus virginiana	RED CEDAR	*Lythrum alatum*	WINGED LOOSESTRIFE
Krigia biflora	FALSE DANDELION	*Maianthemum canadense*	CANADA MAYFLOWER
Larix laricina	TAMARACK	*Maianthemum canadense* var. *interius*	CANADA MAYFLOWER
Leavenworthia uniflora	LEAVENWORTHIA		
Leersia oryzoides	RICE CUT GRASS	*Medeola virginiana*	INDIAN CUCUMBER ROOT
Lespedeza hirta	HAIRY BUSH CLOVER		
Lespedeza virginica	SLENDER BUSH CLOVER	*Menyanthes trifoliata*	BUCKBEAN
Lespedeza spp.	BUSH CLOVER	*Mitchella repens*	PARTRIDGE BERRY
Liatris aspera	ROUGH BLAZING STAR	*Mitella diphylla*	BISHOP'S CAP
Liatris spicata	MARSH BLAZING STAR	*Muhlenbergia glomerata*	MARSH WILD TIMOTHY
Liatris squarrosa	SQUARROSE BLAZING STAR	*Nemopanthus mucronatus*	MOUNTAIN HOLLY
Liatris squarrulosa	SOUTHERN BLAZING STAR	*Nyssa sylvatica*	BLACK GUM
Lindera benzoin	SPICEBUSH	*Onoclea sensibilis*	SENSITIVE FERN
Linum virginianum	SLENDER YELLOW FLAX	*Opuntia humifusa*	PRICKLY PEAR
		Osmorhiza claytonii	HAIRY SWEET CICELY
Lithospermum canescens	HOARY PUCCOON	*Osmorhiza longistylis*	SMOOTH SWEET CICELY
Lithospermum caroliniense	HAIRY PUCCOON	*Osmunda cinnamomea*	CINNAMON FERN
Lobelia cardinalis	CARDINAL FLOWER	*Osmunda regalis*	ROYAL FERN

NAME	COMMON NAME	NAME	COMMON NAME
Ostrya virginiana	HOP HORNBEAM	*Polygonatum pubescens*	DOWNY SOLOMON'S SEAL
Oxypolis rigidior	COWBANE		
Panax quinquefolium	GINSENG		
Panax trifolium	DWARF GINSENG	*Polygonum scandens*	CLIMBING FALSE BUCKWHEAT
Panicum anceps	TWO-EDGED PANIC GRASS		
Panicum clandestinum	DEER-TONGUE GRASS	*Polygonum virginianum*	WOODLAND KNOTWEED
		Polymnia canadensis	LEAFCUP
Panicum depauperatum	STARVED PANIC GRASS	*Polystichum acrostichoides*	CHRISTMAS FERN
Panicum dichotomum	FORKED PANIC GRASS	*Potentilla fruticosa*	SHRUBBY CINQUEFOIL
Panicum implicatum (= *P. lanuginosum* var. *implicatum*, GC)	TANGLED PANIC GRASS	*Potentilla palustris*	MARSH CINQUEFOIL
		Potentilla simplex	COMMON CINQUEFOIL
Parnassia glauca	GRASS OF PARNASSUS	*Prunella vulgaris*	LAWN PRUNELLA
		Prunus virginiana	CHOKE CHERRY
Parthenocissus quinquefolia	VIRGINIA CREEPER	*Pteridium aquilinum*	BRACKEN FERN
Pedicularis canadensis	WOOD BETONY	*Pycnanthemum tenuifolium*	SLENDER MOUNTAIN MINT
Pedicularis lanceolata	SWAMP BETONY		
Phlox divaricata	BLUE PHLOX	*Pycnanthemum virginianum*	COMMON MOUNTAIN MINT
Phlox glaberrima	MARSH PHLOX		
Phlox paniculata	GARDEN PHLOX		
Phlox pilosa	PRAIRIE PHLOX	*Pyrola elliptica*	LARGE-LEAVED SHINLEAF
Phryma leptostachya	LOPSEED		
Picea mariana	BLACK SPRUCE	*Pyrola rotundifolia*	ROUND-LEAVED SHINLEAF
Pilea pumila	CLEARWEED		
Poa compressa	CANADA BLUE GRASS	*Quercus rubra*	RED OAK
		Ranunculus hispidus	ROUGH BUTTERCUP
Poa paludigena	BOG BLUE GRASS		
Poa pratensis	KENTUCKY BLUE GRASS	*Ranunculus septentrionalis* (= *R. hispidus* var. *nitidus*, GC)	SWAMP BUTTERCUP
Poa sylvestris	WOODLAND BLUE GRASS		
Podophyllum peltatum	MAY APPLE	*Ratibida pinnata*	YELLOW CONEFLOWER
Polygala cruciata	CROSS MILKWORT	*Rhamnus alnifolia*	ALDER BUCKTHORN
Polygala sanguinea	FIELD MILKWORT	*Rhexia virginica*	MEADOW BEAUTY
Polygonatum biflorum	SMOOTH SOLOMON'S SEAL	*Rhus aromatica*	FRAGRANT SUMAC

NAME	COMMON NAME	NAME	COMMON NAME
Rhus copallinum	SHINING SUMAC	*Sanicula canadensis*	CANADIAN BLACK SNAKEROOT
Rhus radicans (= *Toxicodendron radicans*, GC)	POISON IVY	*Sarracenia purpurea*	PITCHER PLANT
Rhus typhina	STAGHORN SUMAC	*Sassafras albidum*	SASSAFRAS
		Saururus cernuus	LIZARD'S TAIL
Rhus vernix (= *Toxicodendron vernix*, GC)	POISON SUMAC	*Saxifraga pensylvanica*	SWAMP SAXIFRAGE
		Scheuchzeria palustris	ARROW GRASS
Rhynchospora alba	WHITE BEAK RUSH	*Scirpus acutus*	HARD-STEMMED BULRUSH
Rhynchospora capillacea	HAIR BEAK RUSH	*Scirpus americanus*	CHAIRMAKER'S RUSH
Ribes americanum	WILD BLACK CURRANT	*Scirpus cyperinus*	WOOL GRASS
		Scirpus lineatus	RED BULRUSH
Rosa palustris	SWAMP ROSE	*Scleria oligantha*	GLOSSY NUT RUSH
Rubus hispidus	SWAMP DEWBERRY	*Scleria pauciflora*	FEW-FLOWERED NUT RUSH
Rubus occidentalis	BLACK RASPBERRY	*Scleria reticularis*	NETTED NUT RUSH
Rudbeckia hirta	BLACK-EYED SUSAN	*Scleria triglomerata*	TALL NUT RUSH
Rudbeckia laciniata	WILD GOLDEN GLOW	*Scleria verticillata*	LOW NUT RUSH
		Scutellaria lateriflora	MAD-DOG SKULLCAP
Rumex acetosella	FIELD SORREL	*Selaginella eclipes* (= *S. apoda*, GC)	HIDDEN SPIKE-MOSS
Sabatia angularis	ROSE GENTIAN		
Salix candida	HOARY WILLOW	*Senecio aureus*	GOLDEN RAGWORT
Salix caroliniana	CAROLINA WILLOW	*Senecio obovatus*	ROUND-LEAVED RAGWORT
Salix discolor	PUSSY WILLOW	*Senecio pauperculus* var. *balsamitae*	BALSAM RAGWORT
Salix humilis	PRAIRIE WILLOW		
Salix myricoides	BLUE-LEAVED WILLOW	*Silene virginica*	FIRE PINK
		Silphium terebinthinaceum	PRAIRIE DOCK
Salix pedicellaris	BOG WILLOW		
Salix petiolaris	PETIOLED WILLOW	*Silphium trifoliatum*	WHORLED ROSINWEED
Salix sericea	SILKY WILLOW	*Smilacina racemosa*	FEATHERY FALSE SOLOMON'S SEAL
Salix syrticola (= *S. cordata*, GC)	DUNE WILLOW		
Salix spp.	WILLOW	*Smilacina stellata*	STARRY FALSE SOLOMON'S SEAL
Sanguinaria canadensis	BLOODROOT		

NAME	COMMON NAME	NAME	COMMON NAME
Smilax rotundifolia	GREEN BRIER	*Thelypteris noveboracensis*	NEW YORK FERN
Solidago bicolor	WHITE GOLDENROD	*Thelypteris palustris*	MARSH FERN
Solidago caesia	BLUE-STEMMED GOLDENROD	*Thuja occidentalis*	ARBOR VITAE
		Tofieldia glutinosa	FALSE ASPHODEL
Solidago canadensis var. scabra	TALL GOLDENROD	*Tradescantia ohiensis*	COMMON SPIDERWORT
Solidago flexicaulis	BROAD-LEAVED GOLDENROD	*Triadenum tubulosum*	MARSH ST. JOHN'S-WORT
Solidago hispida	HAIRY GOLDENROD	*Tridens flavus*	FALSE REDTOP
Solidago juncea	EARLY GOLDENROD	*Trientalis borealis*	STARFLOWER
		Trifolium repens	WHITE CLOVER
Solidago nemoralis	OLD-FIELD GOLDENROD	*Triglochin maritimum*	COMMON BOG ARROW GRASS
Solidago ohioensis	OHIO GOLDENROD	*Trillium grandiflorum*	LARGE-FLOWERED TRILLIUM
Solidago patula	SWAMP GOLDENROD		
Solidago ulmifolia	ELM-LEAVED GOLDENROD	*Typha angustifolia*	NARROW-LEAVED CAT-TAIL
Sorghastrum nutans	INDIAN GRASS	*Typha latifolia*	COMMON CAT-TAIL
Spartina pectinata	PRAIRIE CORD GRASS	*Utricularia intermedia*	FLAT-LEAVED BLADDERWORT
Spiraea alba	MEADOWSWEET	*Utricularia subulata*	ZIGZAG BLADDERWORT
Spiraea tomentosa	HARDHACK		
Staphylea trifolia	BLADDERNUT	*Uvularia grandiflora*	LARGE-FLOWERED BELLWORT
Stellaria pubera	GREAT CHICKWEED		
Strophostyles umbellata	TRAILING WILD BEAN	*Vaccinium angustifolium*	EARLY LOW BLUEBERRY
Stylophorum diphyllum	CELANDINE POPPY	*Vaccinium arboreum*	FARKLEBERRY
		Vaccinium atrococcum (= V. corymbosum, GC)	BLACK HIGHBUSH BLUEBERRY
Stylosanthes biflora	PENCIL FLOWER		
Symplocarpus foetidus	SKUNK CABBAGE		
Talinum rugospermum	FAME FLOWER	*Vaccinium corymbosum*	HIGHBUSH BLUEBERRY
Tephrosia virginiana	GOAT'S RUE	*Vaccinium macrocarpon*	LARGE CRANBERRY
Thalictrum revolutum	WAXY MEADOW RUE		
Thaspium barbinode	HAIRY MEADOW PARSNIP	*Vaccinium oxycoccos*	SMALL CRANBERRY
Thaspium trifoliatum	MEADOW PARSNIP	*Vaccinium pallidum*	LATE LOW BLUEBERRY

NAME	COMMON NAME	NAME	COMMON NAME
Viburnum acerifolium	MAPLE-LEAVED ARROW-WOOD	*Viola pubescens*	DOWNY YELLOW VIOLET
Viburnum cassinoides (= *V. nudum* var. cassinoides, GC)	WITHE ROD	*Viola rostrata*	LONG-SPURRED VIOLET
Viburnum lentago	NANNYBERRY	*Viola sororia*	HAIRY WOOD VIOLET
Viburnum prunifolium	BLACK HAW	*Viola triloba* (= *V. palmata*, GC)	THREE-LOBED VIOLET
Viburnum rufidulum	SOUTHERN BLACK HAW	*Vitis labrusca*	FOX GRAPE
Viola lanceolata	LANCE-LEAVED VIOLET	*Woodwardia virginica*	CHAIN FERN
Viola pallens (= *V. macloskeyi*, GC)	SMOOTH WHITE VIOLET	*Xyris torta*	YELLOW-EYED GRASS
Viola pedata	BIRD'S FOOT VIOLET	*Zigadenus elegans*	WHITE CAMASS
		Zizia aurea	GOLDEN ALEXANDERS

Glossary

AGAMOSPERMY	The formation of viable seeds without fertilization.
ANGIOSPERM	Those plants that have (or have the potential for having) flowers (as opposed to non-flowering plants, such as ferns, mosses, etc.).
ANTHER	The pollen-bearing portion of the stamen, typically located at the apex of a column (in orchids).
ANTHESIS	The time period when a plant's flower or flowers are open.
APOMIXIS	Reproduction by asexual means.
AUTOGAMY	Self-fertilization.
BEDROCK	Solid rock that typically occurs underneath the soil surface. In places it appears above the surface to form cliffs.
BILATERAL SYMMETRY	A condition of flowers whereby the right and left halves are identical, like a mirror image. The upper and lower halves are unlike, however.
BULBIL	A bulblike body produced on the above-ground part of the plant. Some bulbils are capable of developing into new plants.
CALCAREOUS	Consisting of, or containing, calcium or calcium carbonate. Such materials are alkaline.
CALCIPHILE	A plant which requires a calcareous substrate.
CAPITATE	Shaped like a rounded head.
CAPSULE	A dry fruit, or seed-pod, that splits when ripe. In orchids the capsules are thin-walled with thousands of minute seeds.
CHASMOGAMOUS	A condition whereby the flower is open and available for cross-pollination.
CHLOROPHYLL	A green-pigmented substance used by plants for the manufacture of food.
CLEISTOGAMOUS	A condition whereby the flower is closed and self-fertilized. Fertilization in bud.

COLUMN	The main reproductive structure of an orchid, composed of fused stamens and pistils (minus the ovary).
CORM	A bulb-like, enlarged, fleshy base of a stem.
CRYPTOPHYTE	Plants which have overwintering buds buried in or submersed in the substrate.
CUNEATE	Wedge-shaped, triangular, narrowing toward the base.
DIANDROUS	Possessing two anthers.
DICOTYLEDON(S)	Flowering plants that typically have net-veined leaves, two seed-leaves (cotyledons), and flower parts in 4's, 5's, or other multiples, but normally not in 3's.
ELLIPTIC	A circular shape, widest at the middle, with margins curving symmetrically and equally toward each tip, as if laterally compressed.
EXTIRPATED	The local absence of an organism in an area where it formerly occurred. Extinct is best used to refer to global absence. Extant indicates confirmed occurrence in an area.
FALCATE	Scythe-shaped.
FERTILIZATION	The sexual union of egg and sperm.
FILAMENT	The thread-like portion of a stamen that supports the anther.
FILIFORM	Thread-shaped.
FRUIT	A mature or ripened ovary that generally contains seeds.
GEOPHYTE	A specific type of cryptophyte, with the overwintering bud buried in soil.
GLABROUS	Without hair.
HEMICRYPTOPHYTE	Plants which have overwintering buds at the soil surface.
HEMIPOLLINARIUM	One of two pollinaria in orchid flowers that possess two distinct viscidia (of the pair, a single viscidium with the attached stipe or caudicle and pollinium [or pollinia]).
HERBARIUM	A storage place for pressed and dried plant specimens.
HYPHA(E)	Individual thread-like segments of a fungus. Collectively, they compose the fungus body (not to be confused with a fruiting body, or "mushroom").
INFLORESCENCE	That part of the plant that possesses the flowers.
JEWELACEOUS	The shiny, crisp, crystalline to bead-like quality of the perianth of some flowers.
LABELLUM	Another name for lip.
LANCEOLATE	Shaped like a lance, broadest below the middle and tapering upward to a slender tip. Much longer than broad.
LIP	The one of the three petals of an orchid flower that is typically larger and different in shape and color

	from the other two. In most orchids, it is also the lowermost petal.
MARL	A whitish to grayish unconsolidated deposit composed of a mixture of clay and calcium carbonate, and commonly also shell fragments. Marl is very alkaline.
MESIC	A moisture condition (of a substrate) that is midway between wet and dry. A mesic substrate is moderately drained but moist for most of the year.
MONANDROUS	Possessing only one anther.
MONOCOTYLEDON(S)	Flowering plants that typically have parallel venation, a single seed leaf (cotyledon), and flower parts three or multiples thereof.
MUCK	A dark-colored, well-decomposed organic soil material.
MYCORRHIZA(E)	A symbiotic relationship between vascular plants and fungi, formed through the connection between plant roots and fungal mycelia.
OBLANCEOLATE	Inversely lanceolate (broadest above the middle).
OBLONG	A rectangular shape, widest in the middle, with essentially parallel margins.
OBOVATE	Inversely ovate (broadest above the middle).
OBOVOID	The form of an egg, with the large end toward the tip.
ORBICULAR	Circular.
OUTCROSSING	Pollination between two different plants of the same species.
OVARY	The lowermost portion of a pistil. In maturity, it becomes a seed-laden fruit.
OVATE	Shaped like an egg, widest below the middle, curving symmetrically upward to a gradually narrowed point. Only slightly longer than broad.
PANDURATE	Fiddle-shaped.
PARASITE	A plant that grows on another plant and derives most or all of its nutrition from it.
PEDICEL	The stem that supports an individual flower.
PERIANTH	The combined total of the sepals and petals of a flower. Basically, the perianth comprises the "showy" parts of the flower.
PETALS	White or colored flower segments located within the sepals.
pH	In general, pH is the measure of alkalinity or acidity of a solution. On a scale of 1 to 14, with 7 being neutral, solutions decreasing from 7 are increasingly acidic, while solutions increasing in pH from 7 are increasingly alkaline.
PHENOLOGY	The study of the seasonal or periodic attributes of an organism, such as flowering dates of plants.
PHYLLOTAXY	The arrangement of leaves or flowers on a stem.

PISTIL	The female reproductive structure of a flower, composed of a stigma, style, and ovary.
PLICATE	Folded, usually lengthwise, such as in pleats.
POLLINARIUM	A unit consisting of pollinium, stipe, and viscidium.
POLLINATION	The application of pollen to the stigma.
POLLINIUM (PL. POLLINIA)	A coherent mass of pollen.
PUBESCENT	Hairy.
QUADRATE	Squarish in shape.
RACEME	An inflorescence of pedicelled flowers attached to a single, elongated stem.
RACHIS	The main axis, or central stalk within an inflorescence.
RANK	A row of flowers within an inflorescence.
RESUPINATION	A condition where the lip is in the lowermost position on the flower (this accomplished by a twisting at the pedicel).
ROSTELLUM	That structure that separates the anther and functional stigma. It is thought to be sterile stigmatic tissue. In some orchids it produces a sticky substance that glues pollinia to a visiting insect.
SAPROPHYTE	A plant that, being unable to manufacture its own food, derives its nutrition from decaying organic matter.
SCAPE	A leafless flowering stem, commonly arising from the ground.
SCROTIFORM	Bag-shaped.
SECUND	Arranged on one side of a stem.
SEPALS	The outermost (closest to pedicel) flower segments. These are normally green, but are white or colored in most orchids.
SESSILE	Without a stalk.
SPATULATE	Broadest at the end, like a spatula.
SPIKE	An inflorescence of sessile flowers attached to a single, elongated stem.
STAMEN	The male reproductive structure of a flower, composed of a filament and anther.
STAMINODE	A sterile stamen.
STIGMA	The apical portion of a pistil that receives the pollen.
STIPE	A stalk that connects the viscidium with a pollinium (pollinia).
STOLON	An elongate, horizontal stem with long internodes, and rooting at the tip to form new plants.
STYLE	In a pistil, the connecting structure between the ovary and stigma.
SUBSTRATE	The medium in which a plant's roots grow. Soil is the principal substrate for terrestrial plants.

SYMBIOSIS	A relationship, or living together of different organisms, in which both benefit.
TAXON (PL. TAXA)	A taxonomic entity at any level; e.g., form, variety, species, etc.
TRIDENTATE	Having three teeth.
TUBERCLE	A small, tuber-like prominence.
VISCIDIUM	A sticky, pad-like structure of the rostellum that is connected by a stipe to the pollinium.
XERIC	An excessively drained, extremely dry condition (of a substrate).

Literature Cited

Aldrich, J. R., J. A. Bacone, and M. A. Homoya. List of extirpated, endangered, threatened, and rare vascular plants in Indiana: an update. Proceedings of the Indiana Academy of Science 95:413–419.

Aldrich, J. R., L. A. Casebere, M. A. Homoya, and H. Starcs. 1986. The discovery of native rare vascular plants in northern Indiana. Proceedings of the Indiana Academy of Science 95:421–428.

Ames, O. 1905. A synopsis of the genus *Spiranthes* north of Mexico. Orchidaceae 1:122–156.

Ames, O. 1922. A discussion of *Pogonia* and its allies in the northeastern United States. Orchidaceae 7:3–38.

Andrews, F. M. 1927. Some flowering plants of Monroe County, Indiana. Proceedings of the Indiana Academy of Science 37:330–334.

Auclair, A. N. 1972. Comparative ecology of the orchids *Aplectrum hyemale* and *Orchis spectabilis*. Bulletin of the Torrey Botanical Club 99(1):1–10.

Baird, J. F., and J. L. Taylor. 1878. Catalogue of phanerogamous and vascular cryptogamous plants of Clark County, Ind. Manual of the public schools of Clark County, Ind. for 1878–9:46–65.

Blatchley, W. S. 1897. A catalogue of the uncultivated ferns and fern allies (Pteridophyta) and the flowering plants (Spermatophyta) of Vigo County, Indiana. Twenty-first Annual Report of the Indiana Department of Geology and Natural Resources 21:577–708.

Bowles, M. L. 1983. The tallgrass prairie orchids *Platanthera leucophaea* (Nutt.) Lindl. and *Cypripedium candidum* Muhl. *ex* Willd.: some aspects of their status, biology, and ecology, and implications toward management. Natural Areas Journal 3 (4):14–37.

Bowles, M. L. 1987. The status of Indiana special concern (endangered, threatened, and rare) vascular plants at Indiana Dunes, Clarke and Pine, Shell, Gibson Woods, Hoosier Prairie, and Tefft Savanna nature preserves. A report submitted to the Division of Nature Preserves, Indiana Department of Natural Resources. The Morton Arboretum, Lisle, Illinois. 147 p.

Bowles, M. L., W. J. Hess, and M. M. De Mauro. 1986. An assessment of the monitoring program for special floristic elements at Indiana Dunes National Lakeshore. Phase II. Threatened and special concern species. A report submitted to the Indiana Dunes National Lakeshore, U.S. Department of the Interior. The Morton Arboretum, Lisle, Illinois. 375 p.

Brackley, F. E. 1985. The orchids of New Hampshire. Rhodora 87:1–117.

Bradner, E. 1892. A partial catalogue of the flora of Steuben County. Seventeenth Annual Report of the Indiana Department of Geology and Natural Resources 17:135–159.

Braun, E. L. 1950. Deciduous forests of eastern North America. The Blakiston Company, Philadelphia, Pennsylvania. 596 p.

Braun, E. L. 1967. The vascular flora of Ohio. Vol. I: The *Monocotyledoneae*. Ohio State University Press, Columbus. 464 p.

Britton, N. L. 1901. Manual of the flora of the northern states and Canada. Henry Holt and Company, New York, New York. 1080 p.

Brunson, M. E. 1942. Distribution of Indiana Orchidaceae. Butler University Botanical Studies 5:173–178.

Camp, W. H. 1940. A new variety of *Triphora*. Rhodora 42:55–56.

Campbell, E. O. 1970. Morphology of the fungal association in three species of *Corallorhiza* in Michigan. Michigan Botanist 9:108–113.

Case, F. W. 1987. Orchids of the western Great Lakes region. Revised edition. Cranbrook Institute of Science, Bulletin 48, 251 p.

Case, F. W., and P. M. Catling. 1983. The genus *Spiranthes* in Michigan. Michigan Botanist 22:79–92.

Case, F. W., with William Schwab. 1971. *Isotria medeoloides*, the smaller whorled pogonia, in Michigan. Michigan Botanist 10:39–43.

Case, L. B. 1881. Hardy native orchids. L. B. Case's Botanical Index 4(2):25–30.

Catling, P. M. 1980. Rain-assisted autogamy in *Liparis loeselii* (L.) L. C. Rich. (Orchidaceae). Bulletin of the Torrey Botanical Club 107(4):525–529.

Catling, P. M. 1982. Breeding systems of northeastern North American *Spiranthes* (Orchidaceae). Canadian Journal of Botany 60:3017–3039.

Catling, P. M. 1983a. Pollination of northeastern North American *Spiranthes* (Orchidaceae). Canadian Journal of Botany 61:1080–1093.

Catling, P. M. 1983b. *Spiranthes ovalis* var. *erostellata* (Orchidaceae), a new autogamous variety from the eastern United States. Brittonia 35(2):120–125.

Catling, P. M. 1983c. Terrestrial orchids in Canada. Pages 87–132 *in* E. H. Plaxton, ed., North American terrestrial orchids, symposium II, proceedings and lectures. Michigan Orchid Society, Southfield, Michigan. 143 p.

Catling, P. M. 1991. Systematics of *Malaxis bayardii* and *M. unifolia*. Lindleyana 6(1): 3–23.

Catling, P. M., and V. R. Catling. 1991a. Anther-cap retention in *Tipularia discolor*. Lindleyana 6(2):113–116.

Catling, P. M., and V. R. Catling. 1991b. A synopsis of breeding systems and pollination in North American orchids. Lindleyana 6(4):187–210.

Catling, P. M., and G. Knerer. 1980. Pollination of the small white lady's-slipper (*Cypripedium candidum*) in Lambton County, southern Ontario. The Canadian Field-Naturalist 94:435–438.

Clapp, A. 1852. A synopsis; or, systematic catalogue of the indigenous and naturalized, flowering and filicoid (exogens, endogens, and acrogens), medicinal plants of the United States. Transactions of the American Medical Association 5:659–906.

Correll, D. S. 1978. Native orchids of North America north of Mexico. Stanford University Press, Stanford, California. 399 p.

Coulter, J. M. 1875. A partial list of the flora of Jefferson County. Sixth Annual Report of the Geological Survey of Indiana 6:230–277.

Coulter, J. M. 1876. An interesting herbarium. Botanical Bulletin (Gazette) 1(3):9–10.

Coulter, J. M., S. Coulter, and C. R. Barnes. 1881. Catalogue of the phanerogamous and vascular cryptogamous plants of Indiana. Review Steam Book and Job Printers, Crawfordsville, Indiana. 38 p.

Coulter, S. 1900. A catalogue of the flowering plants and of the ferns and their allies indigenous to Indiana. Twenty-fourth Annual Report of the Department of Geology and Natural Resources of Indiana. 24:553–1002, 1019–1074.

Crankshaw, W. B. 1989. Manual of the seed plants of Indiana. Monograph No. 6. Indiana Academy of Science, Indianapolis. 278 p.

Crovello, T. J., C. A. Keller, and J. T. Kartesz. 1983. The vascular plants of Indiana: a computer based checklist. University of Notre Dame Press, Notre Dame, Indiana. 136 p.

Cunningham, A. M. 1896. Distribution of the Orchidaceae in Indiana. Proceedings of the Indiana Academy of Science 1895:198–202.

Dana, M. W. S. 1908. How to know the wild flowers. Charles Scribner's Sons, New York, New York. 346 p.

Deam, C. C. 1912. Additions to the flora of the lower Wabash Valley, by Dr. J. Schneck. Proceedings of the Indiana Academy of Science 1911:365–369.

Deam, C. C. 1940. Flora of Indiana. Indiana Department of Conservation, Indianapolis. 1236 p.

Deam, C. C., T. G. Yuncker, and R. C. Friesner. 1951. Indiana plant distribution records XI. 1950. Proceedings of the Indiana Academy of Science 60:82–90.

Dressler, R. L. 1981. The orchids—natural history and classification. Harvard University Press, Cambridge, Massachusetts. 332 p.

Drew, W. B., and R. A. Giles. 1951. *Epipactis helleborine* (L.) Crantz in Michigan, and its general range in North America. Rhodora 53:240–242.

Ettman, J. K., and D. R. McAdoo. 1979. An annotated catalog and distribution account of the Kentucky Orchidaceae. The Kentucky Society of Natural History Charitable Trust, Louisville. 32 p.

Evermann, B. W., and H. W. Clark. 1920. Lake Maxinkuckee, Vol. 2. Indiana Department of Conservation, Indianapolis. 512 p.

Fernald, M. L. 1946. Technical studies on North American plants. Rhodora 48:5–16.

Fernald, M. L. 1950. Gray's manual of botany, 8th ed. American Book Company, New York, New York. 1632 p.

Freudenstein, J. V. 1987. A preliminary study of *Corallorhiza maculata* (Orchidaceae) in eastern North America. Contributions from the University of Michigan Herbarium 16:145–153.

Gibson, W. H. 1905. Our native orchids. Doubleday, Page, and Company, New York, New York. 158 p.

Gleason, H. A. 1952. The new Britton and Brown illustrated flora of the northeastern United States and adjacent Canada. Vol. 1. New York Botanical Garden, New York. 482 p.

Gleason, H. A., and A. Cronquist. 1991. Manual of vascular plants of northeastern United States and adjacent Canada. The New York Botanical Garden, Bronx. 910 p.

Gray, A. 1848. Manual of the botany of the northern United States. J. Munroe, Boston, Massachusetts. 710 p.

Gray, A. 1879. *Epipactis helleborine*, var. *viridens* (*E. viridiflora*, Reichenbach), a North American plant. Botanical Gazette 4(9):206.

Harley, J. L., and S. E. Smith. 1983. Mycorrhizal symbiosis. Academic Press, New York, New York. 483 p.

Higley, W. K., and C. S. Raddin. 1891. The flora of Cook County, Illinois, and a part of Lake County, Indiana. Bulletin of the Chicago Academy of Sciences 2(1):1–168.

Hill, E. J. 1878. A double-flowered *Cypripedium spectabile*. American Naturalist 12:816–817.

Hogan, K. P. 1983. The pollination biology and breeding system of *Aplectrum hyemale* (Orchidaceae). Canadian Journal of Botany 61:1906–1910.

Homoya, M. A. 1977. The distribution and ecology of the genus *Isotria* in Illinois. Master's thesis, Southern Illinois University, Carbondale. 104 p.

Homoya, M. A., D. B. Abrell, J. R. Aldrich, and T. W. Post. 1985. The natural regions of Indiana. Proceedings of the Indiana Academy of Science 94:245–268.

Hull, E. D. 1935. *Arethusa bulbosa*. American Botanist 41:29–30.

Kravig, M. L. 1969. Orchids of the Black Hills. Master's thesis, Black Hills State College, Spearfish, South Dakota. 21 p.

Light, M. H. S., and M. MacConaill. 1989. Albinism in *Platanthera hyperborea*. Lindleyana 4(3):158–160.

Luer, C. A. 1972. The native orchids of Florida. New York Botanical Garden, Bronx. 293 p.

Luer, C. A. 1975. The native orchids of the United States and Canada excluding Florida. New York Botanical Garden, Bronx. 361 p.

Maximilian, A. 1841. Reise in das innere Nord-America in den Jahren 1832 bis 1834. Zweitner Band, Z. 373. Coblenz. Bei J. Hoelscher.

McDonald, E. S. 1937. The life-forms of the flowering plants of Indiana. American Midland Naturalist 18(5):687–773.

Medley, M. E. 1979. Some aspects of the life history of *Triphora trianthophora* (Swartz) Rydberg (three-birds orchid) with special reference to its pollination. Master's thesis, Andrews University, Berrien Springs, Michigan. 45 p.

Mehrhoff, L. A. 1983. Pollination in the genus *Isotria* (Orchidaceae). American Journal of Botany 70(10):1444–1453.

Mohlenbrock, R. H. 1970. The illustrated flora of Illinois. Flowering plants: lilies to orchids. Southern Illinois University Press, Carbondale. 288 p.

Morris, F., and E. Eames. 1929. Our wild orchids. Charles Scribner's Sons, New York, New York. 464 p.

Nieuwland, J. A. 1913. Notes on our local plants. IV. American Midland Naturalist 3:98–125.

Nieuwland, J. A., and T. Just. 1931. New and interesting plant records from northern Indiana. American Midland Naturalist 12:217–223.

Niles, G. G. 1904. Bog trotting for orchids. Knickerbocker Press, New York, New York. 310 p.

Peattie, D. C. 1930. Flora of the Indiana Dunes. Field Museum of Natural History, Chicago, Illinois. 432 p.

Pepoon, H. S. 1927. An annotated flora of the Chicago area. Chicago Academy of Sciences Bulletin. 554 p.

Riddell, J. L. 1835. A synopsis of the flora of the western states. E. Deming, Cincinnati, Ohio. 116 p.

Schneck, J. 1876. Catalogue of the flora of the Wabash Valley below the mouth of White River, and observations thereon. Seventh Annual Report of the Geological Survey of Indiana 7:504–579.

Schrenk, W. J. 1978. North American Platantheras: evolution in the making. American Orchid Society Bulletin 47:429–437.

Schultes, R. E., and A. S. Pease. 1963. Generic names of orchids. Academy Press, New York, New York. 331 p.

Schwegman, J., and R. H. Mohlenbrock. 1968. Notes on the flora of extreme southern Illinois. Transactions of the Illinois Academy of Science 61:317–319.

Sheviak, C. J. 1973. A new *Spiranthes* from the grasslands of central North America. Botanical Museum Leaflets, Harvard University 23:285–297.

Sheviak, C. J. 1974. An introduction to the ecology of the Illinois Orchidaceae. Illinois State Museum, Springfield. 89 p.

Sheviak, C. J. 1982. Biosystematic study of the *Spiranthes cernua* complex. New York State Museum Bulletin 448. 73 p.

Sheviak, C. J. 1990. Biological considerations in the management of temperate terrestrial orchid habitats. Pages 194–196 in R. S. Mitchell, C. J. Sheviak, and D. J. Leopold, eds., Ecosystem management: rare species and significant habitats. New York State Museum Bulletin 471, Albany.

Sheviak, C. J. 1991. Morphological variation in the compilospecies *Spiranthes cernua* (L.) L. C. Rich.: Ecologically-limited effects of gene flow. Lindleyana 6(4):228–234.

Sheviak, C. J., and M. L. Bowles. 1986. The prairie fringed orchids: a pollinator-isolated species pair. Rhodora 88:267–290.

Sheviak, C. J., and P. M. Catling. 1980. The identity and status of *Spiranthes ochroleuca* (Rydberg) Rydberg. Rhodora 82:525–562.

Shull, E. M. 1987. The butterflies of Indiana. Indiana Academy of Science, Indianapolis. 262 p.

Soper, J. H., and L. Murray. 1985. Helleborine—a 30–year update and analysis of its distribution in Ontario. Michigan Botanist 24:83–96.

Steele, W. C. 1881. The Orchidaceae of northern Indiana. L.B. Case's Botanical Index 4(1):4–5.

Steyermark, J. A. 1963. Flora of Missouri. Iowa State University Press, Ames. 1725 p.

Stoutamire, W. P. 1967. Flower biology of the lady's-slippers (Orchidaceae: *Cypripedium*). Michigan Botanist 6:159–175.

Stoutamire, W. P. 1971. Pollination in temperate American orchids. Pages 233–243 *in* M. J. G. Corrigan, ed., Proceedings of the 6th World Orchid Conference. Halstead Press, Sydney, Australia.

Stoutamire, W. P. 1974. Relationships of the purple-fringed orchids *Platanthera psycodes* and *P. grandiflora*. Brittonia 26:42–58.

Stoutamire, W. 1978. Pollination of *Tipularia discolor,* an orchid with modified symmetry. American Orchid Society Bulletin 47:413–415.

Strausbaugh, P. D., and E. L. Core. 1970. Flora of West Virginia. Seneca Books, Inc. Grantsville, West Virginia. 1079 p.

Summers, B. 1987. Missouri orchids. Missouri Department of Conservation, Jefferson City. 92 p.

Swink, F. A. 1966. Orchids of the Indiana dune region. American Orchid Society Bulletin 35:706–710.

Swink, F., and G. Wilhelm. 1979. Plants of the Chicago region. The Morton Arboretum, Lisle, Illinois. 922 p.

Thompson, M. 1892. Geological and natural history report of Carroll County. Seventeenth Annual Report of the Indiana Department of Geological and Natural Resources 17:171–191.

Thien, L. B., and B. G. Marcks. 1972. The floral biology of *Arethusa bulbosa, Calopogon tuberosus,* and *Pogonia ophioglossoides* (Orchidaceae). Canadian Journal of Botany 50:2319–2325.

Van Gorder, W. B. 1894. Flora of Noble County. Eighteenth Annual Report of the Indiana Department of Geology and Natural Resources 18:33–71.

Vogt, C. A. 1990. Pollination in *Cypripedium reginae* (Orchidaceae). Lindleyana 5 (3):145–150.

Voss, E. G. 1966. Nomenclatural notes on monocots. Rhodora 68:435–463.

Wampler, F. 1988. Wildflowers of Indiana. Indiana University Press, Bloomington. 177 p.

White, J., and M. H. Madany. 1978. Classification of natural communities in Illinois. Pages 309–405 *in* J. White, ed., Illinois natural areas inventory technical report. Illinois Natural Areas Inventory, Urbana.

Whiting, R. E. and P. M. Catling. 1986. Orchids of Ontario. CanaColl Foundation, Ottawa, Ontario. 169 p.

Wiggins, I. L. 1980. Flora of Baja California. Stanford University Press, Stanford, California. 1025 p.

Wilhelm, G. S. 1990. Special vegetation on the Indiana Dunes National Lakeshore. Report 90–02 submitted to the National Park Service Midwest Region, U.S. Department of the Interior. The Morton Arboretum, Lisle, Illinois. 373 p.

Withner, C. L. (ed.). 1974. The orchids—scientific studies. John Wiley and Sons, New York, New York. 604 p.

Index

An active member and fellow of the Indiana Academy of
Science and former chairman of the plant
taxonomy section,
Michael A. Homoya
has published over twenty scientific and popular articles
on Indiana flora and ecology. As botanist with the
Indiana Department of Natural Resources,
Homoya spends much of his time searching for and
monitoring endangered plants, and
inventorying and assessing
natural areas.

Book and Jacket Designer
Sharon L. Sklar

Editor
Roberta L. Diehl

Production Coordinator
Harriet Curry

Typeface
Goudy Old Style

Typesetter
Weimer Graphics, Inc.

Printer and Binder
Printed in Hong Kong by Everbest Printing Co. Ltd.
through Four Colour Imports, Ltd.